Maud Beerbohm Tree
Lady of the Stage

LEGENDA

LEGENDA is the Modern Humanities Research Association's book imprint for new research in the Humanities. Founded in 1995 by Malcolm Bowie and others within the University of Oxford, Legenda has always been a collaborative publishing enterprise, directly governed by scholars. The Modern Humanities Research Association (MHRA) joined this collaboration in 1998, became half-owner in 2004, in partnership with Maney Publishing and then Routledge, and has since 2016 been sole owner. Titles range from medieval texts to contemporary cinema and form a widely comparative view of the modern humanities, including works on Arabic, Catalan, English, French, German, Greek, Italian, Portuguese, Russian, Spanish, and Yiddish literature. Editorial boards and committees of more than 60 leading academic specialists work in collaboration with bodies such as the Society for French Studies, the British Comparative Literature Association and the Association of Hispanists of Great Britain & Ireland.

The MHRA encourages and promotes advanced study and research in the field of the modern humanities, especially modern European languages and literature, including English, and also cinema. It aims to break down the barriers between scholars working in different disciplines and to maintain the unity of humanistic scholarship. The Association fulfils this purpose through the publication of journals, bibliographies, monographs, critical editions, and the MHRA Style Guide, and by making grants in support of research. Membership is open to all who work in the Humanities, whether independent or in a University post, and the participation of younger colleagues entering the field is especially welcomed.

ALSO PUBLISHED BY THE ASSOCIATION

Critical Texts
Tudor and Stuart Translations • *New Translations* • *European Translations*
MHRA Library of Medieval Welsh Literature

MHRA Bibliographies
Publications of the Modern Humanities Research Association

The Annual Bibliography of English Language & Literature
Austrian Studies
Modern Language Review
Portuguese Studies
The Slavonic and East European Review
Working Papers in the Humanities
The Yearbook of English Studies

www.mhra.org.uk
www.legendabooks.com

EDITORIAL BOARD

Chair: Professor Jonathan Long (University of Durham)
For *Germanic Literatures*: Ritchie Robertson (University of Oxford)
For *Italian Perspectives*: Simon Gilson (University of Warwick)
For *Moving Image*: Emma Wilson (University of Cambridge)
For *Research Monographs in French Studies*:
Diana Knight (University of Nottingham)
For *Selected Essays*: Susan Harrow (University of Bristol)
For *Studies in Comparative Literature*: Duncan Large
(British Centre for Literary Translation, University of East Anglia)
For *Studies in Hispanic and Lusophone Cultures*:
Trevor Dadson (Queen Mary, University of London)
For *Studies in Yiddish*: Gennady Estraikh (New York University)
For *Transcript*: Matthew Reynolds (University of Oxford)

Managing Editor
Dr Graham Nelson
41 Wellington Square, Oxford OX1 2JF, UK

www.legendabooks.com

LE THEATRE

ABONNEMENT ET VENTE :	PUBLICITÉ :	CONDITIONS DE L'ABONNEMENT :
24, Bd des Capucines. — Téléph. : 242-43	C. O. COMMUNAY, seul concessionnaire 19, Boulevard Montmartre. — Téléphone : 142-06	PARIS : 1 an 40 fr DÉPARTEMENTS : 1 an 44 fr. ÉTRANGER (Union Postale) : 1 an 52 fr.

Maud Beerbohm Tree

Lady of the Stage

Susana Cory-Wright

Modern Humanities Research Association
2018

*Published by Legenda
an imprint of the Modern Humanities Research Association
Salisbury House, Station Road, Cambridge CB1 2LA*

*ISBN 978-1-78188-683-0 (HB)
ISBN 978-1-78188-684-7 (PB)*

First published 2018

All rights reserved. No part of this publication may be reproduced or disseminated or transmitted in any form or by any means, electronic, mechanical, photocopying, recording or otherwise, or stored in any retrieval system, or otherwise used in any manner whatsoever without written permission of the copyright owner, except in accordance with the provisions of the Copyright, Designs and Patents Act 1988, or under the terms of a licence permitting restricted copying issued in the UK by the Copyright Licensing Agency Ltd, Saffron House, 6–10 Kirby Street, London EC1N 8TS, England, or in the USA by the Copyright Clearance Center, 222 Rosewood Drive, Danvers MA 01923. Application for the written permission of the copyright owner to reproduce any part of this publication must be made by email to legenda@mhra.org.uk.

Disclaimer: Statements of fact and opinion contained in this book are those of the author and not of the editors or the Modern Humanities Research Association. The publisher makes no representation, express or implied, in respect of the accuracy of the material in this book and cannot accept any legal responsibility or liability for any errors or omissions that may be made.

Trademark notice: Product or corporate names may be trademarks or registered trademarks, and are used only for identification and explanation without intent to infringe.

© *Modern Humanities Research Association 2018*

Copy-Editor: Charlotte Brown

CONTENTS

	Acknowledgements	ix
	List of Illustrations	x
	Notes on References	xi
	Introduction	xii
1	Miss Hellen Maud Holt 1858–71	1
2	Miss Hellen Maud 1871–81	10
3	Mrs Beerbohm Tree 1882–87	20
4	Trees in Good Voice: The Red Lamp, 1887–90	28
5	Mrs Beerbohm Tree 1892	37
6	Mrs Tree, Sardou, Her Majesty's Theatre, and Ibsen 1895–96	51
7	'That Brutus may be a little missed' 1898	63
8	Philanthropy and 'The Absent-Minded Beggar' 1899	67
9	Midsummer Revels 1900	79
10	Caesar's Wife: Becoming a Wo-manager 1901	89
11	Agrippina 1906	100
12	Paulina and a Fateful Winter's Tale 1906	111
13	'Stand and Deliver': Being Lady Tree 1907–13	117
14	Sir Herbert and Lady Tree 1914–16	132
15	Still Waters 1916	142
16	Herbert and I... 1917–20	153
17	Maud Helen Louise, Lady Tree OBE 1920–29	160
18	The Man Who Could Work Miracles 1931–37	171
	Appendix: List of Theatre Roles	179
	Bibliography	185
	Index	190

ACKNOWLEDGEMENTS

Any research into the Tree family will necessarily involve many visits to the wonderful Theatre Collection at the University of Bristol. The correspondence pertaining to Maud in the Tree Family Archive consists of some 13,500 letters alone. Consequently, negotiating this vast collection would have been impossible without the help of its staff and as ever my thanks go to Catherine Hudson, Bex Carrington, Jo Elsworth, and Heather Romaine. I would also like to thank Sarah Clark, Davina Downes, and Andrew Holt. The holders of copyright pertaining to Gerald du Maurier were equally helpful, as was Merlin Holland as trustee of Constance Wilde's estate.

I would like to thank Donald Roy and Marion O'Connor of the Society for Theatre Research. More recently however, my thanks go to Graham Nelson of Legenda and to Charlotte Brown.

As always, I remember David Cory-Wright whose gift of his grandmother's letters inspired me in the first place.

Once again, however, this book is really dedicated to my mischievous muses Emma, James, and Maximilian, and to Jonathan.

s.c-w., London, December 2017

LIST OF ILLUSTRATIONS

FIG. 1.1. Certified Copy of Hellen Maud Tree's Birth Certificate
FIG. 2.1. 'Maud Tree (in the Nineties)' (Pearson 1988, [n.p])
FIG. 2.2. Letter from Edward Burne-Jones to Maud Tree, undated (MBTC/000121)
FIG. 3.1. Maud as Oenone in *Helena in Troas*, sketches taken at the Greek Theatre, Hengler's Circus (*Queen: The Lady's Newspaper*, 5 June 1886)
FIG. 4.1. Maud Tree (photograph by Raphael Tuck & Sons, no. 29; author's own)
FIG. 4.2. 'Mr. & Mrs. Tree, Ogden's *Guinea Gold Cigarettes*' (author's own)
FIG. 5.1. Herbert Tree and Maud Tree in *Hamlet* at the Haymarket Theatre (*Graphic*, 30 January 1892). From a painting by H. M. Payet
FIG. 6.1. Maud Tree as Mrs D'Acosta and Lewis Waller as her husband Stephen, in *A Woman's Reason* (*Sketch*, 29 January 1896; photograph by Alfred Ellis, Upper Baker Street)
FIG. 8.1. Maud Tree recites Rudyard Kipling's 'The Absent-Minded Beggar' at the Palace Theatre (*Black and White*, 11 November 1899)
FIG. 9.1. Maud Tree as Titania in *A Midsummer Night's Dream* at Her Majesty's Theatre (*Sporting & Dramatic*, 20 January 1900)
FIG. 9.2. Herbert Tree as Bottom and Maud Tree as Titania (Theatre Museum, Victoria and Albert Museum)
FIG. 9.3. Maud Tree as Mary Archerson in *The Likeness of the Night* (*Sketch*, 7 December 1901)
FIG. 10.1. Maud Tree at the Playgoers' Club Ladies' Dinner (*Era*, 1 January 1902)
FIG. 10.2. Maud Tree and Charles Wyndham (*The Entr'Acte*, 5 April 1902)
FIG. 10.3. Maud Tree with her daughter Viola in her new tonneau (*The Car*, 17 June 1903)
FIG. 11.1. Maud as Agrippina (*Le Théâtre*, January 1906)
FIG. 13.1. Letter from Maud Tree to her daughters, 15 February 1910 (SCW, letter 103)
FIG. 13.2. Cast of *Diplomacy* (Rotary Photo postcard 6914; author's own)
FIG. 15.1. The Empire Picture Hall advertising Maud in the film *Still Waters Run Deep*, 1916 (Edwards 1992: Figure 125, [n.p.])
FIG. 15.2. 'France's Day in Aid of the French Red Cross', originally published by the London Committee of the French Red Cross, 1916 (Imperial War Museum Posters)
FIG. 15.3. Letter from Maud Tree to Felicity Tree, 20 June 1917 (SCW, letter 164)
FIG. 17.1. Maud Tree as the Countess of Crewkerne in *Araminta Arrives* at the Comedy Theatre (*Graphic*, 29 October 1921)
FIG. 17.2. Maud Tree in the film *Mayfair to Montmartre* (still from British Pathe Film, Id, 994.21, 27 April 1922)
FIG. 18.1. Maud Tree as Mistress Quickly in *King Henry IV, Part I* at His Majesty's Theatre, 29 April 1935 (photograph by Leadlay-Dallison)
FIG. 18.2. Maud Tree as the Duchess of Stroud in *Our Own Lives* at the Ambassadors Theatre (*Play Pictorial*, 67: 404)

NOTES ON REFERENCES

The following abbreviations are used:

BTC	Beerbohm Tree Collection
HBTA	Herbert Beerbohm Tree Archive:
HBT/R4	Herbert Beerbohm Tree Letters, Lewis Waller Letters, MBT diary
HBT/RA	Maud Beerbohm Tree to HBT America, Pinney letters, Maud to Rudyard Kipling
SCW	Susana Cory-Wright Private Collection
TFA	Tree Family Archive:
MBTC	Letters in the Maud Beerbohm Tree Collection to 1899
MBTC 2	Letters in the Maud Beerbohm Tree Collection 1900–17
MBTC 6	All undated and uncatalogued correspondence
MBTC 7	All letters from Lewis Waller and those pertaining to May Pinney

The University of Bristol Theatre Collection houses two important archives pertaining to Herbert and Maud Beerbohm Tree: One is the Herbert Beerbohm Tree Archive which comprises business records, production papers, financial ledgers, and some sixty-five volumes of press cuttings, the other is the Tree Family Archive. Within the latter is to be found the Maud Beerbohm Tree Collection and other smaller collections. In the 1970s, David Parsons gifted a collection pertaining to his mother Viola Parsons (nee Tree) to the Victoria & Albert Museum which was in turn purchased by the University of Bristol. In an attempt to reduce the volume of papers, David destroyed many of the accompanying envelopes. This of course has only added to the difficulty in accurately dating the correspondence. Although much of the correspondence and ephemera pertaining to the Trees has been catalogued across the archives, there is still a vast amount that has not. In this instance, correspondence is literally bundled in a box and labelled MBTC 6 or 7 etc. (see above). However, if a letter has been catalogued and numbered by the University of Bristol, I have retained their original numbering, these begin 'HBT/', 'R4' and 'RA'. With the exception of the SCW collection, all the above collections are to be found at the University of Bristol Theatre Collection.

Her Majesty's Theatre became His Majesty's on the death of Queen Victoria in 1901.

To avoid confusion, I refer throughout to Viola, Duchess of Rutland, by her maiden name of Lindsay. Her name would change a further three times during her lifetime: on marriage to Henry Manners in 1882, then in 1888 when she became Lady Granby, and 1906 when she became the Duchess of Rutland. Similarly I also refer to Viola who was married in 1912, Felicity in 1915, and Iris in 1916, by their maiden name of Tree.

INTRODUCTION

Some years ago I was given a box of assorted family documents for safe-keeping. These consisted mostly of sepia photographs, school reports from the 1920s, shopping lists, and old theatre programmes. There were also bundles and bundles of letters tied up with string. At first glance the contents of these appeared to be more of the same: instructions to nannies from a distant parent, the chronicling of the minutiae of daily life between the wars bookended by the terrible loss sustained by most families. At first, these sentimental letters — made all the more so with the passage of time — were the ones to capture my imagination. But I was not sure of their wider appeal outside the family and so I bundled them away.

More recently I embarked on a PhD and once again sought inspiration from the contents of the trunk in the attic. This time my focus had altered. I was now less interested in war stories and much more so in the character, the voice that from the many hundreds of letters I scoured screamed for recognition beyond the footlights. Its owner was flamboyant, exaggerated, often hilarious yet always courageous. This woman who was also my children's great great grandmother was none other than the wife of that larger than life actor manager, Sir Herbert Beerbohm Tree.

But who was she really this Helen Maud Holt, Maud Beerbohm, Maud Beerbohm Tree? A woman with as many personas as names? So much has been written about *him*, his sexual exploits, his grandiose Shakespearean productions at His/Her Majesty's Theatre, the theatre he built in the heart of his theatre kingdom, but what about *her*? Who was this woman buried for so many generations beneath the enormous weight of his colossal reputation?

What did become evident was that anyone who was anyone at the end of the nineteenth century and beginning of the twentieth, had corresponded with Maud. She counted artists, members of the royalty, actors, and politicians as close friends and her vast correspondence showed how she was neither the token novelty artist or decorative wife but an actress, working wife, and mother juggling the demands of a family within the constraints of marriage. In possession of such a copious amount of her correspondence, I decided to annotate a selected collection and this, in 2011, formed the basis of my doctoral thesis, 'An Annotated Edition of the Selected Correspondence of Maud, Lady Tree: 1880–1917'. In 2012, I published *Lady Tree: A Theatrical Life in Letters*, and in 2017, a fictitious, highly romanticized novel entitled *The London Wife*, about a Lady Tree but though based loosely on Maud by no means a serious biography. This was still not enough — of all the literature published by and about Herbert Beerbohm Tree there remains very little about Maud. She herself wrote an unpublished memoir entitled 'Our Little Life'. Her published recollections appear as a chapter in a book about Herbert but are far from reliable. This biography of Maud, therefore, is an expanded and reworked form of the 2012 project.

Archival evidence, however, reveals that Maud was an emancipated wife and mother, a working actor atypical of the leading ladies of the day. She was a woman of contradictions who accepted but was not swayed by new ideologies — anti- rather than pro-suffragette. What further distinguishes Maud from her contemporaries is that she was no society actress made good nor of the sinner-to-saint mould. Maud Tree's classical education, of which she was immensely proud, ensured that throughout her career she had an edge over other actresses. A ladylike demeanour and ability to ape the aristocracy also contributed to the seamless transition between drawing-room and stage precisely at a time when there 'was a notable shift' in public opinion with respect to the theatre and women practitioners in particular.[1]

Thus, with the dividing-line between home and theatre blurred, the aristocracy began not only to endorse the theatre but also actively to seek employment in it. Henry James, who later became a close family friend, admitted however at the time that actors 'appear in society and the people of society appear on the stage; it is as if the great gate which formerly divided the theatre from the world had been lifted off its hinges'.[2] And as the biographer Judith Flanders makes clear, British society had always been permeable to money, but now in the nineteenth century it became permeable to talent.[3] This was Maud's trump card. Aristocrats marooned in their vast country houses were desperate for entertainment, and Maud with her lovely manners and ability to pass herself off as one of their own, coupled with her wit and flair for recitation, was a popular guest.

Maud's self-awareness was clearly defined, and archival evidence also reflects the extent to which she valued this hard-won social position as she distanced herself and her daughters from the reputation of an actress. William Charles Macready had declared that actresses were 'trained to proclaim to the world the passions that proper ladies were made to conceal'.[4] In fact in 1896 only three years before Maud gave her solo rendition of Kipling's 'The Absent-Minded Beggar', the *Theatre* of 1896 lamented 'the popular identification of real-life prostitutes with actresses'. But the image that Maud Tree presented to the world was not merely to negate the sentiment behind this. She was acutely aware that she and her daughters were different. True aristocrats could do and behave as they liked; *they* could not. For as she wrote to her daughter Felicity: 'Have lovely manners & never be vulgar [...] be respected before everything: & noone [sic] however much they seem to like one ever really cares for whom they do not respect'.[5]

By the 1890s, Maud was already a celebrity actress, adept at using her influence on playwrights, aristocrats, and politicians alike in order to create professional opportunities for herself and her family. To her contemporaries and friends, Maud was a loyal compassionate friend whose ability to make light of Tree's infidelities, in particular, earned her respect and loyalty in return. Her greatest talent in friendship was her refusal to bear a grudge, and even in the midst of personal anguish, she was able to take the long view. Integral to understanding Maud's character, achievements, and professional legacy is her relationship with her husband, whose posthumous, problematic reputation she would nonetheless zealously guard. It would seem, too, that many of the parts Maud played echoed the real-life heartache that dogged her personal life. Equally, a rigorous self-discipline and willingness to adapt meant that she survived the transition from silent screen to 'talkies', when many of her contemporaries did not.

Maud's life bears witness then to a time of immense social and industrial flux; she saw the aftermath of two great wars, and her own life in the theatre altered beyond recognition. Her ability to embrace rather than fight change, however, ensured her professional and emotional survival, and the challenges she faced as a working mother and wife hold true today, as does the inspiration of her wit and stoicism. It is utterly typical that when Maud gave her first radio broadcast on the 27 February 1926 she should ask somewhat disingenuously: 'Do you think anyone heard me?' The radio host's reply was swift: 'About a million and a half people'.

With her customary wit and fondness for epitaphs, Maud once said that hers should read: 'This is the Life of Little Me, I was the Wife of Herbert Tree'. It was rather more than that.

Notes to the Introduction

1. Vicinus 1977: 9.
2. James 1948: 120. Henry James was godfather to Viola Tree.
3. Flanders 2001: 22.
4. Pollock 1878: II, 266.
5. Maud Tree to Felicity Tree, 20 September 1913 (SCW, letter 584).

CHAPTER 1

Miss Hellen Maud Holt
1858–71

In the 1 July 1926 edition of *The Stage* of London, there is an advertisement at the back of the magazine that reads:

> Wanted Artists
> Aristocratic Lady — Must have personality for Light Comedy.

In 1926, the widowed Lady Tree was in her late sixties and professionally busier than at any time in her life. Although by then she was contributing regularly to radio, theatre was still her mainstay, the need to work as paramount as ever. The above was exactly the kind of advertisement to catch her attention and one to which she may well have responded. Playing aristocratic ladies in comic situations was something Maud had been doing for most of her life. It was a role she had so perfectly honed that the transition from a real-life drawing-room to one on the stage was fluid and faultless. Life with her husband Herbert, on the other hand, had only polished an inherent wit.

But Maud was not born into the aristocracy and her upbringing, no matter how comfortable she would have us believe it, was still a far cry from the lavish Belvoir and Walmer Castles that would become as second homes to her in later life. The youngest of seven children, Hellen (*sic*) Maud Holt was born on 5 October 1858 at 21 South Bank, Marylebone.[1] Maud's mother Emma was forty-five years old and her father William, whose occupation is stated as 'gentleman' at the time of her birth, as it would be at his death, was fifty-four.[2] Over the years, however, William's occupation would change from innkeeper to licensed victualler, and his reversals of fortune seem to have been the one predictable feature of Maud's growing-up. The family moved frequently, a habit Maud would form herself later on. She adopted a particular fondness for renting country houses, which, recognizing them as such, she called her 'follies'.

There is some mystery associated with Maud's upbringing — a mystery Maud did nothing to dispel either in her memoir, which is unreliable and suffers from memory lapses, or in the public speeches she made throughout her life.[3] If anything, she encouraged further mystery by referring only vaguely to circumstances she must have known a great deal more about, while omitting others altogether. Later Maud, like many of her peers in the acting profession, would embellish her background, portraying her father as a Dickensian character who had fallen on hard times. Similarly, as in the memoirs of other leading ladies, these parents, though impoverished, are invariably noble and dwell in rose-clad cottages.[4] What is known for certain is that Maud's father, William Holt (1804–72) and sometime victualler, was also the son of a licensed victualler, marrying Emma Brown (1813–63), a farmer's daughter, at St George's, Hanover Square, on 30 March 1839. It was the same church in which William's father, James Holt from Great Missenden, had married Elizabeth Holloway in 1799 and an ornate family bible marks the occasion.

William and Emma's first four children were born at two- to three-year intervals. There then followed a five-year gap between the births of Arthur (1851–86) and Horace (1856–1932). Maud, born two years after Horace, was thus eighteen years younger than her oldest sibling. This fact is said to highlight the possibility that Maud and Horace were fathered by someone other than William, but there is no evidence to suggest this, nor is it significant that Emma Holt was in her forties when Maud was born. There were frequently large age differences in families at a time when birth control, such as it was, was unreliable and Maud's mother may well have suffered a miscarriage or two after the birth of Arthur.

Whatever the case, Emma was dead by the time Maud was five and thereafter the girl spent an itinerant childhood, brought up by her much older sisters. Emmie the eldest, now in her twenties, had married a London hotelier called John Mayson who was to die young, while Bertha's short-lived marriage to Mr Floyd,[5] an East End merchant's clerk, with whom she had eloped, was over by the time Maud was fifteen. But at least she had spent her happy, early years at 13 Grove End Road, close to Lord's cricket ground, where in the 1860s most of the houses were built on their own plots of land. In a large house with a garden, Maud and her brother Horace enacted sketches from their favourite play. The aptly titled *Maud* by Alfred Lord Tennyson published only three years before her birth was a narrative poem they particularly enjoyed performing. 'O that 't'were possible after long grief and pain | To find the arms of my true-love round me once again!', she would cry strutting between the apple trees. Horace, popping up from behind a lilac bush, would throw open his arms and fix her with 'a beatific stare'. Maud would then call out: 'It is, it is, it is my long-lost husband!' The children's playacting continued indoors if the weather was wet, with Maud rushing down the stairs crying 'Henri de Laguadere!' Horace, running to catch her in his arms would answer, 'I am heeeere'.

The favourite, however, was Justin H. McCarthy's melodrama *The Duke's Motto*. McCarthy dedicated his play to the French dramatist Victorien Sardou, but attributed its inspiration to the 'romantic actor Lewis Waller'. Although she could not know it then, both men would later figure significantly in Maud's life. She would act in a number of Sardou revivals — *Fedora* being the most famous — and she would enjoy an intimate friendship with the matinee idol Lewis Waller. There would be a further connection: neither Waller nor Maud ever mentioned the fact, but her niece Gwendolyn Floyd (sister Bertha's daughter) later became his manager.

Maud's experience of theatre, however, was not limited to childish reenactments with her young brother. Theirs was a household 'steeped in literature', with the

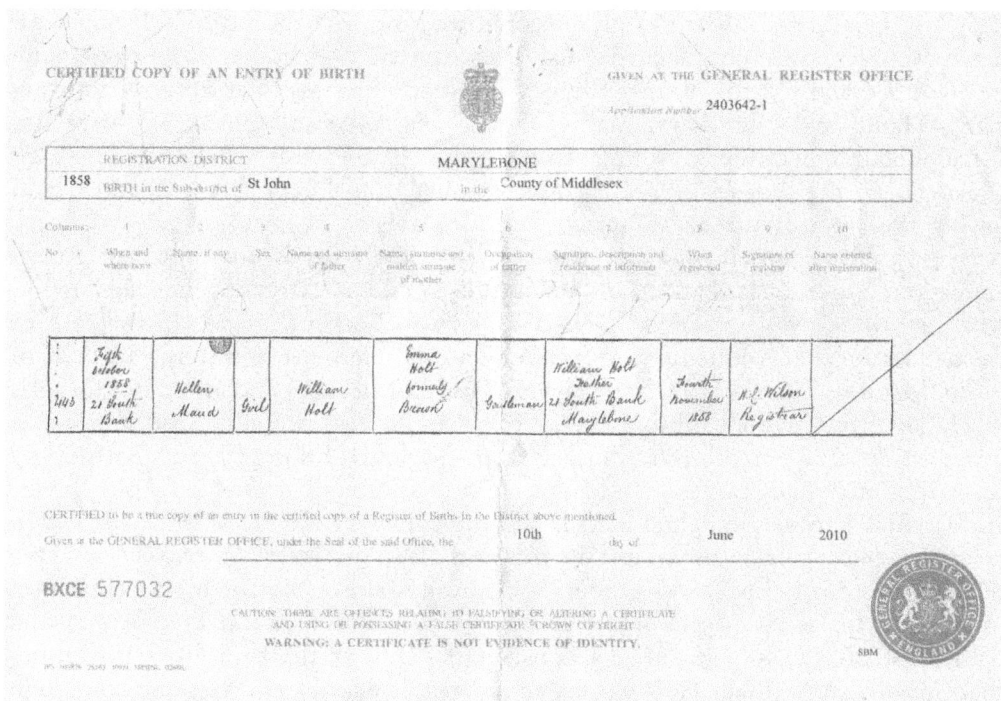

FIG. 1.1. Certified Copy of Hellen Maud Tree's Birth Certificate

two older sisters particularly passionate about theatre. The sisters saw *The Serf* at the Olympic Theatre some 'twenty times', while even more popular was *Our American Cousin* by Maud's future English teacher and later editor of *Punch*, Tom Taylor. This play was later infamous as the one being performed when President Abraham Lincoln was assassinated in 1865, when Maud was seven. Sister Bertha, having left her husband, worked for a Mrs Bateman at the Lyceum and thus Maud's earliest recollections revolved almost entirely around theatre. She learned the names of famous actors and actresses by rote until they were as familiar to her as nursery rhymes. Her sisters, returning from the theatre, would mimic these stars and even her mother, when she was alive, shared this passion.[6]

But the happy childhood at Grove End Road was short-lived and the family had moved several times when William Holt died a few years later. Maud was fourteen and the older sisters now stepped in to take charge of their younger siblings' education, being particularly diligent with Maud. Henrietta, known in the family as 'Harrie', would be of invaluable support to Maud in later years, minding house and offering companionship when she was widowed, but in the very early years it was Emmie and Bertha who appear to have been the most influential. Emmie, who had a special love of poetry, passed this on to Maud, encouraging her to memorize long tracts of Tennyson, Browning, George Eliot, and Swinburne.[7] These would later form the bedrock of Maud's solo renditions, with *Enoch Arden* being the most popular, especially when Strauss set it to music in 1897. Hitherto, her schooling had been far from formal. When Emmie married and moved to Kent, Maud went with her, but any knowledge gleaned outside the theatre and books came principally from nature and playing among the cowslips and chickens. Nature would always bring Maud (and later her daughters) great pleasure, and much of their later correspondence details plans for planting out their gardens or the hearing of the first cuckoo in spring. Emmie would also read to her from Dickens, and Maud would devour the monthly magazines serializing his novels.

By 1872, however, it was clear that Maud was in need of a more structured education. Emmie's husband had suddenly died and she urgently needed to find work, so Maud was uprooted once more back to London. Placed in the care of their older brother William, who was now a civil engineer and living in Pelham Place, Maud was duly enrolled in Queen's College, an independent school for girls in Harley Street, where Emmie and Bertha had also been pupils. Instruction was given in an array of subjects ranging from Natural Philosophy and Astronomy to Arithmetic, Languages, and Musical Composition. The writers Tom Taylor and Charles Kingsley taught English, and the principal was the Rev. J. Llewellyn Davies, whose grandsons would be immortalized in J. M. Barrie's *Peter Pan*. Founded originally in 1848 by Frederick Denison Maurice 'for the higher education of women', it was also a school for wealthy women with an annual fee of £25 (the equivalent of £27,000 in 2017), a considerable sum at the time.[8] It is intriguing that, given that William Holt was an innkeeper/licensed victualler and sometime 'gentleman' of various abodes, his daughters Emily, Bertha, and Maud should all have been educated at this new, progressive establishment. However, at the time of his death, William Holt left an estate valued at £800 (or approx. £870,000 today), which may have been used in part to finance the younger children's upbringing.

There now began for Maud a period of hitherto 'unknown bliss', a decade of stability in which she thrived, and although she found living with her older brother William 'terrifying', she revelled in every aspect of the newly imposed regime. Two hours of study before breakfast was followed by the walk to school through Hyde Park. Lessons were over by 4 pm but she would often linger to have tea in the library with a Miss Grove, loath to go home and leave her 'fairy place'. Of all the subjects she was taught, the Classics gripped her imagination the most, only further enhanced by the exciting discoveries and innovations being reported abroad. From the time that young men and women embarked on the Grand Tour and wrote their accounts of the ancient world, there had been a growing interest in all classical subjects, with an emphasis on and aesthetic reverence for classical mythology. Furthermore, the excavation and display of archeological sites would further fuel a feverish fascination with the people who had inhabited them. The viewing of such statues as de Milo's Venus, exhibited at the Crystal Palace exhibition of 1862, and the Praxitelean Hermes in 1887, became further embedded in Victorian popular culture.

Just as important, and with specific relevance to Maud as she grew up, this national fetish altered the then accepted notion of Victorian beauty. Henry James, Edward Poynter, and Lawrence Alma-Tadema, who would all later become close friends and colleagues of Maud, were only some of the artists who used the sculptural metaphor liberally in their work.[9] Oscar Wilde, too, would liken Lillie

Langtry to Helen of Troy in his poem of 1881, *The New Helen*. The inheritance of this classical imagery is also evident in Herbert Tree's later use of tableaux,[10] while the popular 'Attitudes' influenced not only Maud's but the Victorian actress's notion of movement and dance.[11] In Tree's 1895 production of *Fedora*, Mrs Patrick Campbell whitewashed her arms in an attempt to appear more sculpture-like — with unintentionally comical results. Shaw criticized the practice as 'an intolerable absurdity'.[12] This early immersion in all things classical would leave an indelible impression on Maud. In its efforts to keep abreast of the trend, Queen's College valiantly staged its own Greek tragedy in which Maud was to play her first formal acting role.

And so if Maud's classical education fuelled an enthusiastic imagination, feeding it with dreams of Girton, sister Bertha's well-timed employment at the Lyceum and with it invitations to that theatre, sought to rekindle an earlier interest. What had begun as a pastime to while away the hours with her brother Horace became something much more tangible after seeing *The Bells* at the Lyceum. It was as if, Maud wrote in her memoir, 'the gate of another world' had opened. She quickly developed a crush on the show's star, Henry Irving, in much the same way that aspiring starlets would later do on her own husband. But for Maud it was not just the magnetism of the man that drew her to him but his acting methodology. Maud was a great mimic and she took on board anything that was innovative and instructive. Reminiscing about the event years later, the impact of that first encounter was still vivid. She recalled:

> That strange, lurid drama, the mysterious, compelling personality, the wild satanic beauty of the actor, created for me a new Heaven and a new Earth. I thought of nothing but Irving in The Bells. By Hook or by crook I went to see him over and over again and very soon I knew the entire play by heart, every intonation, every gesture, every thought [...] was burnt into my brain.[13]

The Bells, like so many of the popular nineteenth-century plays performed on the English stage at the time, was a translation from the French: adapted by Leopold Davis Lewis from *Le Juif polonais* [The Polish Jew] by Erckmann Chatrian, it went on to be one of Irving's greatest successes. It was originally performed over 151 nights, catapulting the actor to stardom and inspiring impersonations in smoking clubs and private houses throughout the country. (In 1905, Irving would give his final performance as Mathias the night before he died.) At school, in a room normally used for drawing and one partitioned by heavy curtains, Maud gave one-woman re-enactments during the lunch hour. As she intoned to her schoolgirl audience:

> I welcome the Jew to my tavern: I wait to waylay him on his road. I listen for his sleigh bells: I hear the striking of a distant clock striking the hour. I shout a frenzied cry of relief: 'One! One!' — the Jew has passed: he's gone. Thank God! Thank God! — And fall sobbing with gratitude upon my knees. But no! The Jew has not passed: the eerie, ominous sound of sleigh bells is heard nearer and ever nearer. When they are close at hand, I raise my arms and strike and strike again with murderous ferocity: then, with heavily breathing difficulty, I lift the heavy body and stagger away muttering a tiger-ish: To the limekiln![14]

Swinging from those heavy curtains, Maud would then hurl herself forward before falling, feigning death. She soon became known for her 'prowess at staging a faint', and Minnie Davis, a contemporary of Maud, remembers how:

> On one occasion in the middle of one of her shows, we heard Miss Parry's cough which heralded her approach, and Maud without a moment's hesitation fell on the floor and fainted. A girl was sent for water and she soon came to.[15]

A year later, Maud's teenage passion for Irving had not abated, and when he appeared at the Lyceum in W. G. Gorman's drama, *Charles the First*, Maud saw it several times, sitting in the three-shilling upper boxes. Given that the upper boxes were probably beyond the means of a schoolgirl, it can be assumed that it was Bertha's employment in the theatre that made the better seats available to her. Produced by Mrs Bateman's husband (Bertha's employers) and starring their daughter Isabella as the fated Queen, the play was dismissed by the *New York Times* as 'scarcely historical', and confusing 'petty realism' with 'poetic drama'. Nonetheless, drawing on familiar and recognized visual images, it provoked a burst of applause when Irving first appeared, because 'a painting of Van Dyck's seemed to have started from its frame' (*The Times*, 30 September 1872).[16] Maud thought so too, and on discovering where Irving lived, she began deviating from her usual walk to and from school:

'I learnt that he lived at 15a Grafton Street,' she recounted years later to an audience of old alumnae at Queen's College. 'Quickly reconnoitering I made my way, and, yes, there it was: the door in Grafton Street, the rooms over what is now Vicarya's Emporium [...] Those must be his rooms on the first floor — three long windows... I had tracked the eagle to his eyrie!'[17]

However, in true Maud style there was a humorous follow-up to this anecdote. Many years later, when Maud found herself seated beside her now aged idol, she related these events to him only for him to say, 'Alas that was not my street! Alas those were not my windows!'.[18] The play would, however, continue to be a particular favourite of hers, and, forty years later, Maud was still sending out copies of it to her new idol, Gerald du Maurier, and to Norman Forbes-Robertson.[19]

At school, Maud had no difficulty in making friends. She had a reputation for possessing what she herself called the 'dramatic' spirit — she was effervescent, enthusiastic and wore her heart on her sleeve. With a gift for mimicry and quick epigrams, she was always amusing company. Her popularity then ensured that later she could call on the services of many talented women, alumnae who had succeeded in their various fields. Equally, when Maud was an established personality in her own right, and particularly when appearing on screen and radio, these women turned to Maud to return the favour. But Maud made one friendship outside Queen's College that would last until she died over sixty years later. Apart from her classical education and acting it was the single greatest influence of her formative years. Moreover, this friendship would influence the way Maud dressed, decorated her homes, entertained, and reared her children. It also gave her instant social kudos, helping to establish her own position in society and lending invaluable support to her charitable causes.

After her husband's death, Maud's sister Emmie, on leaving Kent, had become a paid companion to one Marion Margaret Violet Lindsay, an aristocratic beauty and talented artist. At an early age, Violet, as she was known, displayed an inordinate gift for draughtsmanship, but it was as a sculptress that she would later be known. Rodin praised her work, and the cast of her young son Lord Haddon, who died at the age of nine, is in Tate Britain today. She gave her first exhibition at the age of twenty-two and her face is the model for a bronze of St Catherine of Egypt by Alfred Gilbert, completed in 1928.[20] In the 1880s she was a member of an elitist circle of intellectual aristocrats known as 'the Souls' — to be a member you had to possess 'a soul above the ordinary' — being one of its most genuinely unconventional and bohemian members, with her taste not just for theatre but for its actors too. In 1882 she married Lord Henry Manners, who would become the eighth Duke of Rutland, and thereby became doyenne of one of the most ancient estates in the country, Belvoir Castle. She also took lovers, her three daughters reputedly fathered by men — including the dashing Harry Cust — other than her husband. Violet had been born in 1856, at Haigh Hall in Lancashire to a hero of the Crimean war and Member of Parliament, the Hon. Charles Lindsay, and his wife Emilia Browne and was their only child to survive infancy.

As Maud was only a couple of years older than Violet, Emmie thought it only natural to introduce them, feeling that Maud's love of theatre and reverence for classical imagery would appeal to Violet's artistic temperament. She was not disappointed. Like many of her elitist generation, Violet was innately snobbish, but preferred talent or money in her friends to a good pedigree. They were instant, bosom friends. They wrote to each other incessantly to discuss all manner of subjects, from clothes to beaux, poetry to infidelity (generally that of their husbands). Besides which they shared a mutual fascination for new movements and intellectual circles devoted to aestheticism, music, and art. Most importantly, each understood and respected the compulsion in the other to pursue her individual talent. But while Violet, as an aristocrat, could satisfy her every whim, associate with whom she pleased, dress in the draped, Greek-inspired floating gowns that became her trademark, Maud as an aspiring actress could not. If there was an invaluable lesson Maud took from this friendship it was an awareness of the delicate nature of an actress's reputation and that the education of which she was so proud marked her out for something more.

The paradox was that while Violet as an aristocrat wished only to behave as an artist, Maud as an artist needed to conduct herself as an aristocrat. Violet, used to breaking taboos, did so further in extending her friendship to a woman whose would-be profession was still ambiguous in the eyes of many aristocrats. Even a decade or so later, when Maud was long married and a fixture of the London social scene, Lord Curzon would complain of the inclusion of such 'new guns' at Lady Desborough's Taplow parties. It was a list that included the Oscar Wildes, the Asquiths, or the Cosquiths, as these two couples were dubbed, and 'Mr. and Mrs. Beerbohm Tree'.[21]

Men, of course, had long cavorted with actresses — indeed Violet's husband, the future Duke of Rutland, harboured a particular fondness for them and would father a love child with another Violet, Violet Vanbrugh. Throughout Maud's long career there would be many examples of aristocrats even marrying them; in 1913 Maud's friend the Duke of Manchester would write an article entitled 'Do Actresses Make Suitable Wives for Noblemen?' But Maud was not of that ilk, nor was she the destitute wretch as later portrayed in George Moore's sensational and sexually explicit *A Mummer's Wife*. First published in 1885, the novel was deemed so shocking by W. B. Yeats that he forbade his sister from reading it. Maud was determined not to fall into either category. Moreover, now that her formal studies were coming to an end, she was forced to make a decision about her future. She was determined above all to conduct herself with propriety and after some inner debate — she was still tempted by a Cambridge degree — decided on a career in theatre after all.

Notes to Chapter 1

1. This road was later demolished when Marylebone Railway Station was extended.
2. The Holts lived at Upper Baker Street at the time of their marriage in 1839. Subsequently they moved to 3 Wyndham Place, 21 South Bank Street, and Grove End Road. At the time of his death, William Holt was living at 4 Bristol Gardens, Maida Vale.
3. Maud Tree's unpublished manuscript 'Our Little Life' can be found in the Tree Family Archive at the Theatre Collection, University of Bristol (MBTC). See also 'Herbert and I', her account of their life together, written shortly after his death and published in Beerbohm 1924: 1–170. All quotations in this chapter concerning Maud's childhood are taken from 'Our Little Life', pp. 1–15.
4. Irene Vanbrugh writes of the 'low, two-story vicarage opening on to a simple but beautiful garden' (Vanbrugh 1948: 5). Similarly, Maud remembers 'a meandering garden, full of apple and pear trees' ('Our Little Life'). Marie Bancroft, born Effie Wilton, avoided any potential pitfalls in reliving a career that began in burlesque by offering a joint narrative written with her husband Sir Squire Bancroft. Only Ellen Terry is candid by saying hers will give 'a few hints — a few diffused part clues and indiscretions' (although even she cannot resist the description of her father's 'lovely face', an oak bureau, and sunsets of 'violet and primrose'). See Terry 1908: 4.
5. Bertha Floyd acted as Mrs Floyd or Floradyce.
6. Maud Tree, 'Our Little Life' (MBTC).
7. Maud would meet Alfred, Lord Tennyson in 1882 while staying with Mrs Lionel Tennyson, who was married to the poet's grandson.
8. Financial records held at Queen's College indicate that Emily Holt was responsible for Maud's school fees. This figure is calculated in terms of income value of a commodity. See Officer and Williamson 2010. It should be noted that historic conversions are complex depending on what is being measured, for example economic status, income value, or labour cost.
9. In *The Portrait of a Lady* Henry James described Isabel Archer as 'smooth to his general need of her as handled ivory to the palm' (James 1908: III, 11).
10. Tree inserted tableaux in five plays (*Henry IV, Part I, King John, Richard II, Henry VIII,* and *Julius Caesar*) of the sixteen revivals at His Majesty's Theatre. He labelled the setting for the first act of *A Midsummer Night's Dream* in Greek.
11. The legacy of classical sculpture and art in performance, whereby sculpture and drama are aesthetically linked, is further elaborated by Gail Marshall who draws a specific connection between the Greek classical era and the 'Victorian appropriation of the statuesque actress'. Examples abound: Viola Tree (Maud's eldest child), for example, is repeatedly described in statuary language (she was over six feet tall). See Marshall 1998: 170.
12. George Bernard Shaw in the *Saturday Review*, 1 June 1895, in Shaw 1993: II, 353–59.

13. Maud Tree, 'Our Little Life' (MBTC).
14. Ibid.
15. Grylls 1948: 21.
16. More works of art concerning the Civil War were produced than about any other period in British history. One hundred and seventy-five pictures of the War were hung in the Royal Academy between 1820 and 1900. See Richard 2005: 331. The play ran for 180 nights, and Irving would revive it many times with Ellen Terry playing Henrietta Maria.
17. Maud Tree, 'Our Little Life' (MBTC).
18. Ibid.
19. Norman Forbes-Robertson to Maud Tree, 23 May 1914 (MBTC 2).
20. See Lambert 1984: 12.
21. See Davenport-Hines 1988: 58. Herbert Asquith, though brilliant, was considered a self-made man. His wife, Margot Tennant was wealthy in her own right, but her father was a Scottish industrialist.

CHAPTER 2

❖

Miss Hellen Maud
1871–81

At eighteen, Maud was slender, fair and pretty, and a full-time teacher on the staff of the school, with every spare moment devoted to acting. She had also been one of the two models Sir Frank Dicksee (1853–1928), who taught drawing at Queen's College, used for his painting *Harmony*.[1] In the painting, 'Maud' is depicted at an organ dressed in the damask, medieval-inspired robes so favoured by the Pre-Raphaelites. Her bright hair is gathered loosely at her neck, the light appearing to shine straight through it. Beneath a stained-glass casement, a youth sprawls on the window seat beside her, resting his head in his hand and appearing to listen attentively.

During the decade she had lived in London the Pre-Raphaelite Brotherhood was not, however, the only reform movement to herald change, and by the end of it an economic boom would see the mass construction of railroads and new buildings across the globe. The world stage was also in the process of altering dramatically. Garibaldi had fought skirmishes with the French, and the outcome of the Franco-Prussian war, initiated in 1870, would become a factor in the genesis of the First World War. In America, General Custer had died along with 200 of his men at the Battle of Little Bighorn, and in Egypt the Suez Canal was opened to allow ships to travel between Europe and eastern Asia. Closer to home, Queen Victoria, now also Empress of India, was still on the throne (and would be for another twenty-five years), and Gladstone was the Liberal Prime Minister, but there was innovation in virtually every sphere. London and Australia were linked by telegraph at the same time that the Post Office introduced postcards and halfpenny postage stamps. Oxford established two new, women-only colleges — Somerville and Lady Margaret Hall. And although Maud now wore liberating culottes to ride her bicycle, women generally continued to wear restricting bustles consisting of a steel frame attached to the waist at the back while festooning drapery cascaded down the front. But these outward signs of propriety were about to be irrevocably shredded with the introduction of the Married Women's Property Act, which confirmed, at long last, that women might amongst other things possess property of their own.

Maud's first stab at independence was, if not to own property, then to move out of her brother William's house and lease rooms over a shop at 10 Orchard Street. Unlike George Moore's fictitious heroine, however, she did not consider living alone. Friendship with Violet Lindsay opened Maud's eyes to the privileged and lavish lifestyle of the aristocracy. It was a lifestyle that was to be further enhanced when Violet became engaged to Lord Henry Manners a year later. Moreover, as a future duchess, Violet had all the confidence of a beautiful, gifted woman who was soon to marry into one of the oldest (and wealthiest) families in the country. Most of all, Violet had the freedom to act in any way she chose while still keeping her reputation intact. The same did not apply to Maud, who had no great family name behind her, and already one sister (although she did not publicize the fact) had entered the still doubtful acting profession. She had seen how women who were not of noble birth might fare if their reputations were in any way tarnished. She was resolved that scandal would never cloud *her* name, and so for propriety's sake Maud also engaged a paid companion, a Mrs Newman. Earning her own money, living on her own, she was at last free to indulge her interests and tastes, while being ever cautious of drawing just the right amount of attention to herself. It is indicative of Maud's character that while always the first to align herself to new movements — she might use the recently formed Grosvenor Gallery Library, a private club popular with women who supported women's suffrage — she was not necessarily persuaded to change her allegiances.

By January 1881 reviews of Maud's acting were fulsome. With her knowledge of the language she was perfectly placed to play Andromache, in the original Greek, in *The Tale of Troy,* arranged by Professor C. T. Newton of the British Museum. Shortly after, appearing with the amateur group the Erratics, Maud was praised for her 'captivating presence' and 'good voice' in *Shadows* by the barrister-turned-playwright Sir Charles Young, who would achieve fame only a year before he died.[2] A couple of months later, in March, Maud played Olivia in H. G Wells's play *The Vicar of Wakefield,* in which *Era* of 12 March 1881 wrote of her performance:

> Characterized by a charm that was simply marvellous in an actress whose experience, we believe, has been limited thus far with some dozen appearances [...] we can have no hesitation in expressing the opinion that if she goes on as she has begun, Miss Helen Maude [*sic*] will become one of our most accomplished actresses.

It was not only theatre critics who were drawn to observe the young Miss Maude, as she was now known professionally. In the audience at St George's Hall one spring evening, was another aspiring actor who came to see her play Beatrice in *Much Ado About Nothing*. Maud first met Herbert Tree or Herbert Beerbohm, as he was known then, in 1878, shortly before he turned professional. At over six feet tall, with bright red hair, a prominent nose, and blue, pale-lashed eyes, Herbert had overcome paternal opposition to a stage career and abandoned a city desk for the amateur dramatic clubs so familiar to Maud: the Irrationals, the Bettertons, and the Philothespians. Realizing his son was not to be dissuaded, Julius Beerbohm told Herbert that acting was all very well if one reached 'the top of the tree'. By 1877 it appeared that Mr Beerbohm (not yet Tree) would do so. A lanky youth, 'almost sullen and not too proud to borrow an occasional half-crown from a waitress', Herbert appeared on the cover of the *Sporting and Dramatic News*. His skill at make-up and versatility as an actor were being praised, as was his 'grotesque eccentricity' (in the *Illustrated and Dramatic News* of 13 January 1878).

Not at all deterred by the alleged oddity of his character but if anything all the more smitten, Maud instantly switched her star-gazing of Irving in Grafton Street to Tree and the Garrick Club, where she knew him to be a member. However, over the next few years 'sightings' of Tree would be few and far between while he toured the provinces with the Bijou Comedy Company. Increasingly anxious to see him and equally emboldened by her own success, Maud not only asked Tree to come and see her in her next role (an invitation he declined owing to his own theatre engagement in Birmingham) but also asked him whether she was wise to be considering acting as a profession in the first place. He replied, though not immediately:

> My dear Miss Holt,
>   Don't go on the stage unless you feel you must. How are you? We shall meet in the autumn.
>   Yours sincerely,
>   H.B.T[3]

The autumn was still six months away and Maud was not idle. A drawing by Violet of Maud in 1882 (the year in which both women married) shows a slender woman with the frizzled hair known as 'Josephine Curls', a nipped-in waist and sporting the fashionable 'polonaise' apron draped over a frilly underskirt. Their histrionic discussions of clothes ('Mr. Cox is to be married,' Maud wrote to Violet, 'and I am going in [...] don't shriek an apple green bluish gown too lovely for words!') would give way to Violet's aesthetic dress sense when she became an active member of the Souls.[4]

In the meantime, Maud was preoccupied with college teaching and her next engagement. In W. S. Gilbert's three-act fairy comedy *The Palace of Truth* she played Princess Zeolide, in what was to be Gilbert's most successful work before his collaboration with Arthur Sullivan. By 1886, some four years later, the play had earned him £2,200 (approximately £2.4 million by today's standards), a small fortune for the time. It had been adapted from Madame Genlis's original *Le Palais de la verité* and explores the premise that complete honesty destroys both 'dangerous errors and sweet illusion'. Maud was praised in the *Stage* on 27 January 1882 for the fact that 'in every movement of her arms and hands there is grace and her poses are simply exquisite'. The production was a triumph, and also led to a lifelong friendship with Gilbert, who thereafter addressed Maud in correspondence as 'NKL' (Nice Kind Lady), while she him as 'NKG' (Nice Kind Gentleman).

The autumn came and went, and it was not until the winter that Herbert Tree finally visited Maud. After their initial encounter they re-met at a fancy dress party, and Tree's interest was once again piqued as much by Maud's pretty face as by a genuine curiosity to discover whether or not she could act. Tree began visiting Maud in her rooms in Orchard Street and, chaperoned by the redoubtable Mrs Newman, they discussed poetry and in particular Edward Rose's one-act tragedy play, *Merely Players* — a rendition of *Pagliacci* — in which Tree hoped to play Pantaleone. By

Fig. 2.1. 'Maud Tree (in the Nineties)' (Pearson 1988, [n.p])

the time they first appeared together at the Prince of Wales's Theatre on 27 January 1882, in a play by Mr J. Sturgis called *Apples*, Tree had evidently decided that Maud could act after all. Less than a month later he was starring in *The Colonel* and had asked her to be his wife. 'I feel rather light-headed,' he wrote to Maud, 'I suppose it's the excitement and I have been laughing on the stage most disgracefully'.[5]

Tree's large cast of friends and acquaintances were already well known to Maud, but his immediate family now embraced her with open arms. Herbert's youngest brother, only a small boy at the time, remembered Maud with the goddess good looks of the age and as being so charming and amusing because she went out of her way to entertain them.[6] It was this attention towards both young and old and an ability to deal lightly with disappointment and heartbreak that made Maud especially popular. Many of the friendships she made at this time would sow the seeds for future connections, and she was never shy of calling in favours. But her hospitality and generosity were genuine, as was her loyalty to both her family and that of Herbert. She was particularly good with elderly people, and many of her most lasting friendships were with the artists and playwrights who were already old men by the time she knew them. Edward Burne-Jones, for one, was a devoted admirer from the moment he knew she was prepared to travel a great distance by carriage, from London to Brighton, on learning he was unwell. On missing her he wrote dejectedly:

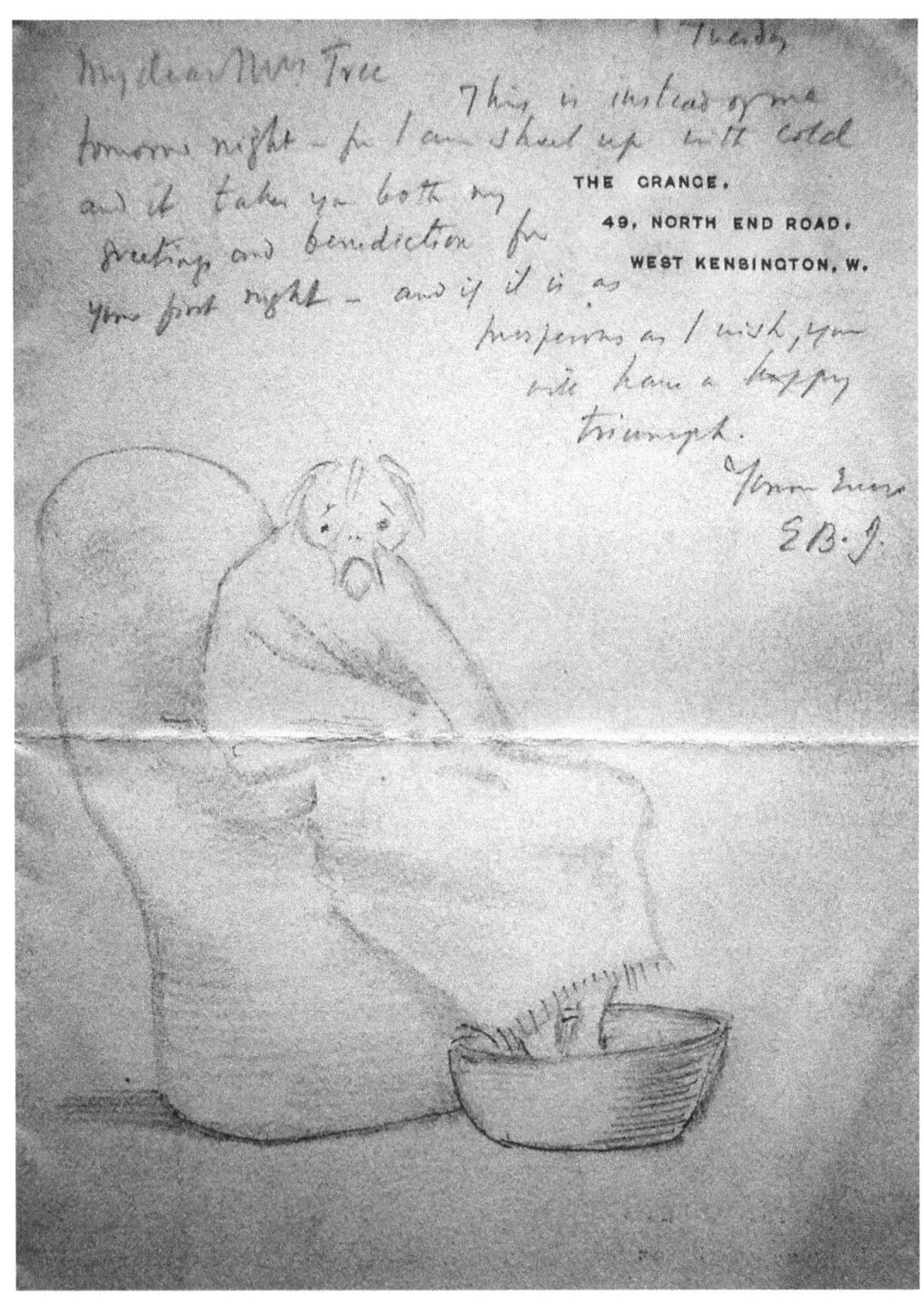

FIG. 2.2. Letter from Edward Burne-Jones to Maud Tree, undated (MBTC/000121)

> What a beautiful but cruel sight I have seen this very minute past my window — you driving past — driving swiftly past as if the last thought on earth was to brighten the little house with your presence [...] Now I shall send a messenger with this to call at every hotel in Brighton for I don't know where you are.[7]

But being so popular with the opposite sex meant she was always immensely careful with women of her own, sending them little gifts and later complimentary theatre tickets to avoid any potential friction. She evaded female rivalry in particular by being self-deprecating. In response to a compliment about her hair she replied, 'sweet of you to say it's mine'. Later her ability to make light of her own misfortune only made women admire her courage all the more. When questioned, for example, about the decade-long gap between the births of her first and second children, she responded that by then she had learned 'to wait in line'. But nor did she miss an opportunity to reveal her own worldliness. Once, protesting at Somerset Maugham's early departure from a party, she said:

> 'But surely, Willie, you can at least stay and have coffee with us?'
> 'No, Maud, I h-have to g-go to bed early — it's the only way I can hope to k-keep my youth.'
> 'But then why didn't you bring him?' replied Maud archly. 'We love those kind of people!'[8]

Maud was no stranger to large families, with the eldest sibling often considerably older than the youngest, as was the case in her own family. However, the large age gap in the Beerbohm household, as Maud soon discovered, was explained by somewhat unconventional circumstances. Of Lithuanian, German, and Dutch extraction, Herbert's father, Julius Ewald Beerbohm was born in Memel and educated in Schnepfeuthal in central Germany, arriving in London to become a corn merchant when he was twenty. He first married, at the age of forty, a pretty, but chronically absent-minded, woman ten years his junior called Constantia Draper. Family reminiscences testify to Constantia's charming feyness — she liked to wander the streets, her shoelaces undone — and was much too disorganized to manage a household, the care of which she left to her younger sister Eliza. Julius and Constantia's union produced three boys, Ernest, Herbert, and Julius and one daughter, Constance. When Constantia died at the age of twenty-nine, Julius promptly married his dead wife's sister Eliza. As at the time such an act was illegal under English law, Julius married Eliza in Switzerland, returning to England to father a further five children, of whom three survived. The eldest of this second union, Agnes Mary, became a friend of Walter Sickert and is the model for his 1908 picture *Fancy Dress,* now in the Athenaeum. Dora became a nun, and the youngest, Henry Maximilian, born in 1872 and thus only ten years old when Herbert and Maud married, would grow up to be the essayist and caricaturist Max Beerbohm.[9]

Every Sunday, once Herbert and Maud became engaged, was spent lunching with the Beerbohms, who lived in Claricarde Gardens. Supper, however, was spent at the home, literally opposite, of the publisher-cum-amateur actor Edmund Routledge and his equally large brood of five sons and three daughters. Maud had already met Edmund when he played Benedict to her Beatrice in the production of *Much Ado About Nothing* Tree had seen her perform in at St George's Hall, but now she had a chance to observe Tree, as he romped with Edmund's children. Throughout his life Tree would express an innocent, inordinate love of children and look to their lack of inhibition as a guide to his own acting, rather than any formal acting training. Max for one revered Tree. From the age of four, the tall red-haired man held an aura of glamour for the young boy and now he saw Maud in equally heroic terms. As the couple disappeared off to dinner at the Routledges, Max Beerbohm remembered being shocked and awed by this in equal measure. Dinner on a Sunday night was an uncommon practice in itself, but Max being sent to bed could see the lights on in the house opposite and — as well as envious of the grown-ups who could stay up late and fascinated by the likes of Oscar Wilde, James Whistler, and William Gladstone — passed through its front door.[10] It was at these Sunday gatherings that Maud also met the exotic writers, actors, and artists who constituted Tree's set.

Love of theatre was what united all visitors to the Routledges, but Tree's passion for Shakespeare in particular was sparked, he would tell Maud, by seeing Ellen Terry as Portia in Squire and Mrs Bancroft's 1875 production of *The Merchant of Venice*. He wrote in his diary that he could not understand how she 'could smile so naturally'.[11] From then on he spent every spare moment rehearsing in plays and travelling to see other professional actors. Soon he could ask Ellen Terry how it was that she achieved such 'naturalness', as Terry would be a frequent Sunday visitor, as would Clement Scott, Dion Boucicault, Hamilton Aidé, Lawrence Alma-Tadema, and George Alexander, with whom Tree would soon share lodgings and who like Tree had shunned a City job for the theatre. But while Maud would become close friends with Ellen Terry — indeed Terry would become godmother to Maud's eldest daughter — she was less enthusiastic about Terry's lover and father to *her* children, E. W. Godwin.

While enthralled by the theatrical world in which she was now involved, Maud never lost sight of her place in it, nor of the importance of safeguarding her reputation. 'A woman's reputation,' says de Neste, a character in *Caesar's Wife*, a play Maud would produce, direct and act in some years later, 'how precious and yet how fragile. It is a thing as light as thistledown as lightly to be scattered by the breath of the night wind, one breath and then piteous bareness'.[12] It was the possibility of this 'piteous bareness' that would most terrify her and every actress hoping to continue in long-term employment. Although fictitious examples abounded of fallen women, Maud needed to look no further than the example made flesh of their own Ellen Terry, who was virtually banished to the country to bring up her young children once her affair with Godwin was made public. By the time she did re-emerge, some six years later, it would be alone and without Godwin. Despite this tremulous start, Terry was considered a darling of the nation, although not to the extent that she did not have to wait some fifty years to be created a Dame, while Irving, Bancroft, Alexander, and Tree were all knighted for services to theatre much earlier in their careers, and despite publicized affairs.

Maud took it upon herself, therefore, to do everything in her power to enhance her family's reputation — both that of the one she had come from and the one she would create. In her memoirs Maud would have us believe that not everyone in her family embraced her impending marriage in the spirit that Herbert's did. She claims to have been nervous of her brother William's reaction to the notion of her marrying an actor — especially an actor with 'frayed cuffs'.[13] Given that according to her earlier recollections the entire family loved theatre, that indeed it was the older sisters who were responsible for her theatre outings in the first place, and that furthermore by the time Maud married, sister Bertha had already been employed at the Lyceum for some time, it seems a little odd that William should have been so opposed to the marriage. Eagerly recording William's disapproval, however, is part of the carefully constructed narrative Maud would promulgate in order to elevate her family's standing, while at the same time distancing it from a profession that still carried negative connotations.[14] In her embellished memoir even the desire to act at all is explained by the Greek word — *diakomodisi* or imitation. She goes to some lengths to explain that all children have the 'histrionic gift', telling us that only 'by imitation does it walk and speak'.[15]

It was with similar conviction that Maud tackled Herbert over his friendship with 'the wicked Earl', as E. W. Godwin was known to his friends, whose amorous affairs were as notorious as was his fondness for donning a large black hat and cloak.[16] But nor could Godwin be easily ignored. The architect-turned-theatre-impresario had designed costumes for Mrs Bateman's 1880 *Otello* (sister Bertha, it will be remembered, was employed by Mrs Bateman), and in founding the Costume Society (of which Herbert had recently become a member) was now consultant and textile designer for Liberty of London. He was also, when Maud first knew him, in the process of conducting a highly indiscreet affair with Ellen Terry. Maud was emphatic that if he loved her, Herbert would renounce this friendship. She told him that her older sister Emmie (who after all spent most of her time with a future duchess) was especially shocked to hear that Tree frequented such company. Prompted by Emmie, Maud now wrote to Tree:

> I have no sympathy with the Costume Society and I am quite opposed to the idea of your engaging in anything that occupies you the greater part of the day. These are minor considerations, however, compared with the intense objection I have to your being engaged in any scheme whatsoever in which you work hand and glove — with Mr. Godwin.

In case Herbert was not prepared to comply she threatened to continue working at Queen's College (which she knew he hated) unless he gave Godwin up. 'I warn you,' she ended, 'you will have to choose between him and me'.[17]

Emmie, it transpired, was not just troubled by Herbert's friendship with Godwin but by Herbert himself, and not least because he was an actor. She sensed disquiet in him and, as with Godwin, an insatiable need to be flattered by women. Her own experience of theatre acquainted her with the pitfalls of marrying into the acting profession. Unwell, Emmie had recently spent time with Herbert and Maud in Aix-les-Bains, where it was hoped that the warmer climate would restore her to health.

Herbert had shown Emmie nothing but kindness, but ultimately her reservations stemmed from the fact, as she told Maud, that Herbert would 'necessarily belong to the Public and not to the home'.[18] It was this observation that would prove the most perspicacious. But if Tree belonged 'to the public', as Emmie put it, he was paradoxically fiercely opposed to the notion that Maud should. 'In regards to your going on the stage,' he had initially written after they appeared together in a one-act play at his parents' home, 'my mind is still filled with doubts'.[19]

Maud's mind was not. If anything, Tree's opposition now to Maud's working at all crystallized much that was unclear and they began quarrelling in earnest as much about her career as about his friendship with Godwin. 'I shall very certainly keep on a great deal of my teaching,' she retorted, 'This I think only the sensible thing to do'. After all he was busy in the evening so why should she twiddle her thumbs waiting for him to finish at the theatre? '*I must be alone at night*,' she wrote to him defiantly, 'I need not be alone in the daytime and shall be really glad, as you know, not to lose my work entirely'.[20] Tree was astounded by her wilfulness. 'I absolutely *forbid* you to take up your college work,' he wrote by return. 'I wish you on no account to take it up again, and certainly I think your threat a somewhat ungenerous proceeding'.[21] The matter was unresolved. 'Possibly you have written in temper,' he wrote the next day in between rehearsals, '*I* don't like you when you act like this — it is not like your own self'. But Tree had underestimated Maud and the matter remained unresolved, with each one wanting the last word. 'Of course you are my first consideration,' he wrote to her later the next day:

> And I would never expose you to anything to which you should not be exposed — you know I love you too well. It so happens that I have avoided Godwin since I have been back except to meet him in business matters. I did not mean that I should devote all my afternoons to business as you threaten to. Maud, I hope you will be sorry for this [...] I send you back your letter, for I don't like to keep it and I don't like to tear it up — but you will do so, will you not? You have grieved me. — I shall telegraph you tomorrow to retract what you have said in regard to College work.[22]

The following morning Herbert wrote again:

> My dearest Maud,
>   I wrote the enclosed during last night's rehearsal, and — although I was very excited at the time — I shall let the letter go as it is. The reflections of the morning leave my mind unchanged, and I am going to telegraph you this morning that the College scheme is out of the question — You understand me, I mean this. I fancy I know the source whence your sister had heard such damaging reports in regard to G [...] But G. has been in many ways a very good friend to me — and I should not like to actually hurt his feelings by 'cutting' him in a heartless manner — you understand me. — Maud, I expect you to allow me to have a certain authority over your actions — or endless misunderstandings may arise — I am to be the breadwinner not you — I should not like you to further worry yourself with my work — and if you once set this precedent, there is no knowing where your whims may lead you to! Now let the matter drop.[23]

Maud's response was to return Herbert's engagement ring. For two weeks Tree raged at her interfering friends and relations, although the urge to make a pun of it was irresistible. 'A little less than kin and less than kind' was required.[24] Meanwhile Maud 'gloried' in his grief, but not for too long. At length one of his letters seemed to hit home. It arrived by hansom and she promptly hopped into the cab, returning to Hampstead to see him. Soon everything was back to where it was before their rift. She continued working at Queen's College and he at the theatre. Maud assured her 'darling heart' of her love and that she thought of him 'every hour of the day' — hours that were, as a result, full of 'buttercups' and 'sunshine'.[25] Herbert melted instantly, convinced too that he would have *his* way. Four days before they married he wrote a final letter and having 'no stamps' promised to leave it at Orchard Street. 'My darling love,' he wrote, 'I feel quite serious tonight and shall think of you and pray for you so nicely tonight... I will *try* to be a good husband.'[26]

Notes to Chapter 2

1. *Harmony* was exhibited at the Royal Academy in 1872 and bought by the Chantrey Bequest on behalf of the nation for £367. See Dibdin 1905: 4–6. It is now (not on display) at Tate Britain. See also Grylls 1948: 21–22.
2. Sir Charles Lawrence Young (1839–87) was a barrister and playwright. *Jim the Penman* ran for almost a year in 1886, starring Herbert Tree, and was performed in New York, Sydney, and London. See Young 1881.
3. Herbert Tree to Maud Holt, 22 January 1882 (HBT/RA/420).
4. Maud Holt to Violet Lindsay, 8 October 1881 (by kind permission of His Grace the Duke of Rutland).
5. Herbert Tree to Maud Holt, [7 February 1882] (HBT/RA/420).
6. See Cecil 1985: 22.
7. Edward Burne-Jones to Maud Tree, [n.d.] (MBTC/000121).
8. As quoted in Moffat 2004: 69.
9. Max Beerbohm (1872–1956), best known for his novel *Zuleika Dobson* published in 1911, was therefore not only Herbert's half-brother but also first cousin.
10. Cecil 1985: 19–20.
11. Ibid.: 11.
12. *Which?*, promptbook for Marquis de Neste (HBT/000131, I.1, p. 4).
13. See Beerbohm 1924: 6–7.
14. Bertha's daughter Gwendolyn would also enter the profession in due course, becoming Lewis Waller's manager. Lewis Waller (1860–1915), born William Waller Lewis.
15. Maud Tree, 'Our Little Life' (MBTC).
16. See Jopling 1925: 289.
17. Maud Holt to Herbert Beerbohm, 28 August 1882 (HBT/R4).
18. Beerbohm 1924: 7.
19. Herbert Beerbohm to Maud Holt, 8 May 1882 (HBT/RA/420).
20. Maud Holt to Herbert Beerbohm, 28 August 1882 (HBT/R4).
21. Herbert Beerbohm to Maud Holt, 30 August 1882 (HBT/R4).
22. Ibid.
23. Herbert Tree to Maud Holt, [1 September 1882] (HBT/RA/420).
24. Beerbohm 1924: 7.
25. Ibid.: 8.
26. Herbert Tree to Maud Holt, [12 September 1882] (HBT/RA/420).

CHAPTER 3

Mrs Beerbohm Tree
1882–87

Maud and Herbert were married on 16 September 1882 — the day chosen by Maud for being Emmie's birthday. Despite the extended holiday in Aix-les-Bains, Emmie never fully recovered her health and would die four months later. The previous summer Herbert's parents had rented Thurnham Court, an Elizabethan manor near Maidstone, famous for having been leased in former times by Byron so as to be near his mistress Lady Oxford. Staying with his parents that August, Herbert wrote to Maud that he very much wished them to be married there, as she would, as it were, 'issue to the church from the bosom' of his family. Maud did in fact spend the eve of her marriage at Thurnham Court, as Herbert was acting and could only get down to Kent on the morning of the wedding. She appears not, however, to have remembered the literary connection associated with the house, referring to it only vaguely as 'a sweet house [...] in whose garden there happened to be a church'.[1] Max Beerbohm was Herbert's best man, and at the age of ten was so excited by his role that he turned up over an hour early to await his brother under a bower of flowers that were, according to the gardener, 'not awful grand but what you might call rustic'.[2] It was a wedding Max was to remember (in greater detail than Maud) all his life, not least for the syllabubs served at the wedding breakfast and Herbert's witty repartee along the lines of 'And Syllabub, the son of Syllabub, reigned in his stead'.[3]

Maud did remember, however, the contrast in their moods in the days leading up to their marriage and indeed on the day itself. Herbert had written to her a few days before, 'only be to me as you are now — and I *know* we shall be happy'.[4] What Maud had not quite appreciated, as she soon discovered, was 'the unguessed, ungauged depths', as she described it, of his temperament, and how opposed to her acting he really was. She considered his resistance nominal, certain that she would win him over. Her great friend Violet Lindsay was suffering equal resistance from her new husband Henry, a fact that only served to strengthen the bond between them. 'Henry is loathsome,' Violet wrote Maud, 'I want to draw and he wants to prevent it'.[5]

Maud considered their responses, wrongly as it turned out, to be of little consequence. She had resigned her teaching job at Queen's College, but more from a desire to concentrate on her acting than to please Herbert. She was also busy finding a home in which they could entertain their growing number of friends —

Comyns Carr (whose wife Alice would design the famous Beetle dress worn by Ellen Terry as Lady Macbeth), Herman Vezin, Claude Ponsonby, and Hamilton Aidé, to name but a few. Maud desired a backdrop against which she and Herbert could dazzle. For the moment the quarrel over her working seemed to have dissipated, besides which in the honeymoon period that followed they were both preoccupied with their work and in love. Indeed Maud wrote to Violet Lindsay, herself soon to be married, that she was 'an old married person in a bonnet', and how fond she was of her new husband, 'I can't tell you how dear and lovely he is — I love him more and more'.[6]

By the time Maud appeared four months later in her first professional stage role in *Sweethearts* at the Gaiety Theatre, however, the old tensions between husband and wife had resurfaced. The Beerbohm Trees (as they were now known) had moved from temporary rooms they had been sharing with sister Bertha in Burlington Street to set up home at 4 Wilton Street. Of her performance as Jenny Northcott, a role formerly associated with Mrs Bancroft, the *Graphic* of 3 February 1883 was encouraging: 'Her face and figure are well adapted for the stage and her performance generally was one of much promise'. Tree was not. 'There is so much else you could do,' he said witheringly. But Maud was not deterred. She was earning real money — £10 a week, which given that the starting salary of an actor averaged £2 was more than respectable, although much of it, as she confessed in 'Herbert and I', was spent on hansoms and flowers, 'little suppers... parties, music, flights by late Saturday night trains to the country or the sea'.[7] She was also busier than ever. She once famously quipped that she never appeared in a role she could not learn in an evening, and now the parts came fast and varied. In the same theatre a few months later she was Mrs Stern in *Knowledge*, followed swiftly three weeks after that by Olivia in *Twelfth Night*. At the Globe on 8 September 1883, and almost a year since she was married, Maud played Barbara Nugent in *Elsie*.

Elsie was a curtain raiser to a play in which Herbert was acting called *The Glass of Fashion*, opposite the comic actress Lottie Venne, and as such it posed him no real threat. Some three weeks later, however, on 27 September 1883, Maud appeared in *The Millionaire* at the Court Theatre, in what was to be her first real success. She took fastidious care in researching her roles, and turning to literature for inspiration she found it in Wilkie Collins's red-haired adventuress, Miss Gwilt, from his sensational novel *Armadale*. Its heroine, according to the *Spectator* of 9 June 1866, was said to be 'a woman fouler than the refuse in the street'. In donning a red wig Maud did more than 'startle' Claude Ponsonby, who wrote to congratulate her: 'The absolute realism with which you invested this psychological curiosity completely carried one away'. He went on to say:

> The slightest suspicion of stageyness in your asides & soliloquies, or the falling short of a grain in your intimation of the all powerful [sic] influences of the love which you felt for Streightly, would have gone far to ruin the piece = [sic] for upon your shoulders rested the chief weight. You came through the ordeal unscathed: & by the great naturalness (if I may use the word) of your acting at times, & at other moments by the polished act which you used to hide the black side of your character from the world, you have made a great success.[8]

Herbert was less enthralled. Reading press reviews in the morning papers, he said to her, 'I hope it doesn't mean that you will be more famous than I! Because I couldn't have that'.⁹

Maud dismissed Herbert's petulant comment, recognizing his professional jealousy for what it was. Besides which, she was more than distracted by their recent house move to Cheyne Walk, a stone's throw from the Oscar Wildes, A. K. Moore, and W. S. Gilbert. As a hostess, she was fast coming into her own, organizing supper parties for the leading figures in theatre of the day. Her soirées were always generous and well-catered, and if the food was not cooked on sight she sent out to the Carlton Hotel for sides of salmon or ham. The decor was original (although she often had to borrow cash from her sister-in-law Constance, not always paying her back in kind but with the odd Sheraton chair), and guests now flocked to the house, especially after seeing Herbert in *The Private Secretary,* Charles Hawtrey's adaptation from a German farce. This, with *Charley's Aunt*, were the two most popular shows on the stage at the time. It was also the first big hit of Herbert's career and due in part to Maud's quick action. Herbert, though later credited with creating the ridiculous character of the Rev. Robert Spalding, had been appalled at having to play such a burlesque-type creature. To begin with the play appeared to fail, until the evening Herbert decided to wear a blue ribbon in his button-hole. (At the time this was the emblem worn by teetotal fanatics.) Maud, watching from the wings, tore a strip from her blouse, dashed to dip it in a pot of blue paint and presented the badge just as Herbert was to enter on stage. For some reason the audience found this hilarious and from then on the show played to a full house.

If Herbert revelled in his new-found success, Maud's was short lived. In her next play, a three-act comedy called *Margery's Lovers* by Brandon Matthews, the four-months pregnant Maud played the beautiful, young, innocent convent-bred Margery Blackburn in what was described as the 'weakest, dullest and most soul dispiriting play' by a man who 'can't write'. In it the heroine was said to be a 'mere walking lady and not good enough for Mrs. Beerbohm Tree' (*New York Times,* 29 February 1887). But a month later she was on more familiar territory at the Prince's Theatre playing in Tree's one-act play *Six and Eightpence.*

It was a dry, hot summer and on 17 July 1883 she gave birth to their daughter Viola. A few weeks later Maud, a nurse, and baby travelled to Ramsgate, while Tree stayed in London playing the audacious Italian spy Paolo Macari in Hugh Conway's dramatic thriller *Called Black*. His subtle, cynical interpretation, coming so quickly after playing the comical cleric Spalding, was the talk of the town and the play ran for months.

The Trees were enchanted with their baby daughter. Viola would always be especially close to them both. Herbert in particular was delighted with her wit, examples of which he carefully recorded in his diaries. For the moment, Maud was content to nurse her baby by the sea, though she missed Herbert. 'Oh darling one,' she wrote, 'I do wish you were here. I do miss you so.' But there was something she missed just as much. 'I do feel the not acting,' she wrote to Violet Lindsay:

> But it is far better not to act at all than only sometimes [*sic*] & I can bear it all

right if I keep away from the theatre & don't see the paint or smell the gas or hear the applause.[10]

And if Herbert harboured any secret hopes that motherhood might put an end to Maud's acting ambition, he was soon disappointed. If anything, Maud was more resolved than ever to return to the stage just as soon as possible.

After Christmas spent at Belvoir Castle with Violet, Maud returned to London to prepare for her next part, as Thordisa in the stage version of Herman Charles Merivale's *The White Pilgrim*, which had been published less than two years earlier. A contemporary of Swinburne at Balliol College, Oxford, Merivale was Permanent Under-Secretary of the India Office, a barrister, and dramatist, and soon to become a close friend of Maud. This 'poetical play' necessitated the kind of rhetorical recitation at which Maud excelled, and the *Theatre* of 1883 for one, recognized her 'intelligent and pleasing' interpretation in what it otherwise considered to be a 'very monotonous role'. But it was the artists and members of the 'Souls' whom Maud met as a result of her involvement with the Merivale play that made the experience invaluable. It also typified Maud's knack for identifying an emerging talent and aligning herself with it. Herman Vezin, the American actor who played Sigurd in *Pilgrim,* was a voice and elocution expert who had helped Tree on occasion. Once again, the experience of acting together would only reinforce their friendship.[11] Merivale himself would not only become a friend but also prove to be an invaluable ally and critic. In turn, he was a close friend not only of Thackeray, W. S. Gilbert, and Dickens but also of Lord Salisbury, who would become Prime Minister some four months later in June 1885. Henry Manners (Violet's husband) was his Private Secretary.

Thus the Beerbohm Trees were becoming increasingly visible on the social circuit and moving in the same circles as politicians, writers, and members of the aristocracy. But they were not mere figures of curiosity as popular actors. Merely by dint of being married, Maud earned the respectability not accorded, for example, to her good friend Ellen Terry or Violet Vanbrugh. Women of the stage enjoyed a perceived freedom, but domesticity was still viewed as incompatible with it. They were generally expected to give up their work when they married. The heroine of *Through the Stage Door,* published the year before, confesses to being 'a hundred times happier' on the stage and that giving up her profession on marrying had been 'an immense sacrifice'.[12] Maud could clearly do both, and well. She was graceful, vivacious, and cultured. Furthermore, and whether Herbert cared to admit it or not, Maud's new friends had tremendous influence. These new friends now flocked to plays in which both Trees appeared, while the press usefully advertised the fact by reporting *their* attendance.

At this time, once again through Violet's Soul 'gang', Maud met another woman whose friendship would open other doors and with whose family Maud's would have links far into the future. Margot Tennant was one of five daughters born to the fabulously wealthy entrepreneur Charles Tennant, whose energy and boldness typified the Victorian self-made man. Margot and her sisters were more than cultured and charming, they were formidably well-educated and gifted, being able to draw, paint, and play musical instruments to an accomplished degree. They had inherited their father's magnetic character and were said, with their colourful personalities, not only to have erupted onto London society but also to have changed it.[13] Together with his wealth and their exuberance, the Tennant household was a mecca for politicians, artists, and friends of all ages. Margot's elder sister Charlotte was married to the rich and fashionable Baron Ribblesdale, while Laura was engaged to Alfred Lyttleton, later MP for Warwick and Colonial Secretary. The latter on impulse invited Maud to their wedding, at which Gladstone was an honoured guest and at which he made a speech. From then on Maud and the Tennant sisters were close friends and became even closer when Margot married the future Prime Minister, Herbert Asquith, a decade later.[14]

Seemingly, there was nothing to deter Maud. Socially she was a success and she used every contact to further promote herself professionally. A month after starring in *The White Pilgrim* she played Marie Graham in *In His Power,* and having cultivated Arthur Pinero's friendship she was his first choice as Charlotte (alongside Herbert as Mr Poskett) in *The Magistrate,* which opened at the Court Theatre in August 1885. That autumn Maud embarked on a very different journey, setting sail with W. S. Gilbert and his wife for Egypt and leaving the one-year-old Viola in Herbert's care. Even by today's standards, leaving a small child with her father while the mother holidays for over a month might be considered somewhat audacious, but Herbert does not appear to have protested. It was no coincidence that, on her return, Maud's next role should be in Gilbert's *Engaged,* in which she played Belinda Trehern. The Gilberts and Trees were becoming very close friends indeed, to the extent that Herbert once urged Viola to greet 'Gillie' with a kiss. For 'Daddy loves Gillie' Herbert told her. The much-quoted response was, 'Then Daddy kiss Gillie'.[15]

The next six months were worked at a frantic pace for both Trees, and then, in May 1886, came an opportunity that, despite her antipathy towards Edward Godwin, Maud could not refuse. In England the fascination for the ancient world had not abated, nor had the challenge to perform Greek theatre in as historically correct a manner as possible. W. S. Gilbert's *Pygmalion and Galatea* had recently taken London by storm, launching the career of the American-born starlet Mary Anderson. In Gilbert's quest for authenticity the painter Sir Lawrence Alma-Tadema was hired to arrange the folds of Anderson's gown in the proper Greek fashion. Edward Godwin, similarly stimulated, had earlier in the year published an article entitled 'The Greek House According to Homer' for *Nineteenth Century,* but it was the play that he subsequently produced, directed, and managed that enabled him to 'transcend archaeological realism'.[16] Maud may not have liked the man, but she could not deny his passion for Greek art or painstaking attention to historical research.

For this latest venture, Godwin hired Hengler's Circus in Argyll Street, not only to stage John Todhunter's *Helena of Troas* but also to recreate an entire Greek theatre within that space. Influenced by recent discoveries — the real theatre of Dionysus had been uncovered on the Acropolis in 1865 — and by, amongst other sources, a plan of a Greek theatre in J. P. Mahaffy's *History of Greek Literature*, Godwin used

Fig. 3.1. Maud as Oenone in *Helena in Troas*, sketches taken at the Greek Theatre, Hengler's Circus (*Queen: The Lady's Newspaper*, 5 June 1886)

the circular performance arena to create an amphitheatre-like environment, laying tiles in geometric patterns over the boarded-up sandy pit and mounting his own altar to Dionysus, from which a fifteen-strong Greek chorus would sing.[17] The women of the chorus, choreographed by Louise Jopling (who also acted in the play), struck a series of attitudes and poses so that even when resting they appeared like a frieze lifted from the Parthenon. More importantly, the chorus added an innovative dimension for the audience: forming sculptural groups within the arena, they were thus fully integrated with the audience.

With his experience of working with textiles at Liberty's and the knowledge gleaned from decorating private homes, Godwin was able to ensure that the costumes were also as authentic as possible. He made numerous detailed drawings of figures he had seen on Greek vases depicting *The Iliad* and *The Odyssey*. Unbleached linen, gauzes embroidered in red, and gold and rainbow-coloured silks were used for the costumes. The chorus wore white sleeveless tunics, their unbound hair held in place by gold fillets. Maud, dressed in misty grey silk, played the river nymph Oenone: she too wore a gold headband, from which flowed a delicate gauze veil. Herbert, as Paris, was majestic in a red chiton belted at the waist. Hermann Vezin, who last starred with Maud in *Pilgrim*, played Priam. Robed in red, with black sleeves picked out in gold stars and a grey mantel with a himation of blue, he carried a long white staff and sported an elaborate scarlet headdress. Alma Murray played Helen, while Constance Wilde, in what would be her only ever stage appearance, was one of her handmaidens.[18] The props were marble, the distant hills purple, and a golden statue of Aphrodite shone out against the painted blue Hellespont. Notwithstanding this visual splendour the plot was unexciting, and Maud provided the only dramatic note to the performance when she leapt shrieking from the battlements. But the audience and the critics were entranced. On 29 May 1886, the *Illustrated Sporting and Dramatic News* published a cartoon of Godwin as ringmaster, while a week later *Queen* produced a series entitled 'Sketches'.

Members of the audience included members of the Royal Family, Henry Irving, Ellen Terry, Oscar Wilde, Frederick Leighton, and of course Alma-Tadema, who would in turn design painstaking sets and costumes for many of Tree's later productions. *Helena in Troas* generated more reviews than any other of Godwin's works and was examined exhaustively by experts and laymen alike. It was, as Wilde declared, sublime, for 'the secret of its beauty was the perfect correspondence of form and matter, the delicate equilibrium of spirit and sense'.[19]

No sooner had Godwin's play come to an end than Maud and Herbert once again played an onstage couple — Sir Peter and Lady Teazle — in F. R. Benson's Bournemouth tour with *The School for Scandal*. On alternate nights they played *Othello* with Tree as Iago, Mrs Benson as Desdemona, and Maud as Portia. Tree was offered half-profits for the week and a guarantee of £10. The only setback that summer was Tree's crippling stage fright, despite once more having engaged Herman Vezin for extra coaching. Herbert in his nervousness was once found in his dressing room nibbling on a stick of greasepaint while attempting to cover his face with a lamb chop. But perhaps there was every reason to be nervous, especially when performing Shakespeare. Throughout his acting career Herbert's critics found particular fault with his peculiarity of speech (some called it almost a lisp) and a voice considered too weak to 'adequately convey the beauty and meaning of Shakespeare's words' (*New York Times*, 31 January 1895).[20] Shaw went further, stating that 'Tree wrote plays of his own which he attributed to Shakespeare, manufacturing unlimited stage business' and 'spoke blank verse unintelligibly'.[21] In between performances Maud sat with Mrs Benson and Viola on the beach, composing odes to her new puppy.

If the summer months had passed at an accelerated pace there was no let-up with the coming of autumn. The Trees were back in London after a particularly frantic period when Tree (still dressed as Iago) would travel from Oxford after a matinée of *Othello* to play the Baron in Charles Young's *Jim the Penman* at a London evening performance.[22] (One of Maud's very first amateur performances had been in Sir Charles Young's *Shadows*.) Maud, meanwhile, played Miss Moxon in another of Pinero's farces, *The Hobby Horse*. The other real husband-and-wife duo, William and Madge Kendal, who also managed the St James's Theatre together with John Hare, played Mr and Mrs Spencer Jermyn. The play premiered on 23 October 1886 and ran for 109 performances.

As the year drew to an end, Maud once again appeared with the Kendals, who also directed, in her former English teacher Tom Taylor's semi-historical drama *Lady Clancarty,* about the Assassination Plot of 1696. With costumes designed by Marcus Stone the lavish production was 'one of the most successful' plays 'offered by the joint managers'.[23] Some critics went further. Although first produced some twenty years before, it had, according to an article that appeared in the *New York Times*, enjoyed 'no success in England or America' until the St James's production of 1887. The characters were said in the *New York Times* of 25 December 1894 to 'avoid most of the exaggerations of melodramatic people' and the part of Lady Betty Noel required the wit and 'life to action' that were beginning to distinguish Maud's acting.

Notes to Chapter 3

1. Beerbohm 1924: 9.
2. Cecil 1985: 22, and also Beerbohm 1924: 9.
3. Cecil 1985: 23.
4. Herbert Tree to Maud Holt, [12 September 1882] (HBT/RA/420).
5. Violet Lindsay to Maud Tree, [n.d.] (MBTC 6).
6. Maud Tree to Violet Lindsay, [4 October 1882] (by kind permission of His Grace the Duke of Rutland).
7. Beerbohm 1924: 21.
8. Claude Ponsonby to Maud Tree, [28 September 1883] (MBTC).
9. Beerbohm 1924: 20.
10. Maud Tree to Herbert Tree, [n.d.] (HBT/RA/420); Maud Tree to Violet Lindsay, [n.d.] (by kind permission of His Grace the Duke of Rutland).
11. Herman Vezin would also play King Priam in *Helena in Troas*.
12. Jay 1883: 20 & 26.
13. Lambert 1984: 17.
14. Viola Tree would enjoy a close friendship with Herbert Asquith and later appear in films directed by his son 'Puffin'. Margot purchased Maud's house *The Wharf* in 1911. Through Maud, the Asquiths became friends with the Duke and Duchess of Rutland.
15. Pearson 1988: 46; Beerbohm 1924: 26.
16. Soros 1999: 342.
17. These drawings had not yet been published in England. Godwin relied upon Thomas Henry Dyer's *Ancient Athens* published in 1873.
18. The play opened on 17 May 1886. Hengler's Circus is now the London Palladium.
19. Wilde 1886.
20. See Pearson and Uricchio 1994: 254.
21. Shaw 1958: 96.
22. Benson had moved *Othello* from Bournemouth to Oxford.
23. Tolles 1940: 239–42.

CHAPTER 4

Trees in Good Voice: The Red Lamp, 1887–90

As adept as she was at acquiring new roles, Maud was just as deft at leasing houses. In the space of a couple of years the Trees went from Wilton Street to Cheyne Walk to North Audley Street to Rosary Gardens before settling on, by Maud's own admission, an extraordinary place in New Cavendish Street. Nicknamed the 'House of the Seven Stables', as it boasted livery for hire beneath, there was as a result a constant, 'nerve- shattering stamp of hooves'. Happily this did nothing to mar the Sunday dinner parties (inspired by the Routledges) that Maud now gave for guests including Oscar Wilde, Arthur Pinero, and Squire and Mrs Bancroft.[1] Her list of influential personages in the theatre world was growing, and would extend even further when Herbert, with the help of Comyns Carr and Stuart Ogilvie, became manager of the Comedy Theatre in Panton Street in April 1887.

Tree kicked off his season with *The Red Lamp* by W. Outram Tristram, a melodrama in which he played the sinister head of the secret police, Demetrius. Unrecognizable even to his friends, Herbert proved a master of disguise, a genius at make-up. The cast included Marion Terry (who would soon spark a jealous tiff between Maud and Herbert) and Janet Achurch, from whom Maud took over the role of the Princess Claudia Morakoff. Tristram wrote to Maud after the opening night:

> Meanwhile let me supplement my telegram of this morning by saying that your performance of the Princess gladdened the author's heart — you made her sympathetic on the prophet side — and on several notable occasions there was Electricity about — (I do not refer to the lighting of the Auditorium). I hope that critics have done you justice and notice this fact.[2]

The critics did indeed notice, and so did the public. Such was the success of *The Red Lamp* that Tree took on management of the Haymarket Theatre, opening with the play on 15 September. Maud was buoyant: Tree was rapidly becoming a personality and actor-manager to be reckoned with, and she was his acknowledged leading lady. Theirs was a lively (if not always lovely) home in which to entertain and further consolidate their rapidly expanding network of friends and contacts. Their professional life, too, was progressing exactly as she had envisioned all those years ago when they first met. Then as now, Maud's focus was on a life in the

Fig. 4.1. Maud Tree (photograph by Raphael Tuck & Sons, no. 29; author's own)

theatre where they shared equal billing. But a conversation that Tree had recently had with W. S. Gilbert should have rung alarm bells. While Maud was always willing to take on any kind of work, falling back on recitation when other parts failed to materialize, Tree was not. Not only that, but earlier he had turned down an engagement that would have earned him £5 5s. od. (approximately £500 by today's standards and half his salary at the theatre) in lieu of more colourful parts. When Gilbert questioned this attitude, given he had a wife and child to support, going as far as to suggest it was 'immoral', Tree replied, 'Possibly, but my ambition is in a different direction'.[3] While Maud's clear agenda was to perform with her husband, ideally in their own theatre, his, as she soon discovered, was quite other and did not necessarily include Maud.

The crunch came when Tree cast his next play. *Partners* was billed as a 'new comedy' in five acts by Robert Buchanan, when in reality it was an old story re-told in three. It was an adaptation of *Fromont Jeune et Risler Aîné,* from the French original by Alphonse Daudet, and was considered risqué in the extreme, as it had to do with adultery, or at least the idea of it. Maud, however, was once again excited at the prospect of playing opposite Herbert and began to prepare for her role as Claire, though he had other ideas as to whom he wanted to play the heroine — the lovely Marion Terry, with whom they had both just acted, for one. When Maud wailed as to why he would not have *her,* he replied, 'You see, the part needs extraordinary sympathy'.[4] It may have come as small comfort that the *Punch* critic was just one of those who did not like the play, commenting that 'Mr. German Christmas Tree had been cut down to a shrub', while *The Times* of 6 January 1888 considered its cast to be 'somewhat eccentric', only to be added to Tree's already 'well stocked gallery'.[5]

This uncomfortable experience, however, clearly demonstrated two things to Maud. One was that if she was going to be taken seriously by Herbert, she was going to have to carve her career alongside his without counting on any favours from him. The other was that her trump card was still her speaking voice. Moreover, the effective execution of a Shakespearean role in particular depended on basic elocution, and ultimately a Shakespearean role was the benchmark for an actor. Maud's classical training gave her the edge over Herbert (which only heightened the professional rivalry between them), and so did her voice. She was all too aware of the recent review in which the theatre critic of the *Leeds Mercury* had said of *Partners* on 14 January 1890:

> For not to waste words, I must state that the average powers of the players in the mastering of blank verse were insufficient and that a performance like that is the strongest argument in favour of those who urge that an improved classical tuition is absolutely necessary in this country.[6]

It was a subject preoccupying theatre critics the land over. In an article entitled 'Theatrical Voices and Elocution', C. H. J. Bistenden argued that:

> Theatrical managers of most of the theatres ought not to wonder why so many people keep away as it's impossible to hear even half of what is said on the stage and therefore the enjoyment of the play is quite lost.[7]

Audiences in the gallery 'had still to complain of the want of properly-trained voices and elocution'. It was a training that was automatically given to actors in France and Italy and to opera singers schooled to project the voice. As a singer, Bistenden wrote from experience and dismissed those 'vocalists who find fault with the acoustics of buildings'. He emphasized the point that he himself could be 'distinctly heard in the galleries by as many as 8,000 people, as in the Royal Albert Hall or the Queen's and Bechstein Halls'.

Elsewhere, on 15 September 1906, the *Dispatch* drama critic 'R. C.' (with Tree specifically in mind) was also of the opinion that:

> If English actors and actresses would pay more attention to the studying of elocution than they do to the invention of stage business it would do much to mitigate the sufferings of present-day audiences who are obliged to 'catch' what they can through inarticulate mumblings of those on stage.

A background in music was clearly advantageous. The actress Lena Ashwell, who originally aspired to be an opera singer, was described by Ellen Terry as possessing a 'fetching voice', while Terry's own was accounted 'a voice that melted your bosom'.[8] Sarah Bernhardt (whom Maud would soon replace in *Fedora*) was famous for hers, which was said to be 'so exquisitely toned and modulated that it realized the fable of the Sirens'. According to the *Era* of 17 June 1899, it acted on the hearer like some soothing, intoxicating 'Indian drug,' as if 'nerve touched nerve, or the mere contour subtil [*sic*] of the voice were laid tinglingly on one's spinal cord'.[9] Maud's voice was repeatedly described as 'sweet', 'delightful', and 'effective'. The *People* (14 November 1899) wrote of her 'appealing looks and accents' and *Era* described 'the musical inflexion of her delivery'.

Moreover, it was not enough to be beautiful. The stellar good looks of the American-born Mrs Brown Potter, for example, in the role of Calypso, were not able to counteract poor diction even on home territory. The *New York Times* of 23 January 1902 reported that she gave a 'new and charming reading of the part, though the acting is regarded as being somewhat marred by defective elocution'. The timbre too of an actor's voice was important. Max Beerbohm described Eleonora Duse's as a 'little shrill voice'.[10] But Violet Lindsay loved it, calling it 'glorious' and 'vivid'.[11]

Critics and audience alike appraised the effect of such a voice, while the 'science' behind it was analyzed by academics such as Dr. H. Hilbert of London University'.[12] There was support available to actors, he further explained, in the art of articulation which would enable them to move their 'articulatory apparatus' efficiently. Effective pronunciation depended on good muscle control and the 'correctness of shape and ability to hold the voice in that shape by efficient control of all vocal forces'. In summary, Hilbert argued the apparent 'instinct' of good acting was one that, if not already acquired, could be learned. He expressed the view that fine acting could be handicapped by slovenly pronunciation or an 'unusual voice'.

Maud was more than confident of her voice but, for her own satisfaction, she was keen to broaden her range, to work alongside playwrights and to become involved behind the scenes generally.[13] Soon there was an opportunity to do just this. By the spring of 1888 the professional rift between husband and wife had healed sufficiently for them to appear together in Haddon Chambers's play *Captain Swift*, which opened at the Crystal Palace. While Maud's performance was considered to be one of her most successful, the play, 'enthusiastically indulging the long arm of coincidence' to begin with, was not.[14] Maud turned to sister Bertha for advice and it was she who suggested the motto 'there is some soul of goodness in things evil' that appeared on programmes and billboards.[15] There were further revisions: Maud not only oversaw costume design but together with the author re-directed Tree's interpretation of his character from comic crook to romantic hero.

The underpinning of this 'cup and saucer' drama in hand, Maud indulged in a role that seemed to have been created for her and one in which, it was said in the *Daily Graphic* of 15 May 1888, she 'retained the delicacy of romantic girlhood'. For the *Sunday Times* of the same date she was 'exceedingly graceful and tender, and for the *Pall Mall Gazette* the role was one of her most rewarding.[16] Elizabeth Robins for one would remember Maud's interpretation for its perfect blending of the requisite 'voice' with refinement and deportment:

> I never before felt so completely the illusion of looking — not in the least at a 'stage set' — but into a private house; overhearing the talk of people like Mrs. Tree's Stella Darbishire, never straining the voice or the point; well-bred, charming and yet so excitingly, the sport of Fate![17]

And Janet Achurch, about to set sail for the Antipodes where she was to tour with her production of *A Doll's House,* requested a picture of Maud as Stella to take with her.[18]

Meanwhile, in an innovative, masterly stroke, Tree initiated the performance of matinees on a Wednesday in addition to the classic Saturday fixture. So while *Captain Swift* continued to run at night, he now produced *Masks and Faces* to run by day. The play was by Charles Reade in collaboration once again with Maud's former English teacher, Tom Taylor. It was also one of the first matinees (that is, one not moved from the evening billing) to run for twenty-five years after its debut, and the play would appear every season at some theatre or other.[19] Originally produced on 20 November 1852, *Masks and Faces* was revived at the Haymarket on 5 December 1888.

As was intrinsic to sentimental comedies of the day, the plot was based on a series of misunderstandings and unbridled desire. The married Ernest Vane has fallen for an actress Peg Woffington much to the annoyance of his rival Sir Charles Pomander. The latter was played by the future Examiner of Plays, Charles Brookfield. According to the *Country Gentleman* of 9 December 1888, Maud was an 'absolutely perfect' Mistress Vane, outstripping her illustrious predecessors in 'freshness, grace and veracity'. Tree played Triplet, a struggling playwright. The *Hawk* of 10 December 1888 said of his acting that he 'evidently intends to take no rest until he has placed himself at the very topmost rung of the histrionic ladder' but applauded his development of matinees. In what the *Evening Standard* of 6 December 1888 termed 'a very sound and excellent comedy', Mrs Tree made 'a delightful Mabel Vane, graceful, earnest and altogether sympathetic'. *Lloyds* of 9 December 1888 went further, stating that 'nothing could be more graceful and truthful than Mrs. Tree's Mabel Vane especially in her scenes with Triplet'. It was just the kind of melodrama whose theme, upholding the 'sanctity of womanhood and home', that was closest to Maud's heart. Playing the injured wife was too, as was the skill required to 'exact laughter at the very moment when the spectator and the listener is getting rid of a refractory fear' (*Era*, 7 December 1888).[20]

As with many of the roles Maud played, art imitates life, as wife and mistress are reconciled. In the final scene, the 'actress' calls the wife 'an angel of truth and goodness', and such is her empathy for her that she finishes by begging to be called 'Sister'. As will be seen later, Maud would indeed befriend her husband's mistress, the actress May Pinney, to the extent that she gifted her money and was still in correspondence with her after Tree's death. But that conciliation was yet to come. For the moment, the *Observer* of 9 December 1888 noted of Maud that:

> There was the ring of true feeling in the tender, entreaty of the neglected wife and something like real passion in the despairing cry when the infatuated husband seems willing to sacrifice honour, home and love for the popular actress.

Little did Maud know how prophetic these words would prove. Unhappily, however, it is only in the play that the actress 'undertakes to restore the affections of the husband to the wife'.

But the most severe marital rupture between the Trees was a little in the future. Maud now took a house for the summer months on Hampstead Heath, when Hampstead was still a village. The house had a garden full of roses in which Viola could play. Maud also had a carriage to take her to and from the theatre. The reality was, though, that neither Tree spent much time in the 'country'. Herbert and Maud were both acting in *Wealth* at the Haymarket, a play by Henry Arthur Jones in which Maud played Edith Ruddock. (One critic writing for the *London Gazette* of 25 June summed up Tree's acting as: 'Act I — dotty, Act II — dottier and Act III — dottiest!'). After the play ended, they travelled to Bayreuth (where Maud was spotted resting her head on Tree's shoulder and he reaching for her hand) to hear *Tristan and Isolde*. Herbert was clearly feeling well disposed towards his wife, as he cast her on their return in the role of Henriette Laroque in Robert Buchanan's adaptation of a French play, *A Man's Shadow,* which roused, as Shaw wrote in the *Theatre* of 1889 the 'usually apathetic Haymarket audience, to a storm'.

In the autumn of 1889, the Trees were still at New Cavendish Street, at least during the week, and were busy with their various projects. Amongst other things, Maud was learning to ride so that she could accompany Herbert on his expeditions around the heath. Working days began late morning and Herbert would often take Viola with him on his drive to the theatre, returning home around 5 p.m. and invariably bringing someone to dine with them or at least, as Maud said, 'someone unwilling to eat at that hour, but willing to watch *us* do so'.[21] As a couple they also enjoyed a period of unprecedented socializing. They were invited by Henry Irving to a small supper party given in honour of the Prince of Wales and attended others at the homes of Sir John Millais, George Watts, and Sir Edward Poynter. They spent Christmas as ever at Belvoir Castle with Violet, who now had four children of her own, but returned to London for a New Year's Eve party given at the home of Sir

FIG. 4.2. 'Mr. & Mrs. Tree, Ogden's *Guinea Gold Cigarettes*' (author's own)

George Lewis. Among the guests were John Singer Sargent (who would later paint Maud's daughter Viola), Lawrence Alma-Tadema, Galsworthy, Ellen Terry, Burne-Jones, Sylvia du Maurier, and Henry James. But the two most important friendships in terms of practical benefit were made with the banker Ernest Cassel, the other with their host, George Lewis, who would become Maud's solicitor and confidant. Both men would prove of immense assistance to her when the time came.

At the beginning of April, spring was depicted by a painted cherry tree, under which the hero sits, in another English adaptation of a French play. Based on MM. Busnach and Cauvin's melodrama *Le Secret de la terreuse* (*The Broken Seal* in America), Sydney Grundy's *A Village Priest* proved so popular that Gladstone and his wife came to see it on the last night. It was a lively production that led to no little controversy, as its central theme dealt with the violation of the confessional. Ardent Roman Catholics were against this portrayal even in a stage play, and there followed a protracted and heated exchange on the Trees' account in various papers. It did not, however, dim the play's popularity and eventually led to the *Catholic Times* of 25 April 1890 'acquitting' the dramatist of 'any intention to attack the [...] priesthood', for, it concluded: 'He has erred in ignorance and his error is also false in art'. Maud played Marguerite, but remembered the play more for the fact that Gladstone, going backstage afterwards, asked about the political opinions of the theatre world. Tree answered, 'Conservative, on the whole; but', he added, noting Gladstone's face darken, 'the scene-shifters are Radical almost to a man'.[22]

Maud could not have been happier. For the time being the arguments to do with her working lay dormant and at last Herbert (if sometimes grudgingly) seemed to acknowledge her talent. Likewise, in a surprising volte-face on more than one occasion, he even cast her as his leading lady. In the autumn he embarked on his first provincial tour, and Maud played Lady Teazle in *The School for Scandal*, followed a few weeks later by the role of Dorothy Musgrave in *Beau Austin*, a play jointly written by W. E. Henley and Robert Louis Stevenson. Both playwrights would become friends of Maud, with the former bringing his wife and baby girl to play with Viola. But a stanza from the Prologue to *Beau Austin* might very well have been composed with the Trees in mind, and with an uncanny insight into the conflicting forces at play within their relationship:

> But then as now, maybe something more —
> Woman and man were human to the core.
> The hearts that throbbed behind that quaint attire
> Burned with a plenitude of essential fire.
> They too could risk, they also could rebel,
> They could love wisely — they could love too well.
> In that great duel of sex, that ancient strife
> Which is the very central fact of life,
> They could — and did — engage it breath for breath;
> They could — and did — get wounded unto death.
> As at all times since time for us began
> Woman was truly woman — Man was man;
> And joy and sorrow were as much at home
> In trifling Tunbridge as in mighty Rome.[23]

For the moment, and on tour herself, Maud was homesick and pined for Viola. One Sunday Herbert surprised Maud by travelling to see her in Birmingham with Viola 'hidden' as luggage. Her tour over, once more Maud was house hunting, once more she looked forward to starring opposite her husband in his next production. Their home life, as she wrote for posterity, was 'very even and entirely happy'.[24]

Notes to Chapter 4

1. Beerbohm 1924: 29–30.
2. W. Outram Tristram to Maud Tree, [September 1887] (MBTC).
3. Pearson 1988: 45.
4. Beerbohm 1924: 32.
5. Ibid.
6. The fact that Tree was not of English origin made him a target for humourists. See Bingham 1979: 38.
7. Bistenden's article, from a lecture given at 105 New Oxford Street on 4 August 1913, was reported in the *Pall Mall Gazette* of the same date.
8. Anon. 1896b.
9. Symons 1903: 27.
10. As quoted in Auerbach 1987: 22.
11. Violet Lindsay to Maud Tree, 1896 (MBTC, uncatalogued).
12. Hilbert 1914.
13. See Beerbohm 1924: 34–35.
14. See Schafer 2003: 110–13.
15. William Shakespeare, *Henry V*, IV.1, l. 4. See Beerbohm 1924: 38; see also the poster for *Captain Swift*, Haymarket Theatre, London (HBT/000035/2).
16. The play was also reviewed on 15 May by the *St James's Gazette, Pall Mall Gazette, Globe, Daily Mail, Daily Graphic*, and *Sporting Life*.
17. Robins 1940: 33.
18. *Captain Swift*, a comedy drama in four acts by Haddon Chambers, was first produced as a matinée by Tree on 20 June 1888. Maud played Stella Darbishire and Tree Mr Wilding. It was so successful that the American rights were bought by an A. M. Palmer and it was seen in New York at Madison Square on 4 December 1888, produced by Dion Boucicault and starring Maurice Barrymore as Wilding and retaining Maud as Stella. On 7 February 1895, Maud once again played the role at the Abbey Theatre, New York, with Lily Hanbury as Mrs Seabrook.
19. Tolles 1940: 94.
20. Ibid.: 89.
21. Beerbohm 1924: 47.
22. Ibid.: 48.
23. Henley and Stevenson 1907: Prologue.
24. Beerbohm 1924: 47.

CHAPTER 5

Mrs Beerbohm Tree
1892

Not surprisingly, this 'evenness' was short-lived. It did not follow from moments of intimacy with Maud that Herbert would automatically cast her in his next production. As proved to be the hallmark of their marriage, such moments were followed on the contrary, by, as Maud saw it, bewildering acts of rejection. And it would seem that the Trees' peculiar dynamic had developed a discernible pattern. Engaged elsewhere, Maud would publicly exert her independence only for Tree, nervous of her success, to reel her back to the theoretical confines of his theatre. Once again, Maud assumed, given their recent closeness, that she would be his first choice as Ophelia in his forthcoming production of *Hamlet,* but once again he had other ideas and chose another actress in her place. There was a compromise: he proposed that she play the role of Ophelia in rep and in Manchester. Depending on her success there, he told her, he would consider her for the Haymarket at a later date. Given that Herbert would not be swayed, and despite seeing the sense in this, it was, as Maud wrote in her memoir, 'the most momentous episode in my stage career'.[1] On the other hand, if Maud could have taken the long view she would have seen the emerging pattern of his rebuttal and her striving even harder, more provocatively, more boldly to turn his attention back to her. Some of her best work came in the wake of exclusion by Tree.

Spurred by his challenge, Maud made such a success of her role in Manchester, where *Hamlet* opened on 9 September 1891 at the Theatre Royal, that Violet Lindsay wrote in her diary, that she was 'the best Ophelia ever known'.[2] Theatre critics were also unanimous in praising Maud, and thus Herbert had no choice but to fulfill his promise and cast her opposite himself in his *Hamlet* of January 1892. But if she had been successful in Manchester it was as nothing to what she was now in London. The *Graphic* devoted a full-size page illustration of the couple painted by H. M. Payet, in which Herbert's eyes appear to 'burn' wildly as he gesticulates to her in a scene from Act III. Her slender figure kneels before him and her red gown trails behind her; her hair is unbound and her waist appears tiny. Elsewhere, Tree's overtly 'romantic' Hamlet was unfavourably compared to that of Irving. Even the theatre critic Clement Scott, reviewing the production for the *London Illustrated News* in 1892, saved the lion's share of his comments for Maud, considering her Ophelia to be among his 'most delightful memories'. As he wrote: 'There was no staginess

FIG. 5.1. Herbert Tree and Maud Tree in *Hamlet* at the Haymarket Theatre (*Graphic*, 30 January 1892). From a painting by H. M. Payet

here, no trick, no artificiality [...] an Ophelia most graceful, most beautiful, most persuasive'. Maud had insisted on having fresh flowers every night for Ophelia to rip up, and this touch, said Scott, gave her acting 'the desired edge'.

In the next few months, with no theatre engagement in the offing, Maud set to work decorating and furnishing the house to which they had moved in the winter. They would live at 77 Sloane Street for the next ten years — a record for the couple — and to this day the house bears a blue plaque to commemorate this occupancy. Misled by the advertisement that suggested the house was to be had cheaply (Maud misunderstood the notice 'Rent without Premium'), she found it proved anything but. Electricity was still a great luxury — Herbert had only recently installed it at the Haymarket — and she now put it in at great cost in Sloane Street. Her decorating bills were notoriously high, but seemingly they could also afford the four servants required to wait on the not one, but two drawing-rooms the house boasted.

Their landlord and immediate neighbour was the English Liberal and reformist politician Sir Charles Dilke, Under-Secretary of State for Foreign Affairs under Gladstone. At the time the Trees moved in, however, he was also the 'scandalous' Sir Charles Dilke, his glittering political career having come to an abrupt end six years after a notorious divorce case in which he was accused of seducing a young bride (not his own). To begin with, the only indication that next door was actually inhabited came from the clang of sabres as Sir Charles fenced with his teacher. One day Viola, drawn by the sound, climbed into the Dilkes' side of the garden and was discovered. Soon Herbert was out riding with Sir Charles and invited to parties where the Trees met Parnell and heard stories about their host's encounters with Bismarck and Napoleon. It was Sir Charles's wife Emilia, the English art historian, feminist, and trade unionist, however, who would become a particularly close friend of Maud. Despite their political differences, the two women would support each other in their respective causes.

Ensconced in this decorative 'nest', hosting stimulating, diverse supper parties Maud was becoming not only a celebrity actress but also a woman of influence. A charismatic character and famous wit made her a popular hostess but in creating and furthering work opportunities for herself and Herbert, her influence was achieved in part, by her prodigious letter-writing. In an age when correspondence was the chief means of communication, Maud's letters were the equivalent of texting or tweeting today. Even when she had a telephone installed she preferred to pen a letter as she was often 'too tired' to go down stairs to make a call. Later when Tree was not at home but 'at dome', Maud communicated with her husband by writing and if they were rowing which was more often the case than not, the letters flew between establishments (and dressing rooms).[3] Maud's technique was simple — she wrote begging favours and/or offered gifts in the form of tickets to her husband's productions. It was not long, however, before aspiring actors and playwrights were writing to *her* with a view to their work being performed either by herself or by Herbert. The playwright Julian Sturgis wrote to Maud: 'I wish to secure your interest — so far that my tragedy of Count Julian shall not be lost under a mountain of neglected dramas which I picture in your poor husband's theatre'; while Ellen

Terry wrote requesting *any* Shakespearean part for her daughter Edy. Violet Lindsay was content simply with 'walk on' parts for hers.[4]

Tree's Shakespearean productions were indeed becoming famous and would take on increasingly ambitious proportions as time went on. The ship in *The Tempest* on its rocking stage would make some theatregoers feel nauseous, while the menagerie of animals required for *Joseph and His Brethren* saw the streets around Her Majesty's Theatre heave with camels, sheep, and goats.[5] But while Herbert's elaborate staging often involved altering the mechanics of production — later he would build the first ever flat stage in England — he had introduced truly innovative gas and electrical devices to facilitate such manoeuvres.

Apart from never having house lights more than half up (while on tour, he provided his own man to manipulate light on the ghost) Tree both experimented and altered lime-light with additional 'focused' or 'flood-light'.[6] The lighting plots for his 1896 *Hamlet*, for example, show that focused light was called for and described as 'box' while flood-light was 'open'. In Act 1.2 where the recreation of a burning log fire is required, two red limes are 'thrown on scene' in addition to lime-light. (Maud would also use this lighting device for her productions at the Wyndham Theatre.) This effective technique to illuminate props and scenery was already in use as early as 1852 in the Sadler's Wells production of *All's Well that Ends Well,* but where Tree was truly innovative was in the reduction of amber limes to half, with the prompt side lime to be raised on the actor's face. The result was very much like what today we could call a cinematic 'close up'.[7] Indeed Tree would go on to be involved with the filming of three of his Shakespeare plays.[8]

Tree's productions also reinforced an uncompromising intent to avail himself of 'all the best archaeological and artistic' effects in order to worthily and 'munificently represent Shakespeare'.[9] But in so doing Tree was not only satisfying his own personal worship of the playwright, but meeting the demands, so he claimed, of his theatre going public. It was a public that in turn, increasingly mirrored the 'developing taste' for luxury and conspicuous displays of consumption. Moreover, the steady rise in purchasing power, as Michael Booth has pointed out, was rapidly creating 'a whole new market for the entertainment industry'.[10] The theatregoer picking his way to the theatre did so along London streets illuminated by gaslight and the sparkling display of goods shining within wide vitrines of plate glass. And once there, theatres with their plush carpets, lavish use of gas light, chandeliers, and mirrors were an extension of the grandeur the theatregoer aspired to, or had come from. Glass in particular with its refracting and reflecting power made the theatre an even more magical place where the theatregoer went expecting 'not so much to hear' as to look.[11]

Tree's spectacular productions then were luxuriant of language, of scenery, and of lighting. The small (but growing) voices of dissent whose complaint about this very realism was that 'it rendered audiences mentally passive and anaesthetized the imagination' were for the moment at any rate, just that.[12] As Tree reminded the critic of *Blackwood's Magazine* who lamented the expense of *The Tempest*, a total of 830,000 people saw the three Shakespeare plays he produced at Her Majesty's

Theatre between 1897 and 1900 and none of the productions had been 'unattended by a substantial pecuniary award'.[13] This 'unity of taste' between actor-manager and spectator would endure as Booth has suggested 'well after critical hostility had been translated into reformist practice'.[14] But in the meantime, as Tree was so resolute in proving, 'illusion' was 'the first and last word of the stage' and the very 'business of theatre'.[15]

For Maud, however, the business of theatre was more complex. She was a wife and mother with a keen sense of responsibility to see these duties fulfilled with decorum. And her ego played less of a role in her relationship with her art than Herbert's did. Of course, as for him, there was the compulsion to act in the first place and the associated delight — the smell of the theatre, the greasepaint, as she described to Violet Lindsay, and the novelty (initially) of being written about in the press. But for Maud, the theatre was a means to an end. Her work quite simply generated an income and she was happiest when she was earning her own money. She enjoyed playing Herbert's leading lady in his much-publicized Shakespearean extravaganzas, but was just as fascinated by the innovative, avant-garde writers of the day, and more in step with the critic for the *Journal of the Society of Arts* (March 1887) who wrote, 'theatregoer need not bring any mind to the theatre at all; it is all done for him', as if indeed referencing Tree's unrestrained productions.

Charles George Cotsford Dick's *The Waif*, an adaptation of François Coppée's *Le Passant*, was by contrast, an elegant and restrained play with the thirty-four-year old Maud playing Zanetto, a very fetching (barefoot) youth. The idea of going barefoot was hers and one she would again deploy when she played Lucius in Tree's production of *Julius Caesar*. (Herbert's Trilby would also go barefoot in his hugely successful production at the Haymarket in 1897.) She later freely admitted to revelling in her first cross-dressing role and to much admiring herself in it. The actress Hilda Hanbury appears to have heartily agreed, for she addressed Maud as 'My dear little Boy' in a letter in which she wanted to tell her how much she enjoyed her 'beautiful performance'. She ended: 'You did look like a dear little boy in the 2nd act — your hair was sweet — & you looked sweet altogether. Please don't think this an impertinent letter — but I felt I must write'.[16]

A few months later Maud's next appearance made the society pages of the daily papers for a very different engagement. On 29 August 1892, Violet Lindsay gave birth to her fifth and last child, Diana Olivia Winifred Maud. The baby's godmothers were Maud and Winifred Cavendish-Bentinck, Duchess of Portland, while her godfather was the future Prime Minister, Arthur Balfour. The Beerbohm Trees then ventured as a family for the first and last time to Marienbad. It was a place Herbert loved and would return to every summer as long as he lived, but Maud never quite 'got into its way of life'. Bored, she began to plan ahead for their next autumn tour, and it was this initial boredom that had a happy result. Once they were back in England, Oscar Wilde came to stay with them, bringing with him a completed manuscript of *A Woman of No Importance*. Having been asked by Tree to write a play for him of the same standing as *Lady Windermere's Fan*, Wilde at first demurred, but eventually wrote the play while staying with Lord Alfred Douglas in Brancaster. After three days, however, Maud found Oscar exhausting and was very happy when he left.[17]

Rehearsals got under way with a break for lunch every day at the Continental Hotel, where Wilde proved to be a much better luncheon companion than houseguest and Maud remembers these gatherings as 'wit-sharpening, intellectual and full of interest'. (He also outlined his idea for three short plays, of which *Salome* was one.) Maud, rather tellingly, was Mrs Allonby, a 'flirtatious woman', as Wilde directed, with 'a bit of a reputation for controversy'. Tree was Lord Illingworth, a role Herbert appeared to be playing so well *off* the stage that Wilde was prompted to quip that Herbert was becoming 'de plus en plus Oscarisé'.[18] After a skittish reception, the play was endorsed by the Prince of Wales, who came to see it on the second night and loved it. In the meantime Wilde's wife Constance, who had acted with Maud almost a decade earlier, wrote to congratulate her on her role as Mrs Allonby and to thank her for her 'exceeding kindness' to her husband through rehearsals. She added, 'I will only say (in the difficulty of putting words to one's emotions) that your courteous kindness has been fully appreciated by us both'.[19]

Over the next year, Maud acted in a couple of plays that were both short-lived but for different reasons. The extravagance of Tree's Shakespearean productions was becoming infamous but this was also the case with *The Tempter*, which, while immensely popular, was also costly to produce. Henry Arthur Jones's four-act tragedy was first performed at the Haymarket Theatre on 20 September 1893. It ran for seventy-three nights and was taken off to a house of £195 3s. 6d., the equivalent of approximately £22,600 today. According to the *Theatre* of 1 November 1893, the nightly expense was therefore 'so great that it could not be continued'. It is worth remembering that by 1899 actors earned, on average, a starting salary of £2 a week while a general servant earned approximately £12 a week. In 1910, Tree's *King Henry VIII* made the headlines not only for its succession of extraordinary pageants, but for the exorbitant cost of its production, which was said by the *New York Times* of 2 September to have been more than $75,000 (approximately $1,816,740 today).

Set in the days of another Henry, the fourth this time, Maud played Lady Avis Rougement in a play she described as being 'part Chaucer, part Goethe'. Tree in the title role was 'practically Mephistopheles' — glamorous, daring and lurid.[20] As in *The Tempest*, *The Tempter* begins with a storm at sea. The Devil or Tempter (Tree) throws the steersman overboard, encourages the crew to drink so much that they slit each other's throats, and befriends the only survivor, a Prince Leon intended for the Lady Isobel. The Devil then encourages the Prince to renege on his vows and instead seduce the more beautiful Lady Avis (Maud). After a complicated denouement, the play concludes with the murder of Prince Leon by Isobel and her subsequent suicide. The lines spoken by Tree — 'Man's an odd animal, much lower than the angels; | Rather higher than the brutes' — might later strike a resonant chord with Maud as would the final words of the play directed to her character:

> Be thou at peace my daughter, too.
> For know, all evil and all wrong that men
> Endure or do, all misery, all despair

> All pangs, all conflicts, all that hurt us here,
> Are but as pebbles thrown into a pond,
> That make a ripple, then are seen no more.[21]

Maud was said to have 'made the gentle Lady Avis a welcome personage' (*Evening Star*, 25 November 1893).

In Robert Buchanan's *The Charlatan* ('A New Play in Modern Life'), Tree once again played the title role and another kind of devil — 'half villain, half-hero'. And while Maud called Herbert's interpretation 'eerie', it was her own acting, according to the *Westminster Budget* of 26 January 1894 that was termed 'eerie' suggesting 'perfectly,' as the *Theatre* of 1 March wrote, 'the manner of one not under her own control'. This time it was not the expense of production that brought about the play's closure but its unpopularity. Dismissed by Maud as a 'pretty enough play', it was considered by *The Times* (19 September 1894) to be a clever satire but 'too strange for the general public'.[22] The play, dealing in theosophy and hypnotism, also aroused protest from the various authors who considered Buchanan to have plagiarized their work. The *Saturday Review* of September 1894 considered Walter Besant's novel *Herr Paulus* (published in 1888) to be 'identical' to Buchanan play, while Stuart Cumberland and Charles H. Dickinson wrote to the editor of the *Pall Mall Gazette* highlighting the similarities between their works — *The Wonder Worker* and *An Unpaid Debt* respectively — and *The Charlatan*.

There was high praise however, for Maud's role and singing in the part of Isabel Arlington, the innocent and sweet heroine whose redemptive love ultimately saves The Charlatan, such as the following in the *Birmingham Daily Post* of 9 March 1894:

> All round the acting was superb, but the honours were carried off by Mrs. Tree. Her acting in the difficult sleep-walking scene was tragic in its intensity, and yet so well subdued that it never seemed unnatural. Grace and winsomeness distinguished her in the lighter portions of the play, and the tenderness of her love avowal could not be excelled.

Punch went further, stating on 10 February 1894: 'Mr. Robert Buchanan owes her more, perhaps, than he does to Mr. Tree for the success of the piece; for indubitably the success of *The Charlatan* is mainly due to these two'.

After a year that closed, as Maud wrote in 'Herbert and I', 'somewhat gloomily', Maud was Mrs Murgatoyd 'to almost sensational success' in *A Bunch of Violets*.[23] Yet another French original, it was adapted by Sydney Grundy from Octave Feuillet's *Montjoye* and opened at the Haymarket in March 1894. (In fact, twenty-five out of the ninety-seven plays produced by Tree, and acted in by Maud, were adaptations of European (mostly French) works). Grundy, who wrote for the Trees at both the Haymarket and Her Majesty's Theatres, would be responsible for 'bowdlerizing and reshaping' several French plays. *Punch* went as far as defining an English playwright as a 'French dictionary on legs'.[24] Grundy was just one of many playwrights freely adapting plays by other authors under their own name and becoming more famous for that adaptation than the original author. Indeed, part of the unpopularity attributed to *The Charlatan* and its consequent short run was as a result of this very accusation of plagiarism. In the nineteenth century dramatists had benefited from fixed payments for each performance but with almost nothing for copyright, and despite the international copyright agreement of 1887 and the US copyright bill in 1891, copyright was still largely unenforceable. There is an ironic postscript to this: Sydney Grundy would *himself* claim to be the victim of plagiarism when Mrs Clifford's *The Likeness of the Night* was performed in 1900 (see Chapter 9 for further discussion of this).

Maud's role in *A Bunch of Violets* came about in an unexpected manner. In despair over the failure of recent productions such as *The Tempter* and *The Charlatan*, one evening though it was already late, Tree was so morose that Maud rang up for a hansom and suggested they visit Sydney Grundy to see if he had any work in the pipeline. As luck would have it, not only was Grundy still up but by pure chance happened to have a new play ready for production. That very evening Tree chose his cast. The actress Lily Hanbury (sister of actress Hilda who had loved Maud's performance as Zanetto) was to be his leading lady, but the part of the adventuress was as yet unfilled. 'Whom on earth,' Tree asked ruefully, 'can we get for Mrs. Murgatoyd?' Maud remembers holding her breath. 'There sits the only actress who can play it,' said Mr Grundy pointing his pipe at Maud.[25]

Florence Bell, with whom Maud would later collaborate, was one of the first to congratulate her, saying that she had 'never seen anything more bewitching in her life'.[26] William Archer, drama critic of the *World*, wrote on 2 April 1894 the play was 'intelligent, daring, original' and that 'Mrs. Tree looks at times like a creation of Mr. Aubrey Beardsley, in one of his more human moods'. The latter in turn felt compelled to write to Maud and say 'how delighted and honoured' he was that '"The World critic" should have found in any of my drawings something to suggest a comparison with you in The Bunch of Violets. I am fascinated by the charm of your impersonization'.[27]

Perhaps Tree thought so too, because by the time the play had ended, Maud was pregnant with their second child, and she now took a three-month break to rest and prepare for her next theatre engagement. But while Maud had much to look forward to, her close friend Violet was all but inconsolable after the death of her nine-year-old son Lord Haddon, who had died from a twisted gut on 28 September. If Maud was solicitous of Violet, Herbert for once was mindful of Maud. From his annual leave in Marienbad he wrote to the ten-year-old Viola:

> I hope you are taking good care of Mother — she is not very strong just now and you must treat her kindly... Don't always think of catching butterflies and enjoying yourself. Think of Mother who has worked so hard this year.[28]

Felicity Tree was born in December, and less than six weeks later Maud accompanied Herbert on his first American tour. An exquisitely dressed Max Beerbohm was in attendance as Herbert's private secretary. Always amusing company, Max on this occasion did not provide much practical help. He was too slow at answering correspondence and was hopelessly ill, finding the sea 'like a lake of glass and the vessel pitching like Hell and the disembarking at the hideous harbour with the statue of Vulgarity towering over us'.[29] The crossing for Maud, on the other hand, had been pure bliss. For the first and last time in their married life, she had

had Herbert entirely to herself. She was once again, if temporarily, his leading lady, enjoying his undivided attention. Once in New York they were entertained virtually every hour of the day by millionaires, theatre critics, and opera singers. From the luxury of their suite at the Waldorf Astoria on Fifth Avenue Maud wrote ecstatically to Violet Lindsay:

> My Darling Comfort,
> No one ever sits down — no one ever pauses. New York is dazzling, dirty, sweat bedraggled, gorgeous — all spit and splendour![30]

The fast pace at which Americans lived their lives was reflected in an exhausting and seemingly endless round of banquets, speeches, and receptions, in addition to the plays being performed and an audience with President Cleveland at the White House. He and it were far grander and more intimidating, Maud felt, than Queen Victoria and Balmoral, where the Trees had performed prior to leaving for America. She expressed feeling 'underdressed and shabby' despite her 'best brocade' and having borrowed all of Violet Lindsay's jewels for the occasion. 'All the grand ladies here are as joyous and full of fun as Margot Tennant,' she recounted to Violet, 'I suppose their climate makes them so lighthearted.'[31]

The Beerbohm Trees opened at Abbey's Theatre, New York, on 28 January with the ever-popular *The Red Lamp,* staged on alternative nights with *A Bunch of Violets.* As had been the case in London, theatre critics were enthusiastic. Maud was described by the *New York Times* of 3 February 1895 as taking 'the part of an adventuress so cleverly as to win repeated rounds of applause. She has rarely done her work more ably'. It elaborated:

> Mrs. Tree has been a surprise. She is an actress of rare personal charm and distinction: graphic, resourceful and forcible. She has played two sharply contrasting characters with excellent effect and although there is nothing much easier for a clever woman of the stage who has been well trained than to portray a heartless adventuress for whom the dramatist has written telling speeches, there was a degree of feline intensity in Mrs. Tree's impersonation of Mrs Murgatoyd that made it noteworthy. I liked her best as the Russian Princess.

Press coverage of the tour was extensive, but attention that began mildly enough with a fan writing to Maud to say, 'I fell so desperately in love with the second dress that you wore in the Red Lamp that I simply pine to have one like it. I wondered if you would sell it to me second hand' now became something else entirely.[32] On both sides of the Atlantic there was a frenzy of interest in every aspect of Maud's itinerary and life style. Columns were devoted to her physical appearance. She was described as 'a striking blonde' with a 'dreamy countenance' and 'plump round shoulders and a handsome neck'. Even her feet were scrutinized, and these were said to be 'small, straight and well shaped'. Simultaneously, in London the *Sketch* featured Maud in an article called 'Mrs Tree in Sloane Street'. But the American press was after something more, and while headlines in the *Pioneer Press* ranged from 'Woman about Town' to calling Maud on 17 February 1895 a 'Versatile Mathematician, Lady and Scholar', it was the latter subject it wanted to examine specifically. The *Nashville American Journal* of 7 February 1895, in stating 'Mrs.

Beerbohm Tree is said to read ancient Greek as well as she does English', was setting up the premise of a debate in which it wanted her engagement. Maud may have tritely dismissed the woman's question, despite stage representations that echoed the growing movements for women's suffrage (Max Beerbohm famously quipped that the New Woman sprang 'fully armed from Ibsen's brain'), but the American press would not let the question rest.[33] The *New York Sun* ran a feature with the title 'Mrs Tree's Opinions', and reported her as admitting to being 'shockingly old-fashioned'. The *Milwaukee Sentinel* of 7 February 1895 was less sympathetic. It said:

> Mrs. Tree is trying to damage her reputation by admitting that she is not the New Woman and doesn't want to enjoy the suffrage. She has never had time for or interest in women's clubs, she doesn't think women are the intellectual equals of men, she 'would like to see the woman who can write a good play [...] she would rather read Homer than Mr. [*sic*] Humphry Ward.[34]

To the *Louisville Post* of 16 February 1895, Maud confessed that she considered the New Woman of no importance, 'a paper & ink individual created by the novelists & a very insignificant figure in real life'. The journalist Janette H. Walworth, however, proved more persistent and in an article entitled 'Garnered in Feminine Fields' doggedly attempted to understand Maud's position.[35] But it was one from which she would not deviate: her stance was that the New Woman movement was nothing more than a fad and that the 'precious type' set by 'Mother Eve' outnumbered that of the emancipated woman. Maud's views on the subject may appear conflicted, complex, and at times contradictory, but in reality she was essentially very much a product of her time while at the same time straddling the divide between two cultures — that of the aristocrat she was so good at aping and that of the middle-class working mother. Underpinning her beliefs on religion, a work ethic, and the class structure was an essential unshakeable belief that men and women really are different, although in every aspect of her life her example would be to the contrary.

Some of the reasons why Maud was anti-suffrage are explained below, but on a practical level, what many well educated, politically active women (especially Maud) found unpalatable was not only the 'unladylike' heckling and raising of the voice required by speakers but the increasing militancy associated with members of the Women's Social and Political Union (WSPU) and (until they split) the Women's Freedom League (WFL) as opposed to the constitutional suffragists.[36] Moreover it was this shift from wanton acts of vandalism to more concerted action that divided women into militants and constitutionalists.[37] For this very reason the Actresses' Franchise League (AFL) Vice-President Irene Vanbrugh resigned after a Drury Lane rally.[38] As the Suffrage movement evolved, few actresses took part in militant protests, recognizing the consequences of such action in purely financial terms for their careers; put succinctly, few leading ladies could afford a night in the cells.[39] But this would come later; if militancy had not been enough to alienate a woman such as Maud from the cause, a day in the life of an ardent campaigner would have done the trick. In the early years, according to one memoir, there was 'an unwritten rule that there must be no concerts, no theatres and sleep to prepare us for more work'.[40]

Maud's social conscience (like that of any actress whose company toured the provinces) was pricked by an awareness of the inequality of working conditions outside London.[41] Her contemporary, understudy, and friend, Lena Ashwell, described such an experience: 'It was the first time that I had been quite alone on tour, entirely on my own and the rooms in which I found myself fill me with terror'.[42] When her daughters were older Maud wrote to them, like Ashwell, bemoaning the grimness of certain towns: 'Never come to vile Torquay! Oh! The cold of this room and the darkness and gloom! My tour is still the same lamentable fiasco — but all in the days work. Colchester tonight! Margate tomorrow'.[43] On Grand Atlantic Hotel headed paper under which Maud has written 'Martyrdom', she says, 'The Tour is a <u>ghastly</u> failure!' And later:

> I am writing in the Black Hole of Calcutta at Hoglake: a village on the Lancashire coast — But this is the last week of my martyrdom. Darlings, I have nothing to write about except the smellery [*sic*] and misery of some of the places we have visited [...] Now I must go on the dirty disgusting platform and do the Merchant of Venice.[44]

Exposure to grim digs while on tour motivated Maud in her support of diverse charities; it did not motivate her to support women's suffrage. Extended stays in the grand country houses of the day (which Maud much enjoyed) revealed rather the extent to which aristocratic ladies exerted control and power as philanthropists and/ or as wives of politicians. Indeed many of the educational and legal grievances raised by women's suffrage had already been redressed — the Infant Custody Act of 1886 being one of the most significant. In 1884 the anti-suffragist James Bryce claimed that 'women already enjoy greater influence in other ways, both public and private, than the franchise would give them'.[45] Most women may have been excluded from political power but others, as was the case with Maud and her daughter Viola, both intimate friends of Prime Minister Herbert Asquith, would become often 'closer to actual power than many a man'.[46] In 1909, Eleanor Cecil wrote: 'The truth is they have so much power and influence already [...] and their instincts of self-preservation make them as Anti [Suffrage] as the men'.[47] Maud's good friend (and fellow anti-suffragist, president of the Anti-Suffrage League) the popular novelist Mrs Humphry Ward, like Maud in emphasizing a 'natural separation of powers', also advocated men's rule of politics 'at the centre, while women's influence should be indirect in proportion to education and character'.[48]

The exact nature of the influence that aristocratic women wielded over their families may be disputed, but the reality of their practical contribution is not. As Pat Jalland has pointed out, 'the management of large households and sizeable estates, with the constant movement of staff, was comparable to running a substantial business'.[49] Maud's closest friend Violet Lindsay was chatelaine of Belvoir Castle. The organization and movement of numerous servants between town and country required immense skill with sometimes up to twenty-five trips a year. Belvoir (with forty gardeners alone) was not the only house Maud visited where it was usual to maintain a staff of up to and above twenty-four servants, and where numbers were often increased to cater for the frequent house parties. These servants also had to be transported to the city with a skeleton staff remaining. Converting women like Violet proved a challenge to the suffrage movement, for they appeared to do and have everything.

Another reason to explain Maud's anti-suffrage position was her deeply conservative nature. She would be a faithful churchgoer all her life, believing in a pre-ordained inequality. Correspondence with her daughters repeatedly advocates the adherence to a spiritual life. She was also profoundly aware of her place in society and later her anti-suffrage stance would become only more entrenched. She would do nothing to rock the boat either socially or professionally. When Tree was finally knighted in 1909 it was the summation of years of behind-the-scenes work during which time Maud had pressured Violet (the Duchess of Rutland) and Margot Asquith (the Prime Minister's wife) to exert their influence. The Asquiths were vehemently opposed to women's suffrage — Margot was opposed to women's political associations of any kind and Herbert Asquith famously withdrew the promised Franchise Bill of 1913.[50] Although independently minded, Maud could not have condoned a cause responsible for the smashing of Asquith's windows,[51] and, like Lucy Cavendish, was of the opinion that the suffragettes were, 'unsexing themselves — not only by disgusting waverers and turning friends against them, but by enraging the masses of people in London and doubtless elsewhere'.[52]

On the question of women's suffrage, Maud was for once of the same opinion as Tree, who in speaking to a reporter for the *London Budget*, said:

> Women on the stage are very independent and their independence has not deprived them of any womanly charm. Actors and actresses hold a unique position, ours probably the one profession in which there is equality between the sexes. The moral is obvious.[53]

For the moment American journalists would have to contend with Maud's revelation that 'the stage' had been nothing but 'an amusing accident', not 'a pre-ordained vocation'. Moreover, she told a reporter (the *Chicago Evening Post*, 2 March 1895), she could 'keep house and tend the babies just as well as if she had given years of study to that aim'. And then in another seeming volte-face she added, 'But the modern woman isn't looking for contentment [...] it's the enlargement of her sphere she is after'.

Notes to Chapter 5

1. Beerbohm 1924: 59.
2. Violet Lindsay, diary entry for 1892 (by kind permission of His Grace the Duke of Rutland).
3. From 1900 onwards Tree was (unofficially) based at Her Majesty's Theatre. His residence consisted of a large fifty-foot banqueting-hall and smaller bedroom-cum-living-room.
4. Julian Sturgis to Maud Tree, 27 October [1893] (MBTC); Ellen Terry to Maud Tree, 15 March [1897] (MBTC).
5. Beerbohm 1924: 152. Her Majesty's Theatre became 'His' on the death of Queen Victoria in 1901.
6. This was the simplest form of lighting since all that was required was a lamp and a reflector in a box — hence the name; however, the absence of adjusting knobs meant there was no control over its focus. It was also limited to its colour mediums. Orange/red was generally used to indicate sunset-sunrise effects and blue/green night time.
7. See Rees 1978: 146, 190 & 198. See also the lighting plots for *Hamlet* in the British Theatre Museum.

8. *King John* (1899), *The Tempest* (1905), and *Henry VIII* (1911).
9. Tree 1915a: 43 & 46.
10. Booth 1981: 4.
11. Fitzgerald 1881: 49.
12. Booth 1981: 16.
13. Tree 1915a: 46.
14. Booth 1981: 17.
15. Tree 1915a: 213.
16. Hilda Hanbury to Maud Tree, [12 May 1892] (MBTC). Hanbury (1875–1961) was an English actress who joined Tree's company in 1892. Her descendants include the acting dynasty of grandsons Edward and James Fox, and their children Emilia, Laurence, and Freddie.
17. Beerbohm 1924: 77.
18. See Production Papers, *A Woman of No Importance*, Haymarket Theatre, London: fourteen promptbooks (three sets of four); seven promptbooks (HBT/000018/1–14, promptbooks; HBT/000018/15–21, promptbooks, some with sketches of character portraits). There is evidence that the material was reused for the 1908 revival at His Majesty's Theatre, from 19 April 1893 to 16 August 1893.
19. Constance Wilde to Maud Tree, [2 May 1893] (MBTC, by kind permission of Merlin Holland).
20. Beerbohm 1924: 82.
21. Jones 1905: IV.
22. Beerbohm 1924: 82.
23. Ibid.: 84–85
24. Rowell 2009.
25. Beerbohm 1924: 85.
26. Florence Bell to Maud Tree, 18 May 1894 (MBTC/000079).
27. Aubrey Beardsley to Maud Tree, 3 April 1894 (MBTC/000072).
28. Herbert Tree to Maud Tree, [1894] (HBT/RA/420).
29. Cecil 1985: 114.
30. Maud Tree to Violet Lindsay, 23 January 1895 (by kind permission of His Grace the Duke of Rutland).
31. Ibid.
32. Anon. to Maud Tree, [1895] (MBTC 6).
33. Quoted in Longaker 1945: 135.
34. Mary Augusta Arnold (1851–1920), was an Australian-born novelist who wrote under her husband's name as 'Mrs Humphry Ward'. In 1908, Mrs Ward was asked to be the first president of the Anti-Suffrage League and was a frequent contributor to the *Anti-Suffrage Review*. She founded adult accommodation settlements, of which the Mary Ward Centre in Tavistock Place, Bloomsbury, continues to exist as an adult education college.
35. Walworth 1895, *New York Mail & Express*, 16 February 1895; *Pioneer Press*, 17 February 1895; and *Chicago Evening Post*, 2 March 1895.
36. Nevinson 1935: 251–53 details the difficulty of speaking 'against the tumult', as quoted in Tylee 1998: 145. The WFL differed from other societies in its refusal to support the two bills then before parliament: one which excluded married women with a reference to coverture and the other that failed to enfranchise married women. (The married woman's status was that of a *femme covert* meaning that her legal identity was subsumed under that of her husband.)
37. See Cowman 1998: 78.
38. See Vanbrugh 1948: 83–84.
39. See Holledge 1948: 56.
40. Kenney 1924: 110.
41. The first-tier tours played the major cities such as Manchester and Glasgow. Lesser ones visited provincial towns where often the transported scenery did not fit onto tiny stages. See Holledge 1948: 14.
42. Ashwell 1936: 60–61.
43. Maud Tree to Viola Tree and Felicity Tree, [n.d.] (SCW, letter 103).

44. Maud Tree to Felicity Tree, [n.d.] (SCW, letter 533).
45. Hansard, House of Common Debates, 12 June 1884.
46. Lerner 1976: 351.
47. Eleanor Cecil to Maud Selborne, 3 November 1909 (MS Eng.Lett.d. 424, Countess of Selborne Papers, Bodleian Library, Oxford).
48. Mrs Humphry Ward's speech in debate with Mrs Fawcett, February 1909, printed pamphlet, Pusey House, Ward papers. See Pat Jalland, *Women, Marriage and Politics 1860–1914* (Oxford: Oxford University Press, 1988), p. 214.
49. See Jalland 1988: 190. Belvoir Castle is a 52,000-acre estate in Leicestershire. Its roof covers 150,000 square feet and to this day costs £500,000 a year to run.
50. Joannou and Purvis: 1998: 160–65.
51. Mary Leigh and Edith New broke two of the Prime Minister's windows on 30 June 1908.
52. Lucy Cavendish to May Drew, 9 May 1912 (Gladstone Drew Papers, British Library, Add. MS 46235, ff. 251–52).
53. Herbert Tree, 1913 (HBT/000062).

CHAPTER 6

Mrs Tree, Sardou, Her Majesty's Theatre, and Ibsen 1895–96

Despite the enormous press coverage of the American tour it had not in fact been a success, financially or otherwise. Theatre critics were not flattering about Tree, described as a 'peculiar actor who does not move the emotions' (*New York Times*, 3 February 1895) and interest in Maud had been over-zealous. On their return, Tree decided to take a break from Shakespeare and produce Herman Merivale's English version of Sardou's *Dora* as *Fedora* at the Haymarket. Victorien Sardou was the most successful playwright in the English theatre between the 'cup and saucer' dramas of T. W. Robertson (1860s) and A. W. Pinero (1890s). Indeed George Bernard Shaw would first use the term 'Sardoodledom' in his *Saturday Review* critique of Tree's revival (1 June 1895). Not only did English managers such as Tree and du Maurier easily 'borrow' from Sardou's plays, but leading English actors also vied to act in them.[1] As long as copyright law was unenforceable, English theatre managers positively encouraged house dramatists to pillage French originals.

Once again, as Maud might have anticipated, given the dynamic between husband and wife, and especially given their recent intimacy, Herbert did not choose Maud for the lead or indeed for any other part. The 'sensation' of the moment, Mrs Patrick Campbell, was given the title role and the recently returned-to-the-stage Mrs Bancroft was allotted the lesser part of the Princess Bariatine, while Herbert played Boris Ipanoff. Maud may have been comforted by the fact that it was an unintentionally farcical performance. Shaw wrote (*Saturday Review*, 1 June 1895):

> [Mrs P Campbell] made a perfect zebra of his (Tree's) left leg with bars across it. Then she flung her arms convulsively right round him; and the next time he turned his back to the footlights there was little to choose from between his coat back and shirtfront. Before the act was over a gallon of benzene would hardly have set him right again. Mr. Tree had his revenge at the end of the play, when, in falling on Fedora's body, he managed to transfer a large black patch to her cheek.

After two weeks of this nonetheless popular slapstick, Mrs Campbell lost her voice and left the production, and Maud seized her opportunity, learning the part overnight 'to perfection' as she writes in 'Herbert and I'.² The *Sheffield Daily Telegraph* of 23 September 1895 commented that if 'the play is Mrs. Tree's opportunity, it is also her husband's', while the evening edition wrote: 'Victorien Sardou's great play riveted most intensely the attention for three hours in an atmosphere approaching the heat of a Turkish bath'. That same day the *Manchester Evening News* publicly recognized Maud's influence, stating that 'Fedora may be taken as Mrs. Tree's contribution'. Praise for her acting was effusive, with the *Yorkshire Post* also commenting:

> It is little more than two months since an audience sat spellbound under the influence of Sarah Bernhardt [...] They would involuntarily compare the one performance with the other but Mrs. Tree's rendering of the part was nevertheless magnificent [...] She has unquestionably succeeded in investing the part with a vivid reality.

Maud had done much to dispel La Bernhardt's ghost, but not so her reputation. Outram Tristram wrote to Maud after seeing 'an extremely fine performance:'

> And believe one who has seen most Fedoras, and weighs all his words, that your playing was instinct with something very much beyond ability of the marked order. Indeed if you would only consent (off the stage) to be eccentric instead of in the mode — kept a tiger cub for instance in the garden and a coffin or two on the stairs, — you would soon come to be considered an actress of genius. The consideration gained in this way would not probably please you. Console yourself. You do not need it.³

The playwright Julian Sturgis (who was still waiting for feedback on the play he had written and sent to Maud) wrote in the interim:

> Dear Mrs. Tree,
> We were very much interested and warmly admired your playing. Frankly it seems encouraging to me that an English actress can be so effective in a part moulded in every detail to the temperament & talent of a particular Frenchwoman. You have a double task, first to act the sort of woman that Bernhardt is by nature, and then to act 'Fedora.' I thought you wonderfully good. From what Gilbert said I expected you to be very clever (as you always are) and (if I may say so with complete frankness) I expected far more inequality.
> There were two moments when I found myself critical. When you tore off your glove at the end of Act 2, it looked too much as if you did it in order to strike an attitude with the bare hand & arm. We both thought that you would throw it down as if you loathed it because he had kissed it. But I don't <u>suggest</u> — that would be cheek. I only mention the effect as to me a little cold & stagy, the one arm pointing after him. In the beginning of Act 4, I wondered if you were not too much the young English bride home from the honeymoon.⁴ I should have liked a more nervous happiness, which she knows is precarious. Still you may like the other as giving a stronger contrast.
> And yet Fedora, knowing that he may find out at any moment that she has been spying on him, could hardly look so [sweet] calm.⁵
> I am not a critic. So forgive me for making comments.
> I was [very] really astonished at your very clever & convincing performance. So was my wife who has a fine instinct for the stage. Please thank your husband.

He must be much pleased with your success in such a task.
Yours,
Julian Sturgis[6]

Indeed he must have been, for Herbert wrote to Maud from Marienbad: 'you will only feel by and by what an enormous impression you made in Fedora'.[7]

Maud's successes, however, were sometimes followed by moments of apprehension over future work. Tree, for his part, could also admit to financial worries and to the 'fits of depression' from which he sometimes suffered. During a rare period when Maud found herself without work, and an even rarer moment when Tree found occasion to encourage her, he wrote from Marienbad:

> Pray don't fancy that you need give up hope — there was never a time when there was so much hope for your future in regard to the stage, for you have made enormous strides during the past year, and especially this season.[8]

Six months later Maud was back in work, this time appearing at the Shaftesbury Theatre which was now under the management of H. N. Morrell and actor Lewis Waller. In another of those plays that would appear to mimic Maud's home life, she was the leading lady in a production which the *Sketch* of 29 January 1896 considered 'very much strengthened' as a result. In *A Woman's Reason* — with its curiously titled three acts 'Because I Must', 'Because I Will', 'Because I Do' — Maud played the Hon. Nina Keith and Waller her on-stage husband, while Florence West (Waller's wife in real life) played her on-stage sister-in-law.[9] The *Sketch* devoted six pages of analysis to it, of which four consisted of fetching photographs of Maud, slender with a tiny post-baby waist, draped in various artistic poses. In all of them she appears wide-eyed with surprise, while in one Florence West says prophetically, 'You've never had a real honeymoon'.

There is no indication that the suave Lewis Waller made much of an impression on Maud at this time. They had played together once before in *Lady Clancarty* and, like Maud, Waller espoused Ibsen plays to the delight of the theatre critic and Ibsen translator, William Archer. While the Trees were touring the States, Waller had also leased the Theatre Royal, Haymarket, in their absence. But while Waller developed his crush on Maud, there is no record that his feelings were reciprocated. Besides which, there was no time to consider a flirtation. Tree may not always have cast her in his plays but he relied on her for advice. But no jibe was intended or anything to foreshadow future jealousy when he wrote to her shortly after the play closed, 'I can't make up my mind as to whether I should do Othello or Iago — I wish you would read the play through again'.

Delighted to be asked, Maud responded warmly, enclosing a list of playwrights with whom she had been corresponding. The list included Rudyard Kipling (whom she had met at a glitzy dinner in Washington), Haddon Chambers, Sydney Grundy, and Henry Arthur Jones. She wrote to the latter requesting a drama on the Indian Mutiny which became *Carnac Sahib*. Despite their sometime marital discord and professional jealousy, the sentiment behind 'all the distance in the world cannot divide our hearts — can it?' with which Maud wrote to Tree was still in place, and for him she remained the one person he could trust ('I have no one else to rely on').[10]

STEPHEN AND HIS WIFE.

"*I know you can't understand.*"

Fig. 6.1. Maud Tree as Mrs D'Acosta and Lewis Waller as her husband Stephen, in *A Woman's Reason* (*Sketch*, 29 January 1896; photograph by Alfred Ellis, Upper Baker Street)

The autumn of 1896 was a period of renewed intimacy between husband and wife, and great professional enhancement as they worked in unison. On their return from America Tree was resolved to achieve two goals: one was the production of *Trilby*, the du Maurier play he had purchased on the eve of his departure from America; the other was the acquisition of his very own theatre. He had identified a site near the Haymarket, upon which three other theatres had already been built, burned down, and re-built. There were further developments. By the time she played the title role in *Trilby* at the Borough Theatre in Stratford, East London, in September, Maud was pregnant again with her third and last child. A month later the play came to London, opening at the Haymarket with the statuesque Dorothea Baird as Trilby and Tree as Svengali, to a success that Maud described as 'historic' and 'beyond our wildest dreams'. It certainly represented the greatest financial gain Tree had experienced to date and for the first time in his life he was 'rich'. When a socialite asked Maud what jewel Herbert had given her out of this success, she did not hesitate in her reply: 'Her Majesty's Theatre, but I'm not wearing it tonight'.[11]

Tree promptly set off on his second American tour, leaving Maud to set up a committee and oversee the theatre's purchase. This was a project she accepted with alacrity, approaching the Anglo-German banker Ernest Cassel in the first instance. It was because she had initially met Cassel at a dinner party some years earlier that she had no qualms now in either asking him to be her unborn child's godfather or to backing financially Her Majesty's Theatre.[12] Maud's own banker, Carl Meyer, also became a significant shareholder in the theatre, which was bought for £26,400 (approximately £18 million today). Nearly all the realizable assets of the company were the costumes, properties, and scenery;[13] a sum of £10,000 was invested in shares and £16,400 in a second mortgage on the property.[14] The accountants Price Waterhouse, who audited Tree's records, indicate that £5,900 was paid annually in ground rent until 1905 when the business was restructured as the Playhouse Trust Limited. By then Tree held £13,893 in the Playhouse.[15]

By the time it was completed, the building, designed to constitute a symmetrical pair with the Carlton Hotel by Charles J. Phipps, resembled the Paris Opera with its canopy over the main ground floor entrances and cantilevered tiers. At its centre, an enormous square, French-style dome, housing Herbert's own banqueting hall and living areas, dominates the whole to this day. Employing the architect W. H. Romaine-Walker, Maud was responsible for the building's interior decoration; it had gas lighting, plush velvet seats, and the first ever flat stage in England. The first-floor dressing rooms were spacious and comfortable — Tree's own had a small drawing-room, make-up room, and bathroom — and were a far cry from a time when these had been dubbed 'nurseries of fever'.[16] It was to be quite the handsomest theatre in London, where patrons would be treated as guests. There was no charge for programmes or cloakrooms and the orchestra, hidden by palm trees, played such quality music that theatregoers actually listened. In the end the theatre costs had exceeded the estimate by only £300.

There was, however, a blot on the horizon. In November, Maud began to receive the first of a series of anonymous letters that she would continue to receive throughout her life with Herbert. The author of the hand-delivered note was 'sorry to say' Tree was seen 'driving with a Miss P'. Maud immediately telegrammed Herbert, who wrote hastily by return to reassure her that he 'was not flirting with anyone' and that she could rely on his 'being good'. He added, 'I have been worrying myself about that horrid letter — if you get any more, do not worry yourself by reading them, promise me, but send them to Webb and to George Lewis'.[17] Maud, willing to be calmed, and supported by the cosy domesticity of Sloane Street, was indeed unworried to the extent that Tree wrote again:

> My own sweet darling Maud, Last night all your letters reached me — I never knew, dearest, how deep and beautiful your love for me was — I will try and be worthy of it [...] Do not worry, sweet one, about that horrid letter — it is evidently some enemy of yours — for what but a cruel and depraved wretch could send such a letter, knowing your condition. Please don't give it another thought — you can rely on my love and my loyalty to you.[18]

What Herbert was hiding from Maud was the fact that he was indeed having an affair, an affair that had begun sometime in the early 1880s and would in fact last until his death in 1917. Furthermore, by the time Maud received the anonymous letter, his mistress May Pinney had already given birth to their son Claude.[19] He would have another five children with her, of whom the film director Sir Carol Reed was one; the actor Oliver Reed would be his grandson through this liaison. But May Pinney was not his only mistress and he had affairs with many of his leading ladies while continuing to visit Maud and his daughters by her, in the 'marital' home. By the 1900s, Tree was living between the Dome of Her Majesty's Theatre and May's house in Putney.[20] But Maud would only discover the extent of Tree's relationship with May later. For the present he wrote again, anxious to reassure her and say that he had gone to bed with pictures of Maud, Viola, and Felicity. A month later, shortly before the birth of Iris in London, he wrote from America:

> Oh my dear sweet Maud, by the time you get this letter all will probably be over — I hope you will not suffer — you know that I shall always be thinking of you and wishing I could hold your hand [...] It was madness to let you stay behind — and I am very sad without you.

In a moment of professional generosity he added, 'everybody speaks lovingly of you here, and they all miss you [...] Kate Rorke played Ophelia very well — but of course she was not near you'.[21]

Iris was born on 27 January and Maud was inundated with good wishes. George Lewis's wife, Edith, wrote immediately: 'My Dear Mrs. Three, That's your name, no longer Tree but three! Don't fret about the son, you have time yet! And oh dear they sometimes break hearts! Of mothers as well as sweet hearts and wives'.[22] The garden designer, Norah Lindsay (Violet's sister-in-law) wanted to know if the 'third time was bad or better than the second or first'. But Violet's husband, who had become the Marquess of Granby in 1888, in expressing his affection also revealed his prejudice: 'I need not ask after you as actresses get through these little events quickly and well'.[23]

Maud did recover quickly, although, as she admitted to Violet Lindsay, she could not 'ride yet'. But there was scarcely time to enjoy her new motherhood; she had pressing matters to attend to. First and foremost was dealing with Tree's current situation in America. This latest tour was not proving any greater success than the first one, but in her own inspired PR strike Maud now wrote to his agent Elisabeth Marbury to suggest that it be announced that the reverse was true. Moreover, Maud identified Tree's urgent need for a manager who could be entrusted with the business side of the theatre, and Henry Dana, who would stay with the Trees until Herbert's death in 1917, was duly employed. And there was more to arouse disquiet. The Trees' new-found riches had been short-lived; the bulk of the profits earned from *Trilby* had been invested in the refurbishment of Her Majesty's and in other outgoing productions, let alone the American tour. 'I am frightfully worried about expenses,' Maud wrote to Tree, 'My last £5 is nearly gone and I don't believe Webb can give me any more'. And his recurrent 'Don't fret about the bills darling' did little to placate her.[24] In Herbert's absence, Maud decided to come to grips with their financial position. She did not reply to her husband, but instead addressed her concerns to his accounts manager, James Graham, with the words 'I always took for granted that you knew the receipts each night', to which he replied:

> I have made the calculation in another way, on the basis of my fees and it works out the same. If your husband will authorize me to supply you with the details I will do so with pleasure. I may say that occasionally he has shown me the weekly profit and I have found it strictly accurate.[25]

Far from satisfied, Maud wrote to the playwright Sydney Grundy himself. 'I was quite correct,' he replied by return, 'Up to and including Friday the 10th, our 138th performance, the gross receipts were £40,634 or £294 per performance'.[26]

The newly appointed and very loyal Dana was more guarded. His letter, arriving a day after Grundy's, said: 'If the details are withheld from you I don't think I have the right to supply them'.[27] It did not matter, as Maud had already found out what she wanted. Taking matters into her own hands, she decided to risk an investment of her own. In due course Carl Meyer replied:

> I am glad to be able to report that the £50 you were good enough to entrust to me have borne fruit in as much as I am enabled to return them to you herewith accompanied by the £150 profit making £200 in all [...].
> Excuse me if I do not send you a detailed account of my operations on your behalf — they have caused me many a sleepless night.[28]

Although Iris was less than two months old, Maud now actively sought work. While heavily pregnant, she had written to Louis Calvert, whose production of *Cleopatra* would open in May at the Olympic Theatre, but there seems to have been a misunderstanding, for initially Calvert offered Maud the role at £40 per week for seven performances.[29] Two days later he admitted to having offered Mrs Patrick Campbell the part and wondered if Maud would now play a nun. Maud was less than impressed, but by January the part had gone to Miss Achurch anyway. Although nothing came of this endeavour, Maud used the opportunity to rekindle her friendship with Janet Achurch, who had contacted Maud almost a year before with a view to performing 'the greatest Ibsen success that London has yet seen'. The play had been on hold for a year because, although Lewis Waller and H. H. Morell (joint managers of Tree's former Haymarket Theatre) had made an offer on the play, it would have meant casting Florence West (Waller's wife), and Achurch did not believe it suited her. 'Not at all events,' as she told Maud, 'to risk the play on that'.[30]

Now almost a year later, the actress Elizabeth Robins, who had taken over this project from Achurch, wrote to Maud to propose she play 'the subtle and extraordinary' Mrs Wilton in Ibsen's *John Gabriel Borkman*. If she agreed to the part, she could be assured that the play was 'certain to be the best cast Ibsen play' Robins had ever had any connection with.[31] Earlier in the year she had set up a subscription society called the New Century Theatre with the writers Alfred Sutro, W. W. Massingham, and the Scottish journalist, drama critic, and translator of Ibsen, William Archer; but she was already well known to Maud. As an aspiring young actress the American Elizabeth Robins first came to England after her husband famously drowned himself in the Charles River wearing a full suit of armour. She had understudied for Maud in *Forgotten* and *A Man's Shadow*, but her association with the Trees, or rather Herbert in particular, had begun before that. Her diary refers to Herbert as 'H' in the recounting of an unedifying experience in which he wined and dined her and even offered to set her up in a flat, while she innocently hoped merely to be offered a part. Nor was he any more helpful in furthering her career as a playwright, telling her that he had never read a good play by 'a woman's hand'.[32] But Tree was soon to have a surprising change of heart. Secretly he was captivated by Robins's (unpublished) historical melodrama *Benvenuto Cellini,* which was set in the French court of François I. In fact, he was so captivated that he was prepared to pay an astonishing £6,000 to produce it. Typically his productions cost between £4,000 and £6,000, while his largest outlay would be for *Darling of the Gods* (1903) on which he spent £9,238 (the equivalent labour cost of that project being £3.5 million). Of course he wished to play the lead character. In the event the project foundered, as Tree wanted exclusive rights and to implement radical alterations to the play before it was placed under contract.

Luckily, Robins did not associate this trying time with Tree's wife, and happily Maud did not feel her future work would in any way be jeopardized by accepting an Ibsen role now. Some actresses associated with Ibsen or Shaw 'achieved a certain notoriety and success' only to discover that it became difficult to find a manager who would cast them 'as a conventional heroine', though once again Maud's elocution and training on which she invariably fell back, set her apart.[33] The challenge lay less in procuring a role later and rather more in executing a successful one now. More specifically, roles created by Ibsen offered an exciting departure from Shakespearean ones as they necessarily demanded the intellectual engagement Shaw had described in a lecture he gave in 1899 called 'Acting, By One Who Does Not Believe in It'.[34] Great acting was not simply a gift for mimicry but called for a 'metaphysical self-realization' — that is, the talent for portraying a well-defined self through the roles interpreted — such as Elizabeth Robins's famous ability to 'send thought across the footlights'.³⁵ Rehearsals began in earnest with Maud as Mrs Wilton, in a part, as William Archer said, 'that might have been written' for her. It was also, Archer said, one of Ibsen's 'most modern'.³⁶ Elizabeth Robins played Ella Rentheim, Genevieve Ward, Gunhild, and W. H. Vernon, John Gabriel Borkman.

On 28 April, however, Maud took leave of the play to participate in the glittering inauguration of Her Majesty's Theatre. Summoning a cast of friends and contacts, she compiled a programme that included her great friend the soprano Clara Butt and Edward Elgar. The Prince of Wales was the guest of honour, to be greeted by footmen dressed in liveries identical to his own at Buckingham Palace. (The Prince was displeased by this detail and the uniforms were subsequently changed.) Gorgeously gowned women were reflected in polished chandeliers and full-length mirrors, their jewels sparkling in the newly-installed gas light (which failed almost immediately), while Maud herself appeared as a lady of the court of Louis XV. She commenced proceedings with an ode composed for the occasion by the Poet Laureate, Alfred Austin, followed by a performance of *The Seats of the Mighty*, in which she played Madame de Cournal.³⁷

The very next day Maud was back in rehearsal, and *John Gabriel Borkman* opened six days later, on 3 May 1897, at the Royal Strand Theatre. The atmosphere of a play deemed to be 'an Ibsenite study of the coldness of the heart' was further accentuated by the naturalistic use of lighting — or lack thereof. In the interests of economy more candles and lamps were used than electricity.³⁸ In the *Saturday Review* of 8 May 1897 Shaw reviewed the stark set in rather less romantic prose:

> The first performance of John Gabriel Borkman, the latest masterpiece of the acknowledged chief of European dramatic art, has taken place in London under the usual shabby circumstances. For the first scene in the gloomy Borkman house, a faded, soiled, dusty wreck of some gay French salon, originally designed, perhaps, for Offenbach's 'Favert,' was fitted with an incongruous Norwegian stove, a painted stair case, and a couple of chairs which were no doubt white and gold when they first figured in Tom Taylor's 'Plot and Passion,' or some other relic of the days before Mr. Bancroft revolutionized stage furniture, but have apparently languished ever since, unsold and unsaleable among second-hand keys, framed lithographs of the Prince Consort, casual fire-irons and stair-rods, and other spoils of the broker.

The ever-loyal Herman Vezin was of the opinion, however, in a letter to Maud, that the desired 'gloom' had indeed been achieved and 'the depression of the performance is attributed to the play. I only know that when I <u>read</u> the play I was intensely interested & felt no depression'. He went on to praise her performance:

> You were simply delightful as Mrs. Wilton. You can't think what a treat it was upon listening as Ibsen (whose dialogue ought to be delivered simply & naturally) spoils by a style of elocution by many people fitted for fustian old fashioned plays & a great deal of which was unintelligible, to hear your clear, resonant voice filling the house without strain or effort & so understand every word & sentence of the part with pleasurable ease. I suppose I know nothing about it for I read in the Telegraph that the acting was superb.³⁹

Elizabeth Robins herself was unsure of its success: 'I go at my work next day with scrap ends of praise & blame flashing thro' my mind & the good things are overdone & the bad things probably worse'.[40]

Alfred Sutro was not, and on the strength of Maud's performance he wrote:

> I am sending you today the MS of Porto-Riche's play 'Le Passé' — also a copy of my translation of Maeterlinck's Aglavaine.[41] I am asking the publishers to send you The Treasure of the Humble — I am sure you will like the book. The first four essays are not so interesting as the last six: and I advise all are strange as is his way of thinking so begin with the fifth.[42]

But there was little time for Maud to dwell on past performance when she was inundated with requests for future ones. There was demand for recitations — George Alexander dropped a note in at the theatre asking her to come straight after her Ibsen matinees and recite Kipling — and discussions for the next season's programme were already taking place. After the usual summer bazaars and curtain-raisers had finished, it would seem that the entire country was caught up with feverish monarchial celebrations. It was Victoria's diamond jubilee year, and for Tree this could only mean Shakespeare, with all the pageantry, spectacle, and glitz he could muster. And of Shakespeare's plays, there was only one that to Tree's mind perfectly addressed the qualities of leadership. On this occasion, however, Maud was less preoccupied with securing a role for herself than in preventing Herbert from casting himself in the one he envisioned. As they both knew (not that it had stopped him before), much of the rhetoric in Shakespeare was far beyond his declamatory powers. By the autumn, however, rehearsals for a play that had not been seen in the West End for half a century were well under way. *Julius Caesar* would run for six months and 165 consecutive performances. Viewed by 242,000 spectators, it would clear a profit of £11,000. In the end, and thanks to Maud's intervention, Tree did not play Caesar, for as he concluded in his diary, 'For the scholar Brutus, for the actor Cassius, for the public Anthony'.[43]

Notes to Chapter 6

1. Leading ladies included Maud Tree, Ellen Terry, Elizabeth Robins, Mrs Patrick Campbell, and Gladys Cooper. Among English actors who appeared in Sardou plays were Irving, Wyndham, Tree, Forbes-Robertson, and Hare.
2. Beerbohm 1924: 98.
3. W. Outram Tristram to Maud Tree, 6 July 1895 (MBTC/000078). Sarah Bernhardt was notorious for sleeping in a coffin and keeping a menagerie of pets, see Gottlieb 2010: 85.
4. In the play, Fedora and her lover Loris Ipanoff have just returned from a stolen visit to Jersey. Fedora has set a trap for Loris whom she believes to be responsible for her fiancé's murder.
5. In the play, despite now having fallen in love with Loris, Fedora is responsible for his financial ruin and indirectly, the deaths of his mother and brother. This will soon be revealed and Fedora, feeling that she has lost Loris's love, commits suicide.
6. Julian Sturgis to Maud Tree, 6 July 1895 (MBTC).
7. Herbert Tree to Maud Tree, 24 July 1895 (HBT). Beerbohm 1924: 98.
8. Herbert Tree to Maud Tree, 24 July 1895 (HBT).
9. On 27 December 1895, *A Woman's Reason* opened at the Shaftsbury Theatre. It was a play about adultery, based on the novel by William Dean Howell, and starred, and was adapted by, the future Examiner of Plays, Charles Brookfield. As a result of her divorce, Nina is socially ostracized.

10. Herbert Tree to Maud Tree, 15 December 1896 (MBTC).
11. Beerbohm 1924: 100.
12. See the first chapter of Beerbohm: 1924, which gives a description of their first meeting. Cassel became godfather to Maud's third daughter Iris.
13. Production Papers (BTC, PRO BT31/4497/29378, and C26/481). See Davis 2000: 225–31.
14. See Pearson 1988: 101, and Davis 2000: 223–27.
15. Herbert Tree to Maud Tree, 8 December 1896: 'Mind you keep up Sir Algernon West and Werner — it is most important now to get strong people at my back even if they put into the general concern, apart from the mere building' (HBT 1, uncatalogued).
16. The 1860s Contagious Diseases Act dictated that barriers were erected to seal the auditorium from 'improper intrusion' and from disease: 73,000 people died in England of cholera in 1849, only nine years before Maud was born. See Archer 1887: 569, and Davis 1991: 99–101. After a fire at the Theatre Royal, Exeter, in 1887, in which 180 people died, theatres with a pit and gallery were required to install three separate entrances. In the same year, Tree was compelled to engage a fireman for every performance of *The Red Lamp* and wrote to *The Times* in defence of electric light.
17. Herbert Tree to Maud Tree, [1896] (HBT/RA).
18. Herbert Tree to Maud Tree, [27 November 1896] (HBT/RA/420).
19. May Pinney (1871–1955) was the actress daughter of William Pinney. In 1904 she changed her name by deed poll to Reed.
20. From the late 1890s, May Pinney lived at Daisyfield, Putney Hill.
21. Herbert Tree to Maud Tree, [5 January 1897] (HBT). Elisabeth Marbury, Tree's agent wrote to Maud that 'Mr. Tree's and Miss Rourke's [sic] performances were far too delicate for an American audience', 25 November 1896 (MBTC, uncatalogued).
22. Edith Lewis to Maud Tree, [1897] (MBTC 6).
23. Norah Lindsay to Maud Tree, January 1897 (MBTC 6); Henry John Granby to Maud Tree, 4 February 1897 (MBTC).
24. Maud Tree to Herbert Tree, March 1897 (SCW, letter 343). Herbert Tree to Maud Tree, 1897 (MBTC 6).
25. James Graham to Maud Tree, [n.d.] (MBTC 6). Production Papers for *Trilby* (MBTC 6: HBT/000054/1–10, lime plots; HBT/000054/11–24, switchboard plots; HBT/000054/25–46, property plots; HBT/000054/47–58, misc. plots; HBT/000054/59–62, gas, electric, and lime plots; HBT/000054/63, notes on music).
26. Sydney Grundy to Maud Tree, [n.d.] (MBTC 6). From 1908 to1909 Tree produced a matinée season of 'new' plays. *An Enemy of the People* was performed only seven times in 1893, whereas the records for the fiscal year 1911–12 show that *Macbeth* was performed eighty-five times, *Orpheus* fifty-one. *Trilby* was seen thirty-six times, *Oliver Twist* twenty-three and the Shakespeare Festival eighteen. Tree's annual expenditure averaged £10,408 and his personal profit was £12,526. In contrast, the Independent Theatre Society, for example, made barely £400 a year during its seven-year existence. Tree was paid £1,000 for five hours work filming *Henry VIII*, while the sale of the rights to *Trilby* in 1914 gave him £1,352. Elizabeth Robins earned £50 weekly for *Little Eyolf*, but the average performer's pay was £2. Maud typically earned £40 for 8 performances.
27. Henry Dana to Maud Tree, [n.d.] (MBTC 6).
28. Carl Meyer to Maud Tree, 3 October 1902 (MBTC 6).
29. The actor-manager Louis Calvert (1859–1923) published *Problems of the Actor* in 1919, an acting manual for aspiring actors. See Foulkes 1992: 112. Calvert played Flute in Tree's 1900 production of *A Midsummer Night's Dream*.
30. Janet Achurch to Maud Tree, 29 February 1896 (MBTC/000009).
31. Elizabeth Robins to Maud Tree, [1897] (MBTC).
32. Herbert Tree to Elizabeth Robins, 24 April 1891 (Fales Library, New York University). See also John 1995: 110.
33. See Holledge 1981: 33.
34. Shaw 1961: 12–23.

35. Campbell 1922: 65.
36. William Archer to Maud Tree, 6 March 1897 (MBTC/00039).
37. The play was later dubbed 'Mighty Few' as it failed to fill seats. See Pearson 1988: 103.
38. Robins 1940: 242. See also John 1995: 101.
39. Herman Vezin to Maud Tree, 4 May 1897 (MBTC B). Herman Vezin (1829–1910) was an actor.
40. Elizabeth Robins to Maud Tree, [n.d.] (MBTC 6).
41. *Le Passé* (1897) by Georges de Porto-Riche (1849–1930). Edward Thomas Maurice, Count Maeterlinck (1862–1949), Belgian writer who won the 1911 Nobel Prize in Literature; *Aglavaine et Sélysette* was first performed in December 1896 and was said to be his first play of character. *The Treasure of the Humble* was published in 1896.
42. Alfred Sutro to Maud Tree, [1897 (MBTC).
43. HBT/RA/420.

CHAPTER 7

'That Brutus may be a little missed'
1898

In the souvenir programme for *Julius Caesar* the 'hero' is hailed as 'the feverish pulsing city' itself — a gorgeous, visual pageant of eight separate sets designed by Lawrence Alma-Tadema.[1] The senators were clad in crimson silk robes, while the foot soldiers were equipped with hand-made spears and shields. Alma-Tadema made each and every individual phalerian, all the armour and insignias himself and designed and draped every toga. Caesar, played by Charles Fulton, wore a robe of claret brocade shot with violet. Tree also insisted he lie supine as the murdered man throughout the entire Forum scene, refusing to have a dummy for the purpose. When Fulton commented that he suffered from colds in winter and wondered what might happen if he sneezed, Tree replied: 'they will call you Julius Cnaesar'.[2] Louis Calvert (who had dithered over casting Maud in his production of *Cleopatra*) was Casca, Tree was Marc Antony, Lily Hanbury in electric blue was Calpurnia, and Lewis Waller, Brutus. Against costumes designed to dazzle, Maud played Lucius skimming barefoot across the stage.

Chaotic rehearsals, witnessed not least by Shaw, ever ready with lashings of criticism, press correspondents, who labelled Maud a 'spirited aide-de-camp and adviser', and Violet Lindsay's daughters, who lathered their arms in pretend blood and stomped grumpily around the set muttering 'yes, we give you our ears', gave way to what was to be one of Tree's most ebullient productions ever.[3] Not only did he cut the play drastically to make way for Tadema's magnificent tableaux but he also shifted the emphasis from an idealized Brutus to himself, or rather Marc Antony. While the critics could not stretch to comparing Herbert to a Macready, there was no doubt that this Shakespeare was a crowd-puller. More importantly, Herbert made Shakespeare approachable. On the back of its success new friends flocked to the Trees, including the former Prime Minister Lord Rosebery, who went as far as naming Herbert and his production in a speech to the London County Council: 'The Roman,' he said, 'was proud of Rome. He should be prouder still of London'.[4]

If the production was praised there was one actor who came out of it even better: Lewis Waller, who in the part of Brutus pushed his famous voice to its limit. Having by now attracted a following of hysterical women — they had formed the 'KOW' (Keen on Waller) brigade — he was enjoying success elsewhere as the dashing hero of romantic plays, and he now claimed to be very much in love with Maud. 'Shall I be very selfish if I hope that 'Brutus' may be just a little bit missed?' he wrote her in between performances.[5] There is still no indication, however, that Maud felt as passionately for Waller as he did for her. She had never fallen out of love with Herbert, even if on occasion she felt betrayed by him, and she was deeply loyal, but she cannot have helped being flattered by Waller's persistence. She was used to the flattery of older men but not the overt adoration of a younger one. Hamilton Aidé and W. S. Gilbert made no secret of their devotion, nor did Shaw, who had to be careful in his communications with Maud as his own wife could be extremely jealous. But Maud's barefoot charm as she glided about the stage singing — she sang Sullivan's *Orpheus with his Lute* — were not enough to appease Tree, who was stung by this flirtation. Edward Burne-Jones for one came to Maud's figurative rescue:

> Phil [Edward's son] told me heartrending stories of the part you take in Julius Caesar — he says you are ordered about & bidden to do things & he agreed it was hard to bear — when I am well I shall go but I trust I may not be carried away by my feelings (as in Pompadour times) & express loud & open indignities.
> E. B. J.[6]

Mild irritation on Tree's part soon gave way to unreserved enmity with Waller's next move. And the next play with which they were all involved would, if nothing else, expose the petty rivalries between leading ladies and the quarrels, histrionics, and outright ambition amongst the players. Tree's ever-faithful playwright, Sydney Grundy, had adapted a play for him based on Dumas's *The Three Musketeers*. Waller had come up with a similar version and, what is more, soon threw up billboards in the suburbs publicizing his own *Three Musketeers*. Both began casting, Waller's wife being given the part of the scheming Miladi. Tree confided to Maud that he was considering offering Waller £500 to quash his version, but it was too late. Waller produced his play and, with his magnificent voice and physique, was a sensation as D'Artagnan. In an article Edward Morton wrote for the *Playgoer and Society Illustrated*, entitled 'A Queen's Love Romance', he would later comment that Waller 'seems even more at ease in silk and satin, in doublet and hose, than the ordinary clothes of our everyday life'.[7]

Tree immediately sent his manager Dana to see the play but it was sold out, and realizing that his own play would suffer from Waller's competition, he offered Waller the part of Buckingham, a three-year contract, and a large salary if he would close his own play and join Tree's company. Jumping at the chance to be near Maud, who played Anne of Austria, Waller duly closed down his production at the height of its popularity.

But Tree's was to be a production from which none of the actors came off well. Despite the grand costumes — Waller's green and pink velvet doublet and Maud's oversized jewels — the company was considered 'insincere'. Mrs Tree, the *Morning Leader* of 19 June 1898 wrote, 'was not taking very much trouble to display any emotion beside the very slight melancholy in her love scene'. That was the least of it. Florence West had been replaced not by Maud (as Maud had hoped) but by the beautiful American actress Mrs Brown Potter. 'Mrs. Potter's cry,' the same paper

CHAPTER 8

Philanthropy and
'The Absent-Minded Beggar'
1899

Maud had experienced the pain of Herbert's infidelity which was an aspect of their marriage she could do nothing about, but being too busy to breathe was something she could achieve. An ingrained work ethic overrode any despondency she may have been feeling, while her recitation and public speaking were becoming powerful tools in raising funds for the charitable causes that were beginning to take up as much of her time as the stage. In addition to ad hoc requests for 'stand-and-deliver' performances Maud threw her weight behind those schemes specifically connected to the theatre world such as the Theatrical Mission and the Actors' Benevolent Fund. Both Trees had been instrumental in the creation of Siddons House, the patrons of which included Princess Mary, Ellen Terry, Arthur Sullivan, and Sarah Bernhardt. It was a private hospital to be used for 'bona fide actors and actresses peculiarly liable to ailments caused by prolonged work'.[1] Maud was also patron of the Rehearsal Club from its inception in 1892, the King George's Hospital, and The League of Mercy, contributions to which in 1899 totalled £600,000, all donated by artisans and tradesmen.[2] A few years previously, Reverend B. Waugh, in thanking Maud Tree for taking part in a charity event, wrote, 'I think actresses are the kindest people [...] they seem to be ready to take any amount of trouble, and are so nice about it'.[3]

But Maud's involvement in these causes was not purely motivated by what Frank Prochaska has called the 'voluntary impulse'.[4] By the late 1890s philanthropy, like entertainment, was a burgeoning facet of Victorian cultural life, the two becoming symbiotically incorporated within the newly respectable image of the fin-de-siècle actress.[5] The role of the middle-class actress in this newly fashionable 'industry' was heterogeneous, reflecting intrinsic contradictions between the domestic ideology, which was held to prompt this kind of philanthropic activity, and the increasingly public and visible role of women. Just as the aristocratic lady, towards the end of the century, was moving away from the practice of personal charity, the middle-class actress began to take over her role, setting herself up as 'a new, challenging, source of authority'.[6]

It was, however, an authority that crucially depended on the endorsement by the very aristocratic lady it displaced. In this instance, acceptance by the highborn woman was the necessary visible sign by which society could suspend its habitual 'revulsion, suspicion and unease about the performer'.[7] Thus, by associating themselves with and acting under the patronage of these ladies, actresses could prove themselves to be agents of social improvement both for themselves and others. Maud, of course, needed never to look further than her dear friend Violet Lindsay. The *Press Bazaar News* of 28 and 29 June 1898, priced at 1 shilling and thus the most expensive 'daily' at the time in the world, ran the motto 'Find a Duchess, flatter her and get £500'.

As competition between charities grew more acute, so did the need for more original venues and more extravagant means of entertainment. Proceeds were collected from pamphlets, the recital of poems, songs and hymns, benefit matinées, auctions, the painting of Christmas cards, and collection boxes and charity balls. Philanthropic events increasingly fused society and entertainment under the patronage of the aristocracy, which was still needed to lend glamour, respectability, and ultimately spending-power to these activities. By the late 1890s the London season not only encompassed debutante balls, dances, and dinners but all manner of gala performances and theatrical initiatives in the name of charity. Social columnists reporting the daily movements of the aristocracy now gave prominence to these charity engagements, thus attracting more press interest than they might otherwise have done.

Nothing, however, matched the excitement generated by the charity bazaar (over a hundred were advertised in Greater London in 1899), which, according to Robert Louis Stevenson, being 'part amusement, part commerce', made the 'exercise of charity, entertainment in itself'.[8] Usually opened with speeches, songs, children, or royalty, this greatest of stages conferred the ultimate seal of approval by the aristocracy on the gentleman manager and the actors and actresses associated with him.[9]

The most ambitious of these bazaars — the *Globe* of 20 June 1899 called it 'the most interesting and most magnificent bazaar which has ever been held in this country' — was the Charing Cross Hospital Bazaar, which took place on 21 June 1899. Opened after six months' planning, the bazaar was held in the Albert Hall, which had been transformed at a cost of £1,000 (the equivalent today of approximately £400,000). Twenty-seven electrically-lit stalls offered gifts, books (Lady Randolph Churchill sold signed copies of novels by Hardy and Zola), refreshments (the 'Miladi's Smile' cocktail was concocted specifically for the event), and souvenirs. Most of the tent-like stalls, representing countries and draped in their national bunting, were hosted by a stellar cast of celebrities. Indeed, the *Morning Post* of 20 June asserted: 'under no banner but that of charity could such a roll of names have been mustered'. Extensive press coverage was given to the fashion, decoration, and entertainment programmed for the two days, as for example in the *Illustrated London News* of 1 July. The *Court Forward* of 3 June kept the public informed of progress: 'the whole force of the Royal Academy, the foremost dramatists, the most popular novelists, and the most acknowledged humorists are helping Mr. Beerbohm Tree in preparing the souvenir which is to be sold at the Albert Hall'.[10]

At the heart of this fantasy creation, and playing a pivotal role on this real-life stage, was Maud.[11] She gave interviews, held meetings, and sourced donations; she also designed the programme. Marshalling her troupe of friends and artists, she began the first day with a concert given by her good friend Clara Butt and the Australian-born Nellie Melba. On the second, an entertainment starring Madge Kendal, Julia Neilson, and Sir Henry Irving took the form of dramatic skits. Together with the actress Marie Bancroft, Maud manned *Stageland,* a stall selling roses at 5 shillings a stem.[12] The *Glasgow Herald* of 22 June reported her in the company of her daughter Viola and of course Violet Lindsay (now the Marchioness of Granby) and dressed in 'artistic draperies of cream lace'. The *Observer* of 11 November went further, bestowing on Maud its own seal of approval:

> Maud Beerbohm Tree always adopts the same picturesque style as her particular friend, the Marchioness of Granby. She is the tea-gown type of woman and never looks so well as when in soft, clinging garments, set off by quaint jewellery and big hats. When you see Mrs. Tree and the Marchioness of Granby together it is often difficult to tell one from the other.

The *Pall Mall Gazette* of 10 June wrote about both Trees: 'actresses, of course, have long since acquired proficiency in the "Stand-and-deliver" business in the cause of charity. Mr. Tree, however, is the first to show with what success it can be worked by an actor'.

This success was indeed 'worked', but it is worth reiterating that it was Maud's behind-the-scenes skill at social networking that ensured the event's success.[13] In its day the type of bazaar characterized by the Charing Cross instance, this masquerade without masks, was the greatest tool in charity fundraising. Intuitively, Maud exploited the established cultural stereotype that connected domesticity and the maternal instinct to philanthropy.[14] In the months leading up to the Charing Cross Bazaar she had given numerous high-profile recitals for charity which saw her performing every other day for several months.[15] Her domestic life was no less well documented, with interviews for various women's magazines on topics ranging from her 'charming home', her favourite 'gown', acting tips, and how to rear children ('make them happy, keep them bright') to the *English Woman's Year Book*'s request for information on 'the dramatic profession and the benevolent societies connected with it'.[16]

By the end of the century Maud Tree was forty-one years old and had been acting in various roles since she was twenty. New friendships and professional contacts continued to be a priority and could be fostered by brazenly sending out tickets on Herbert's behalf to his matinees.[17] In this manner she wrote to Lady Worsley and the Duchesses of Portland and Manchester.[18] With others the quid pro quo was less subtle. A flurry of increasingly persistent correspondence to E. L. Voynich expressed Maud's interest in dramatizing her story, *The Gadfly*,[19] but despite the acceptance of a ticket to *Julius Caesar* Voynich remained evasive:

> Dear Mrs. Tree
> I did not find time yesterday to write and thank you for the ticket to Julius Caesar. I have seldom enjoyed a play so much [...] I have been to Miss Marbury's

office, but the draft of the American version of the Gadfly is not there [...] Miss Marbury herself I understand will not reach London til next month.[20]

The tentative relationship foundered. One month later, on 14 June 1899, she wrote to Maud Tree: 'I am very sorry that you feel I am making a mistake in trying to dramatize the *Gadfly* myself'.[21] The summer before, in August 1898, she had even arranged for two volumes of Shakespeare to be delivered with her compliments to Winston Churchill, on army duty in the Sudan. Her bait in this instance was successful, and a couple of years later having kept in contact with Churchill ever since, the latter would beg for theatre tickets to see Maud in her play, happy to sit in 'a corner in Viola's box or anywhere'.[22]

A year of matinee benefits, one-act play performances, recitations, and concerts culminated, in due course, in the grand Charing Cross Bazaar of June 1899. Maud, behind her *Stageland*, was a living embodiment of what she had achieved both socially and professionally. But her greatest challenge was yet to come and soon she seized an opportunity that would prove pivotal to her career and reputation and raise her profile a notch further still.

The cool relations between Herbert and Maud extended into the autumn, to be tested even further when, predictably, Maud was excluded from taking part in Herbert's next production, a Shakespeare extravaganza exuberant even by his standards. However, the outbreak of the Second Anglo-Boer War soon prompted Maud to act independently anyway and both Trees responded by using their art to mirror and express the wider socio-political anxieties of the day.[23] Herbert revived *King John*, adding to it a tableau of the signing of Magna Carta, intended to remind the audience of the values for which the war was ostensibly being fought.[24] Maud's contribution was no less significant, both in the eyes of the public and for her future career as an actress.

Day-to-day coverage of the war in the press resulted in large-scale philanthropic activity. Various charities, ranging from the Transvaal War Fund Café to the Bons Frères Club, were rapidly set up to minister to the casualties of the campaign. Competition between the societies was rife and the press whipped its readers into a frenzy of activity. News coverage, both at home and in South Africa, also provoked widespread criticism of a war that was rapidly becoming the most expensive and longest in Britain's recent history. This criticism, in turn, generated an increasingly jingoist tone in the popular response to the war. Rudyard Kipling, in South Africa as a military journalist, wrote articles expressing his views on the conflict, while at home 'sub-Kiplingesque' bombast became the staple of music hall fare.[25] A favourite of the time was *A Hot Time in the Transvaal Tonight*:

> There is trouble in the Transvaal,
> And England wants to know
> Whether Mister Kruger or John Bull
> Shall boss the show.[26]

Charitable foundations were not alone in acquiring funds for the war effort. National newspapers competed to devise ingenious ways to attract a wider readership and channel patriotic sentiment. The *Daily Telegraph* alone raised £250,000, but it was

Alfred Harmsworth, owner of the *Daily Mail*, who made it clearest to his readership that his paper stood for 'power, supremacy and the greatness of the Empire'.[27] His paper was responsible for organizing one of the biggest relief funds for families and soldiers involved in the conflict; and Harmsworth, commanding a circulation of 500,000, commissioned Kipling as the leading poet of the day to write a poem on the conflict for publication. This became 'The Absent-Minded Beggar', versions of which were printed on silk mementoes, commemoration programmes, and pamphlets and other memorabilia.[28]

Maud had already recited timely renditions of Kipling's 'Soldier, Soldier', and in a climate where (in the words of *The Illustrated London News* of 2 December 1899) 'there are now so many concerts and other functions being organised on behalf of the war and charitable funds that it is impossible to follow them all', what followed made her achievement all the more remarkable. The understandable interest whipped up by Herbert's *King John* has also tended to eclipse the events leading up to Maud's legendary recitation. Seeing where Kipling's new poem was to appear, on the same day that she had been engaged to recite for charity, and empowered by the memory of having met him in person in America and by her recent high profile success, Maud telegraphed the editor of the *Daily Mail* requesting an advance copy so that she might recite it on the same day as its publication. It was not the editor who replied but rather Maud's good friend Philip Burne-Jones, in turn a close friend of *Daily Mail* proprietor Alfred Harmsworth. As well as being Kipling's first cousin, Burne-Jones acted on Kipling's behalf while Kipling was in South Africa reporting on the Boer War. Burne-Jones now replied by return that 'the poem will be delivered to you to-day [...] (type-written & in absolute confidence)'. He went on to say, 'I have Kiplings' [*sic*] consent & also seen Harmsworth, who is directing that the poem be sent to you at once'.[29]

Further bolstered by this green light, Maud hired a hansom to take her to what, as she says in her memoir, was then 'the most prominent of music halls'.[30] Within minutes of her arrival, in fact, she had negotiated a contract to recite 'The Absent-Minded Beggar' for a six-week solo run in aid of the Soldiers, Widows and Orphans Fund, with half of her salary going to war charities.[31] That part was easy; telling Herbert was less so. Predictably, as she recounts, he was 'angry and horrified'. The reasons for his negative reaction were complex. First, in this instance Maud had not consulted Tree prior to the engagement. Second, she had actively pursued an engagement that while ostensibly a gesture for charity would clearly be of benefit to her both financially and professionally. She had also negotiated her own contract and decided to make a very public intervention in the masculine sphere of war, doing so, moreover, in a way which implicitly crossed the boundary between 'respectable' theatre and music hall. But never had Maud displayed her business acumen or femininity to better effect. And, while the theatre world still reeled from the impact of Herbert's *King John*, (the *Daily Mail* of 21 September 1899 described its 'beautiful and inspiring ending', giving it 'a majestic seal of completion', and Falconbridge's lines as those of 'loftiest patriotism'), Maud made her own specific contribution.[32] With specific reference to the war, the *Sheffield Telegraph* of the same date, noted: 'the theatrical profession, always prominent in deeds of charity, are coming forward nobly on behalf of the soldiers, wives and families. The noblest of all is that of Mrs. Tree'.

Her decision was indeed 'courageous'. Herbert's angry reaction was compounded by the fact that her action could be construed as trivializing and undermining his own *King John*, which had been meticulously devised to generate a rich cultural iconography. Perhaps equally importantly, Maud's choice of venue and subject matter — the jingoistic nature of Kipling's poem — brought to the fore a debate begun almost half a century before with the Parliamentary Commission of 1866 and rekindled at the turn of the century with a proposed County Council Bill. The Parliamentary Commission had attempted to demonstrate that the great difference between theatres and music halls was that the play was the main attraction of the former and smoking and refreshment that of the latter. The County Council Bill, on the other hand, proposed to remove all distinctions between theatres and music halls.[33] Music halls at this time were still authorized by magistrates under a complex licensing system, while theatres were restricted in a different way, with their sale of alcohol reduced for productions during Lent. In 1892, the music hall share of audience in London was two and a half times that of the theatre, which only accelerated competition between them.[34] The areas of repertoire, excisable liquor sales, and smoking fostered further friction. Without an excise licence music halls were simply not viable, whereas Benjamin Webster stated that the profits from alcohol sales at the Adelphi 'were not worth the gas we burn'.[35] Both Henry Irving and Herbert Tree took up the debate in correspondence to the editor of the *Daily Telegraph*, which culminated in Tree's emphatic statement that '[any] attempt to turn the public-house into a theatre would end in turning the theatre into a public-house' (23 February 1898).

The controversy and debate surrounding the Palace Theatre, where Maud was to 'perform', had been more specific. By arguing for smoking to be permitted in its auditorium — '[there] is a great demand, by the respectable classes for a light character of entertainments, where after the business of the day a bright and varied performance may be enjoyed over a cigar or cigarette' — the Palace aligned itself even more closely to the music hall and to repertoire.[36] Its directors argued:

> This Theatre differs from the ordinary Theatre in being specifically devoted to a light and varied form of entertainment, the visitors to which urge the necessity of being permitted to smoke; in fact the objection to their doing so places the management at a very great disadvantage.[37]

The Alhambra Theatre of Varieties, where Maud would subsequently perform, also enjoyed a questionable reputation. In 1882, the manager of the Alhambra was forced to issue a statement to the effect that its dancers 'do not display themselves more than usual'.[38] (Despite a ban, can-cans, known as 'indecent posturing', were still being performed in 1902).[39]

Notwithstanding Herbert's initial opposition, his consent was eventually obtained and an agreement reached. In the end, all of Maud's salary for the performance was to be donated, not merely half — a fact that was much emphasized in the press.

Maud recorded how 'this unprecedented departure of mine [...] helped break down the barrier between theatre and music hall'.[40] The *Daily Chronicle* of 6 December 1899 certainly thought so when it wrote that she had pioneered '[a] new field for Dramatists. Maud Beerbohm Tree by her appearance on the stage of the Palace Theatre has added a brick to the bridge which will soon span the gulf between the regular theatre and the music hall'. And despite the *Bradford Daily News*'s opinion that 'recitation, as commonly practised is a hateful art', it conceded that Maud's showed a rare distinction (30 October 1899).

Criticism of her acting in the recent *Three Musketeers* was rendered insignificant compared with 'lines spoken', as the 'Nice Kind Gentleman wrote', 'as they had never been before'.[41] His comments were just some of the many accolades she received. Evidently, recitation was an area in which Maud was particularly skilled. Without the competition or pressure from a surrounding cast she was able to give inflection to a voice well suited to solo renditions. A classical training and near-photographic memory ensured she was able to rehearse ballads at speed. Her 'stand-and-deliver' experience in theatre prepared her for analogous performance in the sphere of philanthropy. Away from Herbert and in command of her subject, she excelled. Her achievement was recorded in the frenzy of media coverage surrounding the event. The *Daily Mail* gave away with its paper commemoration programmes of the poem printed on silk, and on 19 November 1899 described Maud's first night in rapturous terms:

> The Absent-Minded Beggar produced quite a scene at the Palace Theatre last night. For five minutes, she stood in a shower of money, until Mr. Morton, fearing she might be hurt by a cascade of coins came forward and begged the audience to desist.

As a result, the *Sunday Special* issued a notice with a request not to throw coins. 'Alas!' wrote Maud in her account of the event, 'notices were placed all over the theatre begging that enthusiasm money should be placed in boxes provided for the purpose! Of course this meant a loss of thousands of pounds'.[42] The *Evening News* (3 October 1899) wrote of her 'splendid effort' and advised: 'other artists please copy'. The *World* of 8 October described her 'as the star of the afternoon', the *Empire* of 11 November 'the novelty of the hour', and the *Daily Mail* of 19 November called hers a 'record for individual effort'. For the next ten weeks, Maud recalled, 'for the first and only time in my life, I without aid from anyone but my author [...] drew the town'.[43] Already well known to both the theatre and society through her philanthropic works, Maud became, for those ten weeks, a stellar celebrity. *Era* commented on 11 November: 'all the town is rushing off to the Palace Theatre to hear Mrs. Beerbohm Tree', while *Lloyds Weekly Newspaper* noted the following day that 'The Palace Theatre has never been so crowded as now, while Mrs. Beerbohm Tree is reciting'. But it was Harry Cust, 'that passionate Imperialist' (and Violet Lindsay's current lover), whose praise meant the most. In her memoir, Maud finishes by saying:

> My example of reciting the poem and of giving everything I earned was imitated all over the kingdom and I believe I was responsible directly and

indirectly for mints and mints of money; but then, as I have said, 'The Absent-Minded Beggar'" made irresistible appeal. Of all the praise I had — and I had much — I liked best that of brilliant, all-conquering Harry Cust, who came after hearing me, and said, with tears in his eyes, 'You seemed like a bit of England'.[44]

The legacy of extant archival press reports and other related ephemera testify to what was, indeed, a triumph. Maud's style of 'calculated fragility' as she emerged on to the stage in a scarlet gown was one designed to contrast with the distinctly unfeminine task at hand — which was, as *The Times* described it on 22 June 1899, to exhort 'with outstretched hands, to "Pay, pay, pay!"' Patriotism, philanthropy, and her web of intricate connections and relationships converged on the first night, and the nights to come. 'There were few pessimists on the war topic to be met with in London last night', noted the reviewer in the *Pall Mall Gazette* of 1 November 1899: 'If such beings were in existence, they certainly refrained from visiting the Palace theatre'.

'Absent-Minded Beggar' fever gathered momentum, with renditions of the poem being offered up and down the country.[45] Sir Arthur Sullivan set the poem to music that, Kipling said, 'was guaranteed to pull teeth out of barrel organs'.[46] Kipling and the Boer War became synonymous with Empire, patriotism, and jingoism.[47] Maud was inundated with requests to recite the poem, from charities ranging from the Council of the Society of Women Journalists to military organizations, and her autograph was requested together with her photograph for programmes.[48] She was asked for advice as to how to recite the ballad, together with requests for the name of the publishers of poems she recited after 'The Absent-Minded Beggar'.[49] Others wanted to know if she used 'Stanley Hawley's musical setting with the piece'.[50] Published and unpublished writers approached her: she was sent W. M. Watkins-Pitchford's 'Account Rendered', Angelica Selby's 'Nanny's Protest', Georgina M. de L'Aubinière's 'England's Promises', and Harold Begbie's 'The Incident'.[51] A flurry of fan mail praised her performance, while an anonymous poem, written on a postcard, was delivered to her at her Palace Theatre dressing room. It read:

> Talent Leading — Beauty Pleading
> Interceding — nothing heeding —
> Big results to show —
> Therefore today the only way
> For us most clearly seen
> Is — joyful pay and pay and pay
> To Every Tambourine.[52]

It is clear from fashion news coverage that Maud Tree's impact on that world during those weeks was as great as it was on the charity fundraising circuit. Gradually her dress was altered to reflect the red tunics of the British soldiers — the very red that made the British easy targets for the Boer militia. Descriptions of the velvet gown trimmed with sable that she wore for her performance prompted the fashion editor of the *Illustrated London News* to comment on 18 November 1899: 'Certain it is that never was there so large a supply of costly furs on show, be it where well-dressed

Fig. 8.1. Maud Tree recites Rudyard Kipling's 'The Absent-Minded Beggar' at the Palace Theatre (*Black and White*, 11 November 1899)

women fashionably congregate or in shops, at the moment'. This 'ideal image of femininity' was featured in a plethora of fashion articles such as the one published by *Country Gentleman* on 2 December 1899 entitled 'Frocks for Patriotic Occasions'.

On 8 December an ice carnival was held at the New Niagara in Westminster to raise funds for the war effort. A programme of entertainment included skating displays and performances by Lillie Langtry and Mrs Brown Potter. Once more, cultural and socio-political elements converged at this philanthropic event. Ideas that had proved successful at the Charing Cross bazaar were implemented again on this occasion. An American bar, for example, sold refreshments, but this time with topical iconography in the shape of a skater holding a box with 'Pay, Pay, Pay' marked on it. And the Duke of Marlborough, in declining an invitation, said 'I am going abroad tonight — I am *not* a brave absent-minded beggar'.[53]

With the publication of society pages announcing that the Prince of Wales would attend her performance Maud Tree could justifiably claim that she alone 'drew the town'.[54] Moreover, the acting profession could reasonably claim that it was on the way to gaining the respectability lauded by Madge Kendal in her autobiography: 'Respect the fact that you are called actors. It is a great title if carried with respect to the Art [...] Leave some footprints in the sands of time that others may follow easily along the path'.[55] Above all, in the face of so much public acclamation, Herbert had no choice but to call on Maud for the leading part in his next production.

Notes to Chapter 8

1. *Siddons House*, pamphlet (MBTC).
2. The philanthropic trend was strong in Victorian Britain. A study of twenty-eight middle-class families for 1896 showed they spent a larger share of their income on charity than on any other item, including food. See *Statistics of Middle-Class Expenditure*, British Library of Political and Economic Science Pamphlet, 1896 (HD6/D267). See also Owen 1964: 469.
3. Rev. Benjamin Waugh to Maud Tree, [1895] (MBTC). Benjamin Waugh (1839–1908) was founder and director of the Society for the Prevention of Cruelty to Children (SPCC) in 1884. See Hindson 2008 for identification of the year of Waugh's letter to Maud as 1895, as the royal charter granted in that year is referenced on the charity's letterhead.
4. Prochaska 1988.
5. See Moore 1891: 176. George Moore (1852–1933), the Irish novelist, art critic, and dramatist, was a close friend of the Tree family.
6. Reynolds: 1998: 111.
7. Davis 1991: 71.
8. Stevenson 1929: 2.
9. 'That a Manager should be a gentleman in all senses of the term', quoted in Anon. 1846: 51.
10. Further press coverage of the Charing Cross Hospital Bazaar can be found in the *Globe*, *Morning Post*, *Pall Mall Gazette*, *New York Times*, *Era*, *Daily News*, *Ladies Pictorial*, *World of Dress*, *Sphere*, and *Illustrated London News*.
11. Donaldson 1970: 11.
12. Marie Wilton (1840–1921) was an example of the actress whose trajectory from playing burlesque and boy roles in music hall culminated in the respectability of marriage, in her case to Squire Bancroft and management of the Prince of Wales's and Haymarket Theatres. The Bancrofts developed the 'cup-and-saucer' dramas of the age.
13. When, for example, *Trilby* opened in 1895 at the Haymarket Theatre, it coincided with an exhibition at the Fine Art Society of George du Maurier's drawings. Subsequently, Dorothy Baird in the title role was instantly recognizable from the drawings.

14. See Nelson and Sumner 1997.
15. See Anon. 1899: 535–57, and *Women's Life* of 10 September 1898, p. 35.
16. Anon., 1898 (MBTC 6).
17. See Pearson 1988: 127. He recounts how Maud sent W. S. Gilbert first-night seats to *King John* in the hope that he might revise his opinion of Herbert's ability to recite blank verse.
18. Consuelo, Duchess of Manchester, to Maud Tree, thanking her for the offer of a seat, [n.d.] (MBTC 6).
19. E. L Voynich to Maud Tree, 22 April 1898, (MBTC).
20. E. L. Voynich to Maud Tree, 16 May 1898 (MBTC).
21. E. L. Voynich to Maud Tree, 14 June 1898 (MBTC).
22. Winston Churchill to Maud Tree, [n.d.] (MBTC 6).
23. In London some 170, 000 people saw *King John*. See Tree 1915a: 46.
24. Kachur 1992: 28.
25. Rudyard Kipling (1865–1936), author and poet, was born in Bombay. He was the first ever English language writer to win the Nobel Prize in Literature, best known for his *Just So Stories*, *The Jungle Book*, and his poems 'Dunga Din', 'If', and 'The Absent-Minded Beggar'.
26. As quoted in Smith 1978: 78.
27. Alfred Harmsworth, *Daily Mail*, 4 May 1896.
28. As early as 1892 Kipling created the Everyman figure of Tommy Atkins (son of the Red Earth) and by 1899 Tommy had entered the English language. Maud herself used it in correspondence to her daughters. Within two weeks of the poem's publication Kipling was offered a knighthood, which he refused.
29. Philip Burne-Jones to Maud Tree, 26 October 1899 (MBTC/000141).
30. Beerbohm 1924: 112–13.
31. Ibid.: 112.
32. See also the *Lady's Pictorial* of 30 September 1899 and the *Globe* of 21 September 1899.
33. County Council (Theatres Bill) 28 June 1889. See Davis 2000: 2 & 59. In the mid-1880s 'a popular low comedian' could earn as much as a Lord Chancellor. By 1912, the number of music halls in Great Britain had peaked at 391.
34. The nightly capacity of music halls was 158,013 people, while theatres held 65,859 (Select Committee figures (1892), Appendix 9: 450–51).
35. See Davis 2000: 61.
36. Augustus Harris to the Lord Chamberlain, 7 December 1892 (TNA LC1/ 538).
37. Palace Theatre Company directors to the Lord Chamberlain, 19 January 1893 (TNA LC1/601).
38. William Holland to Ponsonby, 10 July 1882 (TNA LC1/399); Edward Pigott to Ponsonby, 10 July 1882, (TNA LC1/399). See also Davis 2000: 399, and Davis 1992.
39. See Davis 1992: 132.
40. Beerbohm 1924: 113.
41. W. S. Gilbert to Maud Tree, [n.d.] (MBTC 6).
42. Beerbohm 1924: 113.
43. Ibid.
44. Harry Cust (1861–1917) was the lover of Violet Lindsay, father of Lady Diana Manners, and member of the intellectual, aesthetic group known as 'The Souls'.
45. It was recited at the Brighton Aquarium, Theatre Royal and Prince's Theatre, Bristol, New Theatre Royal, Croydon, Theatre Royal, Portsmouth, Empire Theatre, Bradford, Tivoli and Metropolitan music halls in London, and the Palace Variety Theatre, Aberdeen. It was performed at the Alhambra Theatre, Leicester Square, set to music by Arthur Sullivan. It appeared in the *Aberdeen Weekly Journal*, *Pall Mall Gazette*, *Illustrated London News*, and *Gentlewoman and Ladies Pictorial*.
46. Kipling 2005: 150.
47. 'Jingo' (a euphemism for Jesus) was a word that had been dormant for 150 years before it was taken up in G. H. Macdonald's lines written during the Russo-Turkish war. 'We don't want to fight, but by jingo if we do, we've got the men, we've got the ships, we've got the money too'.

48. The manager of the Croydon Theatre requested her photograph for his production, *A Woman's Reason*.
49. Janine Griffiths to Maud Tree, 31 December 1899 (MBTC).
50. Florence Marks to Maud Tree, [1899] (MBTC).
51. I am grateful to Catherine Hindson for this reference in Hindson 2008.
52. J. Charles to Maud Tree, 6 December 1899 (MBTC).
53. Charles Spencer-Churchill, 9th Duke of Marlborough, to Maud Tree, 27 November 1899 (MBTC).
54. By November 1899, however, the Charity Organization Society had shown grumblings of dissent at the assertion that 'The Absent-Minded Beggar' was 'the most prominent figure on the charitable horizon at present'. Its striking success had served to highlight the financial difficulties of other charitable institutions. The *Pall Mall Gazette*, for example, published a front-page article supporting the work of the SPCC. The funds set up by the *Daily Mail* for a relief corps of the same name were colossal — amounting to £100,000 by March 1900 and reaching a total of £250,000 by the end of the year.
55. Kendal 1933: 300–01.

CHAPTER 9

Midsummer Revels 1900

On 11 January 1900 the *Northern Whig* announced that 'Mrs. Tree, after pleading so long for *The Absent-Minded Beggar* at the Palace, is welcomed back to her husband's theatre as Titania'. The production, in which Tree played Bottom, Lewis Waller, Lysander, and Julia Neilson, Oberon, was seen by almost 220,000 spectators in London alone.[1] Once again Tree's 'lavish naturalism' concentrated on a seemingly escapist revival: *A Midsummer Night's Dream* was Tree's sixth Shakespearean production and his third at His Majesty's Theatre.[2] As the century closed on an era in which territories equal to twenty-four times the area of Great Britain were added to the Empire, Tree's reversion of ancient Greece, Gary Jay Williams suggests, was deliberate.[3] The disastrous defeats suffered in the Transvaal a month earlier made Britain's hitherto unshakeable monopoly on the world stage suddenly fragile and finite. The parallel drawn between comforting images of England and the cradle of civilization that was Greece piled 'simulacra upon simulacra in scenic rhetoric' that was 'emptied of its imperial mythology'.[4] And as *Punch* of 24 January 1900 described the first set as 'the Pantheon [...] on the Necropolis', once more Tree's rationale was calculated to unify a scenic text that conflated England with ancient Greece. Once more brand recognition (as we would call it today) came into play: Victorian children were familiar with such works as *Stories from Shakespeare* by Dr Thomas Carter, whose description of Athens was visually interpreted by Tree, and Julia Neilson as Oberon wore a spiked crown not unlike that of Britannia.

It was a sumptuous production. Athenian views were recreated by Hawes Craven and Walter Hahn, while interiors included a mosaic-painted floor with Grecian border motifs running the width of the ceiling.[5] Mechanical birds sounded in fruit trees heavy with blossom, and below a carpet of thyme was strewn with wildflowers. Bottom was able to see his reflection in a simulated stream as dozens of children dressed as imps and elves were suspended above a moonlit sea. These 'portals of fairyland' were punctuated with fairies sporting battery-operated lights (like those which illuminated Oberon's breastplate and crown and Titania's wings and robe), and a bran-strewn woodland featured real rabbits nibbling real foliage.[6]

The notion that spectacle was detracting from rather than enhancing the bard's texts, however, was expressed by the *Westminster Gazette* (January 1900) when it commented that it was 'wicked to treat Shakespeare as a powder to be taken with a great deal of jam'. In America, the same sentiment was echoed in the charge that 'If spectacle be the main objective to be achieved in performances of a Shakespearian

Fig. 9.1. Maud Tree as Titania in *A Midsummer Night's Dream* at Her Majesty's Theatre (*Sporting & Dramatic*, 20 January 1900)

work, the Hippodrome is always accessible to those who take such a view of theatre'.[7] There was a certain irony in this observation, given Tree's horror of variety halls, his opposition to Maud's performing in them, and the possibility that his work could be trivialized in this way.[8] Sydney Lee in *Sand and Water* (13 January 1900) extended still further the battle lines of a debate that would run unabated for much of the early 1900s. Fervently opposed to the 'modern practice of obscuring Shakespeare's plays by excessive mounting', he found much to criticize in Tree's production. As did the critic of the *Westminster Gazette* of 11 January 1900 who said:

> Nothing whatsoever is left to the imagination, not even the wire suspending Puck [...] nor the cord which makes Oberon inseparable from his electrically lit sceptre, though it is true that nothing is seen of the box ottoman, in which the Queen of the Fairies keeps her various costumes. Was it present to Shakespeare's mind that Titania changed her dress three times in one night? What does it matter? It is impossible to avoid the comparison of the midnight revels of the sprites and elves with a ballet scene in panto.

Indeed, nothing was left to the imagination and Tree might have been piqued by this comparison, but it is difficult for the modern-day theatregoer to appreciate how impressive the Victorians would have found Tree's meticulous and laboriously painted stage-wide pictures. For example, as Oberon touched each of the nine pillars of Theseus's palace, they lit up from within. The *Athenaeum* of January 1900 saluting Tree's achievement, wrote: 'no spectacle equally artistic has been seen on the English stage'. Tree's own half-brother and critic, Max Beerbohm, found the production charming, while J. T. Grein was enthralled, saying its beauty brightened 'these troubled times when there is so much sorrow in the land'.[9]

No amount of spectacle, however, or debate generated as a result could deflect from the domestic drama unfurling behind the scenes. As ever, after an absence during which Maud asserted her independence from Herbert, she had been lured back to Her Majesty's Theatre with the promise of a Shakespearean role. But while critics acknowledged the visual extravaganza of *A Midsummer Night's Dream*, they found fault with its Titania. The effective execution of a Shakespearean role depended not only an ability to act but, as has already been discussed, on basic elocution. The *Western Mail* of 12 January 1900 viewed Maud's performance as 'a piece of acting if not elocution'. Her voice was described as 'sweet', 'delightful', and 'effective'. The *People* wrote of her 'appealing looks and accents' (11 January 1900), while *Era* of the same date described 'the musical inflexion of her delivery'.

All this was well and good, but as with Maud's interpretation of Anne of Austria, when personal discord had adversely affected her acting, it impinged upon it now. Maud had long suspected Tree of infidelity, as anonymous letters as far back as 1895 had intimated as much, but one she received during rehearsals of *Dream* — 'Dearest Maud, I forgot to tell you Miss P was seen about with a man the very image of Herbert' — could not have premeditated the pain it inflicted.[10] Maud, of course, makes no mention at all of this in her memoir and claims to have no diaries (or memory) of the time. After Tree's death in 1917 she and Max Beerbohm destroyed many of his private papers found in the Dome. In the TFA in Bristol, however, a slim, seemingly empty diary for 1900 carries entries for four days in April. 'For the first time since Worthing,' Maud wrote, 'concern myself with MP. They meet near bridge and talk 20 mins. Herbert slips out at night, returning about 4'. The following day, Saturday: 'MP + Herbert meet + talk for a few minutes'. On 22 April: 'H & MP dine together from Grafton St to Garrick at 10.45'; and on 23 April: 'H & MP meet as usual — they are prevented from conversing'.[11] Maud's suspicions were aroused and with reason, as she soon discovered, and the knowledge that May Pinney was indeed Tree's mistress, and that furthermore he had two children by her, impacted heavily on Maud's emotional and professional life.

Transposed, therefore against the complex, composite, multi-layered cultural iconography that was the *Dream*, Maud's true self remained well and truly hidden for the duration of the production, and so did her talent. The contrast between the performance of Kipling's poem and Shakespeare's play could not have been greater. Some critics felt she should have remained in the former. The drama critic for *Sand and Water* wrote on 14 January 1900:

> The Titania of Mrs. Tree was graceful, though it was scarcely worth the while to take her away from the Palace and her praiseworthy task of earning £100 a week for the War Fund for what many others could have done just as well.

It would seem to the critic of the *Observer* that the strident, all-conquering, independent woman who was welcomed 'back to her place in the company had little to do in *Dream*' (15 May 1899). Equally the resonance of her 'Pay, Pay, Pay', that had become an advertising tool and the nation's call to arms, was now muffled

FIG. 9.2. Herbert Tree as Bottom and Maud Tree as Titania
(Theatre Museum, Victoria and Albert Museum)

in a delivery that was strained. In fact, as the *People* pointed out on 14 January 1900, she could not be heard in a part that 'lacked the imagination which distinguished her Ophelia'.[12]

There was more criticism of her role pointing to this very absence of imagination. The *Echo* of 14 January 1900 wrote: 'It must be confessed that Mrs. Tree, monotonous in speech and not too poetical in conception, hardly made an ideal Titania, save from a pictorial point of view'. The *People,* too, identified a lack of imagination, while the *Morning Post* of 15 January 1900 described the feverishness of her gestures, saying 'she indulged too freely in those wiles and lines which, however necessary to women, a fairy can scarcely stand in need of, and the contrast of the human element and the fairy element was so much weakened'. Her famously pleasing voice also let her down. In the most damning of all the critiques the *Pall Mall Gazette* of 14 January 1900 wrote:

> As Titania, Mrs. Tree plays prettily but is scarcely fairy like. It is a fairy from South Kensington, whose revels are limited to Queen's Gate and whose rings are to be found in Kensington Gardens. Mrs. Tree gives one notion that Titania has smart friends somewhere and is only out in the wood because it happens to be for the time a society fad. Nor need a fairy wear quite so fixed a smile; and its constancy makes one suspect the Fairy Queen's true amiability.

The *Society*'s critic also questioned her clipped accent and *fin-de-siècle* air, warning: 'We are not out of the 19th century yet Titania!' It added, 'I may be unduly exacting but I have been brought up to expect the tones used in speaking Shakespeare's lines to be other than those employed in a light drawing room chat' (14 January 1900).

Titania may have been sung to sleep in a honeysuckle bower by forty-seven fairies (one of whom hovered in the air directly above her), while Bottom checked his reflection in a simulated stream, but behind the carefully painted, stage-wide pictures, Maud's life had imploded onto a set which was anything but 'light'. She was not at all concerned by the adverse press — her Titania, if inanimate, had still been exquisitely beautiful — but behind the scenes, she would direct her energy into trying to discover the truth behind the mounting suspicion, innuendo, blackmail, and correspondence that all pointed to a house in Putney. Boldly taking the initiative, Maud wrote to both May Pinney, with whom it was alleged Herbert was having an affair, and to May's mother, with whom May claimed to be living. Receiving no immediate reply and wound up in a frenzy of disbelief and hurt outrage, Maud took the even bolder step of visiting May in person. There followed a fractious interchange that did nothing to appease Maud. And although May's mother wrote:

> The subject of your visit last Sunday has caused infinite pain, but I have since seen your husband, & had a long talk with my daughter, & I am utterly convinced that the friendship which I have always known to have existed between them is only <u>friendship</u> & not that which you would have me believe.[13]

Maud had no option but to reply: 'I am very glad that my husband and your daughter have succeeded in dispelling the unhappiness that I unwillingly caused you on Monday'.[14] But she was not deceived. At the time of writing that letter Mrs Pinney must have been well aware that her daughter had one, if not two sons by Herbert and was pregnant again. She was clearly lying and Maud knew it. Tree's reaction was also ambiguous. In response to her sense of outrage he suggested they should not see each other, but if she changed her mind he would nonetheless endeavour to make her 'comfortable and happy' and 'could always rig up another bed in the sitting room'. He admitted to being terribly distressed by her own distress, 'I can sincerely say I wished that you should have as much joy as your life can procure — but I don't always think you have always had the wisdom to distinguish between pleasure and happiness'. Her frustration was increased hundredfold by his final note: 'Do not imagine,' he wrote, 'I do not blame myself — I do always but do not imagine either that my attitude towards you has been due to my relations with another'.[15]

Living more or less permanently now between the dome of his theatre and, Maud had no doubt, May's house in Putney, Herbert wrote again unnecessarily that he felt 'it best for us both that we should not be together too much for some time'.[16] But a letter Maud received from May really stung:

> Miss May Pinney,
> Presents her compl. [sic] to Mrs. Tree & begs to say that she is at a loss to understand why Mrs. Tree will persist in talking of her husband's affairs to people who give her no sympathy but merely relate these stories to others in exaggerated manner. Miss Pinney regrets that it has lately reached her ears that Mrs. Tree's extraordinary boldness in talking in this way to Mr. Waller who in turn has entertained various members of the company at Her Majesty's Theatre with the scandal. Miss Pinney cannot realize in what way Mrs. Tree's position is improved by this indiscreet behaviour and sincerely trusts that before it is too late, Mrs. Tree will grasp the fact that she is merely holding herself up to ridicule when she mentions subjects of a delicate nature to members of her husband's company.[17]

Maud retaliated and the spat escalated:

> Dear Miss Pinney,
> I should feel inclined to ignore the silly and impertinent letter which I received from you this morning were it not for both our sakes, [sic] it may be better that the misapprehension under which you are laboring should, if possible, be removed. [...]
> In conclusion, my 'position' is according to me an absolutely satisfactory one, and you must not, please, give yourself the trouble of trying to realize in what way I may hope to 'improve' it.[18]

Writing those words, Maud was indeed mindful of her position and mindful that it was not one she was prepared to relinquish. Her ultimate tool, her greatest strength, lay in the fact that she was still Herbert's wife. Divorce was not something to embark upon lightly. In fact, she knew very well that she and Herbert would never contemplate it. Reassured only that Tree would never change, Maud promptly hired a private detective, appropriately named 'Littlechild', to inform her of the births (a further three were recorded) to Herbert and May.

Henceforward *A Midsummer Night's Dream* would enjoy a popularity not realized in Elizabethan times or since, but for the time being London and its stage had lost all appeal for Maud.[19] As she often did when Her Majesty's became a hostile hub rather than a welcoming one, she removed herself from the theatre completely. This time she did not even tell Violet Lindsay that she was leaving London, and arriving in Paris in early January 1901 she would embark, voluntarily, on several months of self-imposed exile.

Paris did Maud much good. Despite being caught between two polar opposites — a husband who did not want her and an infatuated lover who claimed he did — Maud threw herself into distractions, devoting her time to social and philanthropic activities, recitations, and speeches. The press, however, continued to trace her activities and the *Pall Mall Gazette* allotted pages of analysis to a speech in which she called herself an 'after dinner optimist' and the opposite sex, 'humbugging men'.[20] Correspondence between Violet Lindsay and Maud's daughter Viola, however, indicates the level of concern both felt with regard to this career isolation.[21] Waller's persistent letters to her reveal frustration:

> Oh my dear [...] how we torture ourselves and why? I only know that I love you and you only. I want you and mean to marry you. If Pansy [his nickname for Maud] wants exile, the self-imposed exile — I who have left his — want a little love.[22]

But Maud was not convinced by Waller's sweet talk. Her deeply rooted religious belief, her love of her children, and the rigour she showed over their education even from afar, drove her more than the notion of any romantic attachment. Innate self-discipline and courage saw her through this 'bitter' period when, as she would later recount to her friend and lawyer Charles Russell, her spirit 'bled' as she travelled 'a lonely and defeated road'.[23] But the luxury of the Ritz, where she was staying, went some way to restore her optimism. She extolled its virtues in a letter to Viola, but in the same letter castigated little Felicity for not being more conscientious about her studies. The 'mask and faces' she was able to adopt professionally, she now applied to her private life. It was a mask she maintained even to her children, referring to Tree as 'Darling Daddy', and she was quick to defend his reputation even over the most minor accusations.[24] She would, as she vowed to Charles Russell, bring up Herbert's children in love and reverence while she herself was forever lost to him. If there was one thing Maud came to terms with during her time away, it was that, at long last, she had shaken off, as she phrased it, 'the dust of her long dying love' for Herbert.[25]

At length, the turmoil in Maud was quelled, and as a result her acting resumed its stellar quality. Seeking new challenges, she would soon experiment with roles undertaken away from Her Majesty's Theatre but in October 1901, on her return to London, there was controversy if not turmoil surrounding Mrs Clifford's play *The Likeness of the Night* in which Maud played Mary Archerson.[26] Sydney Grundy, no stranger to plagiarizing other playwrights' work, (as discussed in Chapter 5) now claimed to be the victim of plagiarism himself. He accused Mrs Clifford of copying his *A Debt of Honour* which had opened at St James's Theatre exactly one month previously. Mrs Clifford refuted the accusation by stating that her work had first been published — albeit in a different form — some fifteen years earlier. In both *A Debt of Honour* and *The Likeness of the Night* there is an Australian born character but while the former has a happy ending, the latter does not.

Despite Sydney Grundy's comment that adultery only 'takes place in Paris: nobody pretends such things happen here', this play could not have more closely mirrored the Trees' off-stage domestic situation.[27] Nor would the parallels between it and the action have been lost on Maud or anyone else, for that matter, who knew them and went to see the show. Maud not only played the role to the best of her ability, drawing on life experience and a newly gained perspective, but she also made sure she looked sensational. An article entitled 'Letters of a Worldly Woman' in *Country Gentleman* of 2 November 1901, chose to remind its audience almost apologetically that it was 'the acting of Mrs. Kendal and Mrs. Tree that people will go and see'. The *Playgoer* of December 1901 detailed her every costume, with one gown in particular being described as 'a gown typical of sunshine and happiness', and she herself was in her element, as the critic of *The Sketch* of the same date affirmed: 'Mrs. Tree has never done so well or shown to greater advantage'. Notwithstanding detailed descriptions of her now trademark flowing gowns, *Pullman's Western News* of 10 December 1901 said 'Mrs. Tree as the mistress scores a tremendous success', while *Country Life* praised her acting instinct as possessing 'the spirit of the character as conceived by the author'. Maud appeared on the cover of *Illustrated Sporting and Dramatic* magazine of 7 December 1901 with the accompanying article concluding: 'Mrs. Tree's appearance as Mary is of great advantage to the play'. The flattering comments must have gone some way to boost Maud's confidence as the text required the actress to be a twenty-eight-year-old: Maud was forty-three at the time and Mrs Kendal, who wanted the role for herself, ten years older than that.

In rehearsal, Mr and Mrs Kendal played Bernard and Mildred Archerson, while Mary Archerson was played by Madge McIntosh, but Maud subsequently replaced her when the play opened. Mary Archerson is not, of course, the Archersons' daughter, but Bernard's other 'wife'. And not only is Mary his mistress but also the mother of Bernard's two children — a fact obliquely referred to in the play. In effect Mrs Clifford's play appeared to mimic every turn in the Trees' ongoing domestic drama. The irony was that, in this instance, Maud played not a wronged wife but a mistress, and to great effect. In the play Mary says: 'Yes — Yes; we can walk together in the sight of other men and women and not feel that at any moment we may be made ashamed'.[28] And her compassion lends Mary a greater understanding of the other woman (who also happens to be the wife), a paradox not lost on Maud. Correspondence documents Maud's visits to May Pinney from 1900 through to 1917, during which time she offered Pinney financial assistance. Eventually both women did enter into a fragile truce, understanding that ultimately their reputations depended on it, for, as Mary states in the play, 'Whatever happens, the world will forgive him; it is only hard on the woman'.[29] It was a lesson Maud was beginning to learn for herself.

FIG. 9.3. Maud Tree as Mary Archerson in *The Likeness of the Night* (*Sketch*, 7 December 1901)

Notes to Chapter 9

1. Tree cited this figure in Tree 1915a: 46. See also Booth and Kaplan: 1996.
2. Williams: 1997: 130–33.
3. Ibid.: 132.
4. Ibid.
5. Pearce: 1995; see also Williams 1997: 131.
6. Tree promptbook and production papers (HTA).
7. The New York Hippodrome was the largest theatre of its kind from 1905 to 1939. It could seat up to 6000 people and was used primarily for circuses and historical re-enactments. It did not have the same licensing issues that London had.
8. Untitled, undated from Herbert Tree Scrapbooks in the Robinson-Locke Collection, New York Public Library for the Performing Arts at the Lincoln Centre.
9. Grein 1900: 140.
10. Anon. to Maud Tree, [1900] (MBTC 7).
11. Maud Tree, diary for 1900 (MBTC 7).
12. On 9 September 1891 Maud played Ophelia at the Theatre Royal, Manchester. This was repeated at the Haymarket Theatre on 21 January 1892.
13. Henrietta L. Pinney to Maud Tree, [27 December 1900] (MBTC 7). In 1904, May Pinney changed her name by deed poll to Reed. Claude Reed was born 1891, so would have been about nine years old when his grandmother wrote this letter.
14. Maud Tree to May Pinney, 28 December 1900 (HBT/RA/267).
15. Herbert Tree to Maud Tree, 2 August 1901, 2 August 1901, and 17 September 1901 (HBT/RA/420).
16. Herbert Tree to Maud Tree, [n.d.] (MBTC).
17. May Pinney to Maud Tree, [n.d.] (MBTC 7).
18. Maud Tree to May Pinney, 28 December 1900 (HBT/RA/267).
19. There were only two known performances of the play under its own name between 1660 and 1816.
20. *Era* recorded various philanthropic and social events for the period 18 May 1901 to 22 June 1901, e.g. a meeting of the Committee of the Women's Fund in connection with the Queen Victoria nurses, Charing Cross Hospital Committee, and Women's Memorial to Queen Victoria. Maud also attended dinners hosted by Alfred de Rothschild and in turn gave a supper party that included Irving, Bernhardt, and Paderewski, as recorded by the *Ladies Field* of 20 July 1901.
21. Violet Lindsay to Viola Tree, [n.d.] (by kind permission of His Grace the Duke of Rutland).
22. Lewis Waller to Maud Tree, [n.d.] (MBTC 7, RA/420).
23. Maud Tree to Charles Russell, [n.d.] (MBTC 6).
24. Two years after his death, an article in the *Daily Mail* (17 November 1919) discussed Tree's financial affairs much to Maud's displeasure.
25. Maud Tree to Charles Russell, [n.d.] (MBTC 6).
26. The title of the play is from Swinburne's 'A Ballad of Burdens', in Swinburne 1866: 144–47. The original lines are: 'And where the truth was, the likeness of a liar | And where the day was, the likeness of the night' (ll. 69–70).
27. Grundy 1880: 9.
28. See Clifford 1900: 115 & 135.
29. Ibid.: 65.

CHAPTER 10

Caesar's Wife: Becoming a Wo-manager
1901

The society pages for Christmas Eve 1901 recorded Maud once again in Paris, fresh from her success as Mary Archerson, staying at the Ritz. The *Lady's Pictorial* wrote that for a dinner with Lilly Langtry and Nelly Melba Maud wore a 'much remarked gown [...] a kind of Reynolds affair'. But the foreign and national press also devoted pages to speculation as to the true nature of her visit. The *Athenaeum* of 22 December 1901 hinted at a financial arrangement in which she had secured acting rights to a play called *L'Énigme*. The *Morning Leader* of the same date ventured that Maud was 'likely to be an actress manager' and was contemplating 'taking over a theatre in her own right'. If there were to be any voices of dissent, *People* magazine of 20 December 1901 was swift to defend her: 'why should she not set forth upon a stellar career as the Americans call it? We can't always have her before us at Her Majesty's. She has a distinctive manner and style'. The *Weekly Dispatch* of 16 February 1902 confirmed that 'Mrs. Tree, who would rather act than eat and who had never played a part that she could not learn by heart in a day, has been induced to take the Wyndham Theatre for a short time'.

This next phase in Maud's career came about as the result of a chance encounter with, perhaps awkwardly, Lewis Waller's wife. Florence Waller, who acted under the name West, also happened to be staying in Paris with her sister-in-law Mrs Scott, wife to theatre critic Clement. The fact that Florence's husband harboured such strong feelings for Maud does not seem to have come in the way of their friendship, and on this occasion Florence invited Maud to join her at the theatre. The play in question was Paul Hervieu's *L'Énigme,* and Maud was instantly captivated by this innovative, controversial piece of theatre, not least by its central theme of adultery. She needed a new challenge, and producing and acting in her own play seemed just the answer. Bringing the project to fruition, rallying the public's interest, however, would not be straightforward.

On her return to London, Maud tackled her new venture with relish even though there was a series of hurdles to overcome. To begin with, she needed to secure financial backing and a London theatre. Maud had a particular talent in amassing social and professional contacts but securing funds for a project, by a woman,

Fig. 10.1. Maud Tree at the Playgoers' Club Ladies' Dinner (*Era*, 1 January 1902)

was almost always impossible. As Tracy C. Davis has pointed out, the practices of 'gentlemanly capitalism' allowed men to raise money in a 'wide occupational and social spectrum' of which gentlemen's clubs formed a good part. (Davis has stated by way of example that between 1890 and 1914, eight per cent of the Reform Club's members were in banking.) Clubs' socializing hours also complimented male actors' working hours but excluded women's whose appearance anyway in such an establishment would have been misconstrued. Networking by way of the dinner party, for women, in Davis's opinion, rates as 'a poor alternative'.[1] This was not the case with Maud. The dinner party was a medium at which she excelled, and with her extensive network of acquaintances she was relentless in her approach to Russell Spokes who gave the £3,000 (the equivalent of £75,000 today) required to finance the production. Hiring a London theatre was more problematic and there was also the small issue of having the play translated into English. In addition to all this there was a problem with a title for *L'Énigme:* initially it was announced as '*Which?*', but there was already another play in existence under this title by a Mr Edward Terry. Moreover, its treatment of the subject of adultery might have a bearing on the granting of a Lord Chamberlain's Licence.[2] Maud once again consulted her extensive contacts list before engaging her own brother-in-law Max Beerbohm and Frank Harris to adapt the original as *Caesar's Wife*.

Along with two other plays, *Heard on the Telephone* (also adapted from the French, *Au téléphone*) and *Irish Assurance,* the play opened at Wyndham's on 1 March 1902. Under the heading *Sensational Triple Bill*, the *Daily Express* of 11 February 1902 posed the rhetorical question:

> Mrs. Tree as manageress? Why not? Nothing has been more common of latter years than to find a lady at the head of players and Mrs. Tree will adventure only a short season at Wyndham's. She made a striking success of The Likeness of the Night and is one of those actresses far too valuable to be allowed to remain idle.

Most telling of all were the critics who did not pass up the opportunity to denigrate Tree by genuinely praising Maud. There was never going to be room for two stars on a Tree stage, as countless ditties, anecdotes, and straightforward criticism attested, and the *Sunday Chronicle* appeared fully to understand the dynamic between the Trees writing on 10 February 1902:

> Plays that accommodate and aggrandise him cannot be expected to equally accommodate and aggrandise another artist of entirely different distinction and so it has rarely happened that Mrs. Tree could do justice to her genius in the productions at Her Majesty's. So she proposes to make a bid for fame on her own account [...] She is a brilliant and fascinating actress whose opportunities have been lessened by the fact that her husband is the manager and magnet of a great London theatre.

Maud had acted swiftly. Between Christmas Eve 1901, when she had seen and purchased the play, and the end of February 1902, she had leased a theatre, had two plays translated, engaged actors for three, and learned the roles of two parts to be played on alternative nights. Newspaper clippings testify to her success. The *Onlooker* of 1 February 1902 called her 'the bravest actress of the English stage', and 'plucky', producing 'variety and good art all round'. But the greatest attraction, claimed the *Evening Standard* of 11 February, was the 'appearance of the delightful actress herself', reminding the audience 'in her nervous force and excitability of her Ophelia — quite one of her best performances'. The *Era* of 8 March, almost a month later, highlighted the feline quality to her acting, but went further: 'It is pleasant to be able to place on record the fact that Mrs. Tree's first venture as a manageress has been associated with an artistic triumph of no ordinary kind'.[3] An 'end-to-end study of first class acting' is repeatedly praised, while the *Sunday Times* (9 March) went as far as to deem *Caesar's Wife* 'one of the most perfectly acted plays ever seen in this country'. And in America, the *New York Times* of the same date reported the opening night with the headline: 'French plays thrill London'. With the *Lady's Pictorial* of 15 March 1902 recording the presence of the King, first alone and then in the company of 'five men', and a visit by the Prince of Wales, the success of Maud's directorial debut was assured.

But of all the press releases, social commentaries, fashion updates, and contemporaneous notes, the most valuable was the review written by the *Daily Telegraph* critic and Maud's ever-loyal supporter, Clement Scott:

> I have seen it and admire it for the excellent acting that it contains. As a general rule, in the case of a triple bill, one generally expects to find the third portion not quite up to the standard of the remaining two. Managers reckon on this with cheerful pessimism and prepare to face the worst with a sublime confidence in the drawing powers of the rest of the programme. But in the case of Mrs. Beerbohm Tree's venture at Wyndham Theatre, all three pieces are of that order which bespeaks success, individually and collectively. Mrs. Beerbohm Tree has an opportunity of showing the genius that is in her in a manner as striking as it is gratifying to those of her admirers who always maintained that she is an actress to her fingertips [...] Mrs. Beerbohm Tree rises to heights that are as artistic as they are welcome. Everyone should go and see this really unique and clever show.[4]

It was much more than a clever show and Maud brought more to it than a novelty factor. Once more she had used her extensive network of contacts to realize an ambitious project, and during her short term as director of the Wyndham would also develop her business acumen. In this instance she was a kind of 'wo-manager' (a term originally applied by Leigh Hunt to Madame Vestris when she took over the directorship of the Olympic Theatre in 1830) and her ability to secure funds was crucial.[5] Without a personal fortune it was virtually impossible for a woman to acquire the guarantors for the notes of credit required. Maud was exceptional in being socially and professionally on good terms with the bankers Carl Meyer and Ernest Cassel and often dealt with them in place of her husband.

However, the challenges of producing her triple bill were not just financial. Historically, Maud excelled at the interpretation of wronged or duplicitous women as directed by a theatre manager. In this instance, as director herself she was under particular public scrutiny for her treatment of adultery in the case of *Caesar's Wife*, and both the translation and interpretation of the sensationalist *Au téléphone*. Her astute and opportunistic eye not only perceived the continuous need to re-invent herself but also, in a wider, global sense, showed how much more aligned to the theatre critic's way of thinking she was than Herbert. The argument of realism versus spectacle begun decades before, continued to divide critics and if Tree's 'culinary theatre' was being criticized for turning plays into 'commodities' and the audience into their 'consumer', then Maud, in identifying these new plays, was quick to anticipate the changing tastes of her audience.[6] Plays from the Théâtre Antoine, as John Corbin (writing for the *New York Times* on 16 February) said, explored the:

> Nooks of human existence, the particular nook presented may or may not be pleasant to contemplate, but as the idealists have already squatted in most of the pleasant and wholesome nooks, the plays at the Théâtre Antoine are necessarily such as seem on the whole unwholesome to normal appetite.

Maud opened her triple bill with an *English* play and the most digestible of the three. The *Observer* announced *Irish Assurance* as 'something terribly dramatic and weird from France', when it was actually a revival of *His Last Legs*, a farce in two acts written by the American-born London playwright William Bayle Bernard (1807–75). Bernard who was born in Boston, helped popularize the stage type of the eccentric rural American and had adapted Washington Irving's *Rip Van Winkle*, which Tree produced at Her Majesty's Theatre directly after his *Midsummer Night's Dream*. *His Last Legs,* first published in 1840 and performed at the Queen's Theatre, Dublin, in 1866, takes its title from an allusion to the leading character in the play: in published texts and playbills the play was announced as 'A Man of Genius on his Last Legs'. The protagonist, O'Callaghan, is described as such and dressed in 'a shabby genteel suit' (the *Observer,* 12 January 1902).[7] The Irish actor Leonard Boyne (1813–1920) was praised for his brogue, and 'E. A. B.' writing for the *New York Times* in an article entitled 'London Theatrical Topics' said Maud's 'well-worn little play is put on the stage carefully and proves really entertaining in spite of its old-fashioned air'.[8]

By contrast, the second and shortest in the billing, *Au téléphone* was anything but old-fashioned. This play dealt with the novel technology of communication and the equally new and tentatively explored fields of psychology and what we now know to be Freud's vision of psychic trauma. Written by André de Lorde (1869–1942) and Charles Foley (1861–1956), but based on a short play by Charles Foley, it was first produced at the enterprising, non-commercial Théâtre Antoine.[9] André de Lorde was the chief playwright of the Théâtre du Grand-Guignol, an offbeat playhouse in Montmartre which specialized in programmes of short, naturalistically-staged plays aimed at generating a frisson of excitement-cum-shock for blasé Parisian theatregoers.[10] The more than one hundred plays that he presented there were all predicated on the dramatic exploitation of fear, autosuggestion, nerve-racking tension, or mental imbalance, factors underpinned by his interest in the study of clinical psychology.

Another distinctive feature of his work was the incorporation into the action of aspects of new or relatively new technology — in this instance the telephone. After leaving his home in Scene 1 to pay an overnight visit to old friends, a husband receives a call from his wife in Scene 2 that begins conversationally, then descends abruptly into panic when she hears the sound of intruders breaking in, and finally into utter silence, leaving him to imagine that she has been assaulted and killed, as he collapses into raving hysteria. The horrific irony of this instrument of communication becoming a measure of their separation and of his powerlessness to act, or even to see what he can hear, is inescapable.

In producing the play in order to represent the tension between what Jacob Smith calls this 'physical absence and vocal co-presence', Maud used the ubiquitous curtain to mark the distance between husband and wife, an inexpensive device she had seen used to maximum effect in Elizabeth Robins's production of *John Gabriel Borkman*.[11] She had also learned from Tree's innovative use of lighting and in this play she modified limelight by employing additional focused or flood-lighting. The play was a success, as was her own performance in it. The *Evening Standard* of 10 February 1902, for one, said she gave a 'remarkably natural and sympathetic sketch of Marie Marex, the victim of the murder, giving a peculiar charm to this highly ingenious play'.

As with her appearance in music halls to recite 'The Absent-Minded Beggar', and her early support of playwrights such as Ibsen and Elizabeth Robins, Maud's triple bill once again initiated public discourse on the very nature of theatre itself. The critics found in favour of Maud's choice of plays and the simple manner in which she represented them:

> 'What really matters in a setting,' wrote one, 'is not the truthfulness of its details but rather the effectiveness of its mood and the emphasis it throws on the important underlying motive of the play. We have become weary of imitating actuality represented for itself alone and have begun to look for an interpretation of the abstract thing, the medium of stage pictures and effects. Late in the 19th century, productions were satisfied if they succeeded in making their spectators believe what they saw, now, by means of visual suggestions, they try to induce their audience to imagine more than they can actually see'.[12]

With this shift towards the more abstract interpretation of theatre, Tree's extravagant productions were not unanimously acclaimed. Indeed, his later production of *The Tempest*, was disparaged on many levels — the scenery was considered 'irrelevant', the orchestra 'hidden under a mass of vegetables', and he was accused of over-abridgement.[13]

Antagonistic, professional rivalry did not end there. Shortly after Maud's triple bill concluded, an anonymous writer for *The Times*, pointed to the 'evils of the actor-manager system'. More articles followed including another by John Corbin, who once again praised such privately-managed theatres such as the Théâtre Antoine and the Théâtre Libre de Paris. The referencing to the actor-manager underpinned the debate — that of 'fringe' versus national theatre and one that became necessarily entwined with the role of the theatre manager. Corbin continued to vent his resentment writing that 'the actor manager is quite ready to cease being a star, provided he may become the centre of an all-inclusive solar system' (*New York Times*, 16 February 1902). At times flippantly treated, it was a criticism that had already been directed in particular at Herbert whose critics delighted (erroneously as it happened) in reporting that His Majesty's Theatre was under threat.[14] Ditties aimed at him personally such as the ones below that appeared in *Umpire* in 1901:

Wail of the Actor Manager

A Tree — or not a Tree? I ask the question!
Whether t'is nobler in the manager
To yield the foremost place in his new play
Unto an actor
other than himself?

And:

A propos d'arbres

Mrs. Tree had been 'lent' to appear at the S. Theatre during the Lewis Waller season.
   One night a lustre fell between Mrs. Tree and Mr. Waller on the stage.
   Afterwards, said Brookfield to Mrs. Tree: 'Awkward accident yours; if your husband had been on the stage you would have been a widow.'

'What do you mean, Mr. Brookfield?'
'Well it fell in the centre of the stage.'
'Yes.'
'Well Tree wouldn't have been anywhere else!'

It was always Maud's opinion that there was 'too much Tree at His Majesty's'. Anecdotes aside, Charles Wyndham owner of the Wyndham Theatre, responded to the seriousness of the actor-manager issue by claiming that the 'subventioned theatre' was in such 'a parlous state' it would have died altogether within thirty years.[15]

In response to and disagreeing with this possible 'demise', John Corbin in his *New York Times* article of 16 February 1902 praised the Théâtre Antoine where dramatists 'rejoice in a new found freedom'. And meanwhile the public continued to flock to the play whose 'emotional dynamic' was 'stupendous', as described by Corbin. Testament to Maud's success apart from the obvious presence of the King was the standing ovation she received night after night and the critic for the *Whitehall Review* (13 March 1902) who wrote: 'Mrs. Tree deserved the ovation for she has ever striven to climb the heights. She always kept her eyes fixed earnestly upon the upward slope of Art where sits ambition'.

The third play in the triple bill was *Caesar's Wife*. The original *L'Énigme*, written as a prose poem in two short acts by a former barrister Paul Hervieu (1857–1915), has been described as 'Racinean in scope and modern in sentiment'.[16] Like *Au téléphone*, this play was controversial as it raised 'the double enigma', that is: whether a man who has caught his wife's lover is bound to kill him. As the critic for the *Western Times* wrote on 10 March 1902, 'both pieces are being talked about and that means success'. It also meant debate. Various issues were raised, ranging from matters of translation and questions of morality to the very real and taboo subject of adultery. 'Magnificent draperies,' wrote 'NKG' to Maud after seeing the play, 'Adultery is committed often! And we are getting used to the fact!' It was a dilemma acknowledged by the critic who recognized the absurdity of producing a play that dealt with this contentious subject if it could not be referred to on the English stage 'except at the Gaiety, between a wink and a laugh'. But it was equally a skilfully crafted piece written for 'six characters of equal importance; and each in turn absorbs the whole flood of the limelight'.[17]

This element of a 'unique triple bill of unique variety and strength' (*Daily Express*, 11 February 1902) which 'contrary to the expectations of most of the critics, is enjoying marked popularity' (*Western Times*, 10 March 1902), was commented on as much before it opened as it was during its run. Everything, from the title of the play to its translation, was analyzed. Altercations with the censor over the English version, which 'E. A. B.' called 'a perversion', ended in an attempt to downplay the moral element and simplify its meaning for the 'obtuse playgoer who here, as in New York, is in the majority'.[18] When the third in the triple bill opened on 1 March 1902, illness prevented Maud from acting in it for the first ten days. Lena Ashwell stepped in at short notice with a performance of 'conspicuous value' (*Daily Mail*, 3 March 1902), waiving her fee, a fact which was noted in the press and which was also rewarded by Maud with a gift of jewellery.[19] Thereafter, Maud played Léonore de Gourgiran (*Caesar's Wife*) and Marie Marex (*Au téléphone*) on alternate nights.

Caesar's Wife is about two brothers, Raymond and Gérard de Gourgiran, who, together with their respective wives, Giselle and Léonore, are in their country house with two guests, the old marquis de Neste and the young Monsieur de Vivarce, for a weekend's hunting. From the outset it is known that the Gourgiran brothers are obsessed with hunting and have proven to be ruthless killers. Consequently, having spotted Vivarce leaving the guest annexe late at night, the marquis is certain that one of the Gourgiran wives is having an affair with Vivarce and concerned for his safety, attempts to warn him. But which is the wife betraying which brother? That is the question and a question that generates a passionate debate.

Raymond declares:

> Our religion teaches us that the vow of fidelity is binding even into death. After all, the right of the husband to do himself justice has never been actually struck out of him. The lying wife whose soul is all deceitfulness is not worthy of the name of wife; killing is too good for her. Caesar's wife must be above suspicion.[20]

And therein lies the enigma of the play and Frank Harris in translating the play from French was thus inspired to call it *Caesar's Wife*. Returning to a summary of the plot: the brothers are suspicious and attempt to trap their wives but the women continue to deny any wrongdoing. Vivarce however, knowing that his lover will never leave her husband as this would mean also abandoning her children, shoots himself. Initially, it is thought that Vivarce has been accidentally wounded, but on learning that he is dead Léonore can no longer pretend and admits her guilt.

Caesar's Wife is a play full of innuendo, moralistic hypothesizing, and reflections on the frailty of human nature, all of which would have appealed to the Edwardian theatregoer for whom theatre had come to represent 'a newer moral realism' and one that prized 'truthfulness even at the cost of pleasantness of subject or tidiness of dramatic construction'.[21] Related to this, as Joseph Donohoe has so aptly put it, the Edwardian theatregoer also enjoyed a heightened 'appreciation of and appetite for pleasure — hedonistic, intellectual, innocent, or guilty'.[22] The play may have succeeded in entertaining while at the same time expounding its salutary message, but once again for Maud, the ironic parallels to be drawn with her personal life could not have been greater. While the knowledge of Tree's affair had preoccupied Maud during the run of *A Midsummer Night's Dream*, keeping Waller's unrelenting passion for her at bay, and secret, would have been of the utmost importance during the production of *Caesar's Wife*. It was after all at the instigation of Florence Waller that Maud had seen *L'Énigme* in the first place, and perhaps, just perhaps, Florence's friendship was not as transparent as Maud may have believed. Waller was still writing letters in which he declared:

> I do think that it was so loving and gentle of my love to send me that message'; and later, in hoping for a reunion in Eastbourne, 'I know it is impossible to love someone really and still treat them as you are treating me. In all the years you have never done this and I won't have it now [...] I can't continue to think of you every minute of the day and long for you and ache to be with you'.[23]

But an 'ache' for Maud was all it could ever be. Maud knew very well that

FIG. 10.2. Maud Tree and Charles Wyndham (*The Entr'Acte*, 5 April 1902)

FIG. 10.3. Maud Tree with her daughter Viola in her new tonneau
(*The Car*, 17 June 1903)

she would never divorce Herbert and that Waller could never divorce his wife. Although divorce existed in England, prior to 1857 (only a year before Maud's birth) it could be obtained only through a private Act of Parliament. In 1890 there were 369 divorces and by 1900, there were just 560. However, while a man could divorce a woman merely on the grounds of adultery, a woman had to prove her husband guilty of adultery in addition to either cruelty, bigamy, incest, or bestiality.[24] Waller talked of marrying Maud, but they would both have known that this was an impossibility — professionally, financially, and socially. Besides which Maud still loved Herbert. She was hurt by his infidelity but he would always be her best love. It is telling that even on the day he died in 1917, and even though they lived in separate abodes, Maud was still tending to his laundry.

With the proceeds gleaned from her triple bill, Maud bought herself a smart new motorcar. She was pleased with her purchase and proud of her achievement. And more importantly, her position, as she wrote to May Pinney, was exactly as she wanted it.

Notes to Chapter 10

1. Davis 1996: 112–14.
2. See the *Daily Mail*, 21 and 22 December 1901, and the *Glasgow*, 20 December 1990; also the preface to Shellard 2004 for background to censorship rulings in Britain at the time. The

Licensing Act of 1737 introduced censorship, but the Theatre Regulation Act of 1843 established a nationwide system of licensing. Theatre files from 1902 are housed at the National Archive at Kew. Edward Hyde Villiers, fifth Earl of Clarendon (1846–1914) was Lord Chamberlain from 1900 to 1905.
3. For further analysis of the feline quality to Maud's acting, see Chapter 11.
4. Scott 1902: 15.
5. James Henry Leigh Hunt (1784–1859) was a British essayist, playwright, contributor to the *Tatler*, and editor of the *Examiner*. T. C. Davis differentiates between managers and lessee/entrepreneurs, see Davis 2000: 275, 303–04. She terms both Vestris and Lena Ashwell 'lessees', as they purchased the leases of the Olympic Theatre (in 1830) and the Kingsway Theatre (1907) respectively. Mary Moore was lessee of the New Theatre but manager of the Wyndham. From 1882, women owned and controlled property, inheritance, and gifts but became liable for contracts and torts according to their separate property. Loans to married women with separate estates were not binding.
6. See Davis 2000 and Kennedy 1996. Bertolt Brecht (1898–1956) coined the phrase 'culinary theatre', see Brecht 1965.
7. Pomeranz 1971: 136–38.
8. Baughan: 1902a. 'E. A. B.' was actually E. A. Baughan (1865–1938), music critic for the *Daily News* from 1902, and its drama critic from 1904.
9. The play was based on a short play by Charles Foley.
10. The Théâtre du Grand-Guignol (literally, 'theatre of the big puppet') was founded by Oscar Méténier (1859–1913), a playwright and Zola acolyte, at 20 rue Chaptal, Paris.
11. Smith 2008: 213.
12. Richard Silvester, 'The Shakespearian Stage and the Stage Today' (1916), as quoted in Pearson and Uricchio 1994: 214–22.
13. Ibid.
14. On 21 May 1901 the *Evening Standard* ran the headline: 'Theatre Threatened: Mr. Tree won't Sell!'
15. Charles Wyndham (1837–1919), born Charles Culverwell, trained as a surgeon and joined the Union Army in that capacity during the American Civil War. He returned to England to a life on the stage and in 1899 opened the Wyndham Theatre. He was knighted in 1902.
16. Chisholm 1911.
17. Symons 1909: 27–30.
18. Baughan 1902b.
19. For Lena Ashwell see Leask 2000.
20. This idiom originates in fact: Julius Caesar married Pompeia (his third wife) in 67 BC, and four years later he was elected to the position of Pontifex Maximus, that is, chief priest of the Roman state religion. A year after that, Pompeia hosted a female-only festival of the Bona Dea [the good god]. She was a famous beauty and a young Patrician called Publius Claudius Pulcher, who wanted to seduce her, was able to gain admittance disguised as a woman. He was caught and prosecuted for sacrilege. Caesar gave no evidence against him at his trial and he was acquitted, but he divorced Pompeia declaring 'my wife ought not even to be under suspicion'.
21. Donahoe 1996: 14–17
22. Ibid.
23. Lewis Waller to Maud Tree, [n.d.] (MBTC 7/RA/420).
24. Cerasco 1993: 30.

CHAPTER 11

Agrippina
1906

Maud's contentment, however, did not last long, and she attempted to allay her feeling of restlessness by moving house. Now, after a decade at 77 Sloane Street, in June 1904 Maud moved to the romantic Walpole House in Chiswick, for which the Trees paid £110 rent per annum. It had a high-walled garden, an orchard, and 'graceful iron gates'.[1] It also claimed both literary connections in the shape of Thackeray, who had made it the scene of Becky Sharp's school days in *Vanity Fair*, and historical in that it was rebuilt by Charles II for his mistress Barbara Villiers. Villiers was said to haunt the place and Maud claimed to have seen and heard this unhappy phantom wringing her hands and sighing at the loss of her beauty. Moreover, hers was not the only ghost from the past rearing its oracular head. Precisely nine months after moving into their new house, Mr Littlechild (the detective hired by Maud so many years before) begged to present his compliments with another copy of a birth certificate: May Pinney had given birth to Herbert's third son. Tree's response to Maud's accusation that this latest event had killed her love for him was that she was wrong: her love had simply 'committed suicide'.[2]

Since learning of Herbert's affair Maud had in fact come to terms with his infidelity. This had, in part, been helped by the conjecture that relations had since cooled between May and Herbert, and she had even gone as far as to help May financially, feeling sorry for her young children. However, this recent birth proved that his estrangement from May was far from final. Maud felt the sense of hurt and betrayal afresh. She had come to accept Herbert's cavalier treatment of her, and even come to expect it, but she was stung by May's treatment of her. Having gone out of her way to befriend the woman at the expense of her own feelings she now responded to a sharp note from May, replying tartly:

> I think, in writing as you do you are little mindful of the consideration and generosity that has been shown you. — If grief and bitterness wrung no betrayal of your secret from me five years ago, I am not likely to [deal lightly with it] now, when time has been kind to me in teaching me to forget.[3]

Maud had not of course forgotten, and as she always did in times of trouble she turned for comfort to Violet Lindsay, who responded immediately:

Saturday [1905]
23 Bruton Street. W.

Poor darling,
Your account is <u>too</u> heartrending. I wish I were with you to comfort you —

I begin to wish for your sake, that the whole thing, when it came to your knowledge could have <u>killed</u> your real love at one blow — like with me. It would have been better for your peace of mind — and very likely, as in my case, you could have dissimulated enough for Herbert never to have discovered the truth — or notice the poetry & loveliness that was missing from the ordinary every day wifely care that one can bestow — from a sense of duty & kindness —

I can't bear to think of yr <u>wonderful</u> human kindness, & unconventionality towards M.P [May Pinney] & towards the Baby, should have been so misunderstood so grossly, narrowly mightily misunderstood — you were so happy that last day I saw you — feeling that it was a comfort to you to feel the girl was very straight — & that you could use your energy to help her — use your money to help with the baby now it is all dashed in your teeth! & most cruelly [...].

Darling, yr wonderfulness, yr charity, yr large heartedness, is wasted on Herbert, [these] & on these people. Ugh! [...] Don't let yr precious health be hurt by such needless heartaches — I shall soon be back.

Don't be extravagant or <u>save</u> any more now, except for your own <u>Viola —</u> <u>Don't</u> help in <u>any</u> way any more —

They are not worth it — & it is your <u>duty</u> to think of Viola's future — does <u>any</u>one else do so?[4]

Violet's letter hit home in too many ways. While Herbert showed himself capable of begetting three 'little Johns' with May Pinney, it was clear there would be no more children for Maud, and certainly not the longed-for son. Furthermore, she had spent her hard-earned money on May to no avail; if anything, her generosity had been misconstrued. Once again, Maud turned to her work for solace. Walpole House was enchanting, if isolated, and perhaps because she was spending so much time there, she thought of producing her own version of *Becky Sharp*. Maud's close friend James Barrie had written a one-act play based on the last three chapters of Thackeray's novel, which had not proved a success, the *Stage* of June 1893 had called it a 'stupid and vulgar farce'. This novel without a hero was notoriously difficult to dramatize, as Tom Robertson also discovered before admitting defeat. In 1901, however, Cosmo Stuart and Robert Smythe Hichens presented their own version at the Prince of Wales Theatre. Marie Tempest (who was married to Stuart) had played Becky to great acclaim, and Maud now fancied herself in the title role. A flurry of correspondence ensued with the playwright Robert Marshall, who, it was hoped, would write the script with Clement Scott, who had reviewed the play on occasion, but Marshall was hesitant, and although Maud found backers, the project came to nothing.

Violet's closing comment had also hit a nerve. Maud was very attentive to all three of her daughters' education, but she was especially preoccupied with that of Viola. Whatever differences might exist between Herbert and Maud, husband and wife were nevertheless united in their ambition for their precocious daughter. Although she had made her acting debut in 1904 as Ariel in Herbert's production of *The Tempest,* Viola really wanted to be an opera singer. Margot Tennant, for one, had recognized her lovely voice when Viola was quite young. Much energy as a result had been spent in sending Viola to Italy to learn Italian and study with a series of singing teachers, and Maud now concentrated on fostering Viola's singing career by transforming an outbuilding at Walpole House into a music studio. She also drew on her extensive pool of gifted friends in the music business to assist in furthering Viola's career. Sir Thomas Beecham was the long-term lover and companion of Emerald Cunard, whose daughter was Iris's closest friend both at primary school and later at the Slade. A few years later he would lease His Majesty's Theatre for an opera season. Clara Butt and Elgar were also close friends, as was the pianist Paderewski. In such an environment, as *Tatler* of 19 March 1901 put it, 'the daughter of the poplar Trees cannot fail to develop some talent'.

Once again, after a 'cooling off' period Maud and Herbert resumed a cordial correspondence. Apart from their need to communicate about Viola, both were experiencing problems with their respective siblings. Julius Beerbohm, Herbert's brother, the explorer, engineer, and travel writer who wrote about his adventures in Patagonia, was perhaps too much the adventurer at heart, embarking on mad, money-losing ventures. He was now broke again and in bad health, and would die later that year. Maud's own brother Horace was also in financial difficulties. After twenty-six years employed as an engineer, Horace was also out of work and looking to Maud to supplement his income; he wrote to her to acknowledge receipt of a loan for £209, a considerable sum given that she earned £40 per theatre engagement. She was also lending money to sister Bertha and to Harriette, who sometimes kept house for her. The necessity of finding another engagement was thus paramount. As a stopgap, therefore, in 1902 Maud performed in a series of roles culminating in the Coronation revival at His Majesty's of *The Merry Wives of Windsor.* It was a production in which Herbert was to be called 'Tree the Trigamist', his 'wives' (*Punch* of 25 May 1902 said 'there can't be too many for us!') being played by Madge Kendal and Ellen Terry, while Maud was Anne Page, a part she learned in just twenty-four hours. In a further gibe the magazine said Tree, as Falstaff, had reserved the 'fat part for himself'. Maud quipped, in *Dramatic Notes* of 14 May 1902, that he was appearing not in the midst of two stars but two 'ancient lights'.

In the winter of 1906 Tree would once again contrive to carve a 'fat part' for himself; in fact he would attempt to construct his new production entirely around his own role, but the endeavour would have very different and unexpected results, especially for Maud. Much to her surprise, Tree chose her to play Agrippina in the historical drama *Nero*. Written in blank verse by Stephen Phillips, it was the third play by this author to be produced by Tree at His Majesty's Theatre but the only one in which Maud acted. Four years before, in 1902, she had been snubbed when Tree overlooked her in casting Constance Collier as Pallas Athene for his *Ulysses*. Maud had dyed her hair and picked out her costume in anticipation of the role (given her knowledge of classical Greek), only for Herbert to choose his current mistress. (Even Collier was embarrassed by Tree's choice. She confessed to stumbling and stuttering 'over the awful Greek names', and imagined that 'the rest of the cast giggled because of her'.)[5] This latest and lavish production, ostentatious even by Tree's standards, would run for 127 performances over thirteen weeks. It grossed £37,000 and cost £24,000 to produce (£2,000 each went on costume and scenery), so that Tree cleared a profit of over £8,000 at a time when the average middle-class income was £300 a year.[6]

The sumptuousness of Tree's productions with their scores of supernumeraries, elaborate props, tableaux, and painted scenery testified to his wealth as a producer, but the scale of 'gorgeous magnificence' lavished on the scenery and dresses for *Nero* made the theatregoer literally gasp in awe.[7] There were six separate stage scenes and three-dimensional sets, designed by Percy Macquoid,[8] depicting sprawling views of urban Rome and the purple Bay of Naples. Cedar trees, live horses, jewels, and braziers were only some of the extraordinary props deployed to satisfy the Edwardians' 'craze for spectacle', while huge feasts and dishes recreated 'dream worlds of consumption'.[9] Over a hundred supers delivered platters of food and gallons of wine in a banqueting scene lasting ten minutes. A fanfare of trumpets announced a huge stuffed peacock and boar's head, just as rose petals fell from the recreated heaven. Macquoid, in an interview with the *Daily News* on 24 January 1906 prior to the opening of the production, promised the scene would be:

> One of the most magnificent that has ever been produced on any stage. With its profusion of roses [...] its groups of musicians and dancers, its rich carpets and marble columns, it will doubtless recall the famous description of Trimalchio's supper at the 'Satiricon'.

In *A Midsummer Night's Dream* (and in *King John,* although Maud did not act in the latter) Tree had consciously exploited the anxieties surrounding the conflicts then unfolding outside the theatre, namely the possible dissolution of the British Empire as England fought two Boer wars. In *Nero*, however, he relied on the current political, cultural, and economic mechanisms of bourgeois England, which were familiar to the Edwardian spectator, actively to heighten its dramatic tension. As David Schulz has put it, it was 'a thinly coded representation of British Imperial Culture masquerading as Roman fantasy'.[10] And at the centre of this carefully constructed representation of Imperial Rome, in one of the most spectacular theatres in the city, *owned* by its own celebrity actor-manager turned urban gentleman, verily embodying the whole business of conspicuous consumption, was to be Tree (as Nero) himself.

What Tree did not anticipate, however, was the extent to which *women* in the play, by challenging male authority, would engender a response amongst its female (and male) audience. The gender conflict continued to preoccupy Edwardians and the external disruption of traditional patriarchal institutions in the form of the 'New Woman' only reinforced the growing agitation of women in the play and on the stage. With the growing politicization of women's suffrage, women were generally blamed for disruption in society. As David Schulz says, 'in *Nero*, at least, most of the conflicts used to heighten the dramatic tension can be traced to a feminine agent challenging the masculine order'.[11]

Sexually independent New Woman characters such as Mrs Erlynne in Wilde's *Lady Windermere's Fan* or Pinero's Paula Tanqueray in *The Second Mrs Tanqueray* tended to be represented sympathetically by their liberal, male authors. The character of Agrippina does not debate in this New Woman tradition but rather threatens calamity and chaos. Pitted against the sexual adventuress Poppaea (played by Constance Collier, Tree's ongoing, offstage mistress), Agrippina is portrayed as monstrous, and 'almost unstoppable'.[12] By contrast, Poppaea is first displayed being painted by her handmaidens — a scene rooted in female subjectivity. She is the embodiment of sexual desire, as ambitious as Agrippina but acting within a female role. It was not, however, an interpretation that commended her to the critics. The *Daily Graphic* of 26 January 1906 said Collier was 'obvious instead of subtle and human'. It went on to say that Poppaea's character was that of a woman 'as drawn by Mr. Philips, and played by Miss Constance Collier [...] the old-fashioned wicked beauty of melodrama, whom one despises Nero for loving', presumably Maud did too.

The play opens with Agrippina hovering over the dying body of her husband Emperor Claudius, thereby establishing her character's thirst for power. The final scenes depict not only her escalating rage but also her renunciation of Nero. Significantly, the expression of her anger is counterbalanced by a troupe of barely audible female slaves. As she draws a sword, the crowd erupts. She is no longer merely a mother in rebellion against her son but a real and credible threat, actively challenging the emperor's authority. But her ultimate strength as Schulz also points out, is just how difficult it is to kill her. While both Pinero's and Wilde's heroines accept death quietly (or quietly remove themselves from the society they have disrupted), Agrippina refuses to die easily. Having survived a sinking boat, she rises Venus-like.

While performing in *A Midsummer Night's Dream* some six years earlier Maud had been overcome by her emotional life, by the knowledge of Tree's other family, by the overwhelming strictures society placed on the 'respectable woman', strictures Maud felt and continued to feel keenly. That had not changed, but she had lived so long in the shadow of her aristocratic friends that nothing would induce her to risk or endanger her hard-won position in a society that was nevertheless changing. During the run of *Nero* however, she was no longer a victim of chance, subject to its whim, but rather like Agrippina, an architect of its design. She had learned only recently of the birth of yet another child to May Pinney; she would also play alongside Constance Collier, who she knew continued to be Tree's mistress. She had been passed over once before because of Collier, but now she was invited to share a stage. In the six years or so since *A Midsummer Night's Dream* Maud had learned that May Pinney was only one of many women with whom her husband shared an intimate relationship. It did not mean that he did not feel affection towards her, but it did mean that it would never be exclusive. Maud had at long last begun to accept this and the fact that, like Nero, Tree was 'a gorgeous butterfly lost in the night' (*Pall Mall Gazette*, 24 January 1906).[13]

There was also the question of her own relationship with Lewis Waller. The Bristol archive catalogues an extensive collection of correspondence pertaining to Maud and while there are several letters from Waller to Maud, as is to be expected, there are none from Maud to Waller. Searches of further archives and libraries have produced no billet-doux. It can only be concluded that any correspondence from Maud to Waller has long vanished or been destroyed — accidentally or otherwise.

There is no doubt that the correspondence that does exist from Waller to Maud is passionate, reading very much in places, like that of a frustrated lover's. Maud's 'relationship' was unquestionably close, although perhaps not the full-blown affair that his letters might suggest. Olivia Truman, who began writing fan mail to Tree at the age of twelve (Tree was forty-five at the time) and claims in her book that Tree 'made love quite beautifully' to her 'like a boy' (a claim that in itself paves the way for all kinds of other allegations), is not in my opinion a reliable source, but she does offer contemporaneous notes.[14] Truman recounts an incident where Maud had moved her dressing room next to Lewis Waller's when they were acting together at Her Majesty's. In her account, Truman quotes Tree as saying, 'This is *too* disgusting — do you want the whole theatre to look on you as nothing but a common harlot?' Maud is said to have replied, 'Oh Herbie dear — what *is* a harlot?'[15] For Maud, therefore, the need to tread the tightrope of propriety was as challenging as ever. Sexual tension and rivalry were added to the play, said *The Times* on 26 January 1906, by the emperor's (Tree's) mistress Poppaea (Constance Collier) in a clash of artistic temperaments where the crescendo is 'the wild ravings of megalomania'.

Against this actual but no less dramatic backdrop, and to its real-life protagonists, the play must have come as a welcome distraction. And although it is clear that at its core is a character soon to display 'an unexampled propensity for evil', it is Agrippina as the non-domesticated woman who will soon come to embody the urban decay and dissolution that is such a threat not only to patrician Rome but also to Edwardian society.[16] But when she first stepped on to the stage, Maud's slight stature and the 'calculated frailty' of her 1890s appearance elicited much commentary. Her robes were said by the *Daily Telegraph* of 21 January 1906 to drown her, her physique incompatible with the 'masterful qualities of this reckless queen'. It was soon apparent, however, that her acting had risen 'to a tragic intensity [...] carrying the house with her'. It was a rendering considered by William Archer, in the *Tribune* of 21 January 1906, to be 'one of the triumphs of the play [...] a thing to dwell in the memory'.

But this success was not entirely due to having learned to channel emotion or to a newly-gained pragmatism in her dealings with Tree. Formerly, some critics had questioned a 'metallic ring' to her voice (for example the *Whitehall Review* of 6 December 1888), and in an attempt to correct this Maud had engaged Joe Comyns Carr, who had taught her to develop 'a new low voice'.[17] It was this new voice that brought results. The *Evening Standard* of 26 January 1906 wrote that 'Mrs. Tree's voice had its mellow notes which were new to us', and one that grew 'stronger with dignity' and 'virility'. The *Pall Mall Gazette* of the following day, claimed that 'her distinctness and incisiveness of utterance is a lesson to some of her associates' while

FIG. 11.1. Maud as Agrippina (*Le Théâtre*, January 1906)

the *Morning Advertiser* (27 January) praised Maud's skill as an elocutionist, as 'the speeches she is given to declaim need a mistress in the art'. It was hailed as 'one of the triumphs' of her career. An article entitled 'Superb Theatrical Art' that appeared in the *Evening Standard* on 27 January 1906 went further:

> Here let us pay tribute to the actress who so finely interpreted the poet's conception. Mrs. Tree, as Agrippina, provided the surprise of the evening. She reached a splendid height, here and throughout. Great, deep notes in her voice painted the tragic depths of the play; gentle caressing tones showed us the mother. Wild laughter rang real and true; broad and sweeping gestures brought again before us the grand manner of other days. A physical strength quite remarkable sustained her throughout; a keen intelligence and perception illumined the text. Here was Agrippina indeed, a queen of tragedy, an Empress of Rome. Mrs. Tree 'took the stage' as it should be taken and held it and us. The power of her acting at this fine exit to revenge thrilled the audience and established the actress on a plane she has not hitherto even suggested being able to reach.

Maud had indeed succeeded in thrilling her audience, had achieved that psychophysical objective that had become the objective of all actresses, of sending 'thought through the footlights'.[18] But it was one that provoked complex reactions from the spectator, not least from the Victorian/Edwardian male, who seems often to have recoiled in panic.[19] It was one thing to be captivated by the scantily-clad performer that troubled and titillated audiences throughout the nineteenth century, it was another to be presented with the disturbing passion of a serious actress. The response generated by such an actress could be physical, with one critic feeling as though he'd been seized 'by the throat', left 'gasping for breath' as if his life was 'imperilled'.[20] Thus the sexuality represented on stage overstepped the narrow margin of respectability and moved into the public domain to become something intangible and no longer wholly feminine. Criticism of Constance Collier as Poppaea was that her interpretation was too conventional and not human enough. Yet it was this very 'human' quality in a powerful, moving woman that proved so dangerous, and the greater the actress, the more animal-like the comparisons. Shaw, in comparing the actress Eleanora Duse to Sarah Bernhardt, described 'a vampire face whose acting produced the mixed enjoyment of a public execution, or any other spectacle in which we still take hideous delight'.[21] Bernhardt in turn, was described as 'tearing the words with her teeth [...] like a wild beast ravening upon prey'.[22]

Maud as Agrippina was described in similarly feline terms. *The Times* of 26 January 1906 called her instincts 'those of a tigress rather than those of a human being', while *Umpire* of the same date wrote that the scene where 'the mother (Maud) shrieks in a frenzy of rage is the strongest act in the drama'. Her acting is repeatedly described as 'passionate', 'ferocious', 'tiger-like', with energy that is 'feline in its ferocity'. Even Tree at his best is described in terms of animal behaviour, giving 'queer little grunts and snorts of rage; in his worst moments his very nostrils twitch'. His best scene (and Maud's) was said by *The Times* to be the quarrel with Agrippina, 'the tiger turning and trying to rend the tigress'. For an actress to be truly remarkable she must exert 'an almost unbearable' magnetism, 'skinning emotions alive', or, as Maud had duly done, 'thrill' the audience with an instinct closer to that of a wild beast than a human being (the *Layman*, 26 January 1906).

On the opening night, before an audience that included among the guests Winston Churchill, Lawrence Alma-Tadema, the Bancrofts, J. M. Barrie, W. S. Gilbert, Lena Ashwell, A.W. Pinero, Violet Lindsay, and other members of the aristocracy, Maud was never more conscious of the fact that there was a balance to be struck between the actress who appeared inhuman, lustful, and triumphant, and the overtly 'statuesque' actress who showed little sign of life (as in the case of Constance Collier's Poppaea).[23] In addition to this, in order for an actress to create a 'respectable self' she had also to create a womanly self.[24] Her rendition of Agrippina was more virago than New Woman and, true to form, an anti-feminist representation. But even now, giving one of the greatest performances of her career, her interpretation of Agrippina was designed not to challenge the New Woman's criticism of marriage as being a woman's only option for a fulfilling life, but to make her position compatible with it.

All through her life, Maud was particularly preoccupied with this conundrum and all too aware of the precarious position of the actress in society. 'Be dignified and careful' was a prevailing note to her daughters.[25] It was a preoccupation that never left her, but she negotiated this dilemma, and achieved an ultimately respectable self within her diverse acting roles in two ways. Firstly, she accentuated the maternal aspect to her acting. When at its best, her acting might hint at 'troubling sensuality', but even while described as a tiger she is praised for being 'womanly and maternal'. In other words, ferocity and passion are still 'respectable' when they are also maternal. In assessing her talent, Madge Kendal wrote that Maud always tried to bring out the 'maternal side' of every part she played.[26]

The second way in which Maud ensured respectability in her acting was by the simple fact of being married. Edward Gordon Craig, Ellen Terry's son, in assessing his mother's acting abilities, acknowledged that most roles were within her grasp, 'if only she had not been so frightened of the British public'.[27] Maud was equally fearful of the British public, but chose to act within the very social constraints that some actresses found irksome. Every role exposed the complex dynamics, contradictions, and conundrums with which Maud as a working wife and mother was confronted. The Victorian or Edwardian actress would simultaneously arouse those 'two demons that threatened the family: aspiration and sexuality'.[28] Theoretically, the respectable woman should admit to neither, but ultimately egoism posed a more obvious pitfall for the actress.

Craig, in writing of the egoism of actresses, identified the very duality in her personality for which the modern woman is praised today. Ellen Terry's son too wrote of the two selves of his mother: the actress who was always encroaching on the space of the parent with unhappy results. 'E. T.,' he wrote, 'was always getting in the way of my mother [...] I continue to speak of them as two, because although one and the same person, they were leagues apart and agreed to differ on almost every subject'. He continued: 'I don't see how you can rock the cradle, rule the world, and play Ophelia perfectly, all in the day's work'.[29] But this is precisely what

Maud could do. Maud believed in a work ethic, over and above any muse that might have driven her. Correspondence testifies to her multiple roles and an ability to adapt them to the conventions of motherhood and marriage. What Victorians and Edwardians viewed with suspicion was the actress for whom the stage became 'a Svengali' but who in turn and with simarly magical power, succeeded in seducing an audience.[30] But, flitting among the multiple selves so in conflict with the required constancy of a wife was the necessary deception implicit in the skill of acting.[31]

In Tom Taylor and Charles Reade's *Masks and Faces,* in the 1888 revival of which Maud had played Mabel Vane, the heroine exclaims: 'Have we not the theatre, its triumphs, and full-handed thunders of applause? Who looks for hearts beneath the masks we wear?' Following that performance, Ellen Terry, detecting a sadness in Maud that she could not on that occasion disguise, wrote to her friend. 'I wonder,' said Terry, 'were you in pain — or worried when I saw you last night — you have a sweet smile and lovely teeth but the curves of your little face were for a moment thus [...] but you mustn't really you mustn't'. She urged Maud to smile in the face of disappointment; she drew a sad face and a smiling face and assured Maud of her 'affection of the heart'.[32] Now, so many years later, Maud had learned to contain emotion triumphantly and she would remember the four months of *Nero* in which she 'lived only for the theatre'. As she wrote in her memoir, 'Everything else went by the board. The cup of my existence brimmed'.[33]

The opening night of *Nero* did not proceed exactly to plan. Shaw, of course questioned the efficacy of blank verse in the first place for a stage play in which the drama, he said, was smothered and 'you couldn't see the wood for the Beerbohm Trees' (*Umpire,* 28 January 1906). The burning of Rome, which undoubtedly represented Tree's greatest expenditure, almost did not happen at all as the fire refused to take. (By contrast, during subsequent performances the fire was so realistic that members of the audience began to flee.) Tree in his nervousness plucked air rather than his lyre as his attention was diverted to the wings, and Constance Collier (supposedly long dead as Poppaea) opened her eyes once too often, provoking titters from the audience.[34] Only the final scenes did justice to the vanity of the artist. Nubian slaves carried Tree's litter while two gladiators guarded his corpse. Tree (clutching his lily) and Nero were completely intermeshed.[35] Maud, on the other hand, was sprung free from her own character, robed in hand-woven crimson silk where the light and shadows made 'the surface seem alive' (*Morning Advertiser,* 28 January 1906). Years of experience and personal anguish were now channelled into a performance that was, according to *The Queen* of 27 January 1906, 'full of energy and intelligence'.

Notes to Chapter 11

1. Beerbohm 1924: 121.
2. Herbert Tree to Maud Tree, [n.d.] (HBT/RA/420).
3. Maud Tree to May Pinney, [n.d.] (MBTC 7).
4. Maud is reminded to think of her daughter Viola's marriage prospects, which would be damaged by the scandal of Tree's illegitimate children coming to light.
5. Collier 1929: 90. Maud would be further humiliated as Tree had a portrait of Collier as Athene

displayed at His Majesty's along with two other pictures of her. There was only one of Maud out of the ninety pieces of art work distributed around the theatre, in her role as Agrippina.
6. His Majesty's Theatre ledger, 1904–06 (BTC). See also Reed 1994: 399.
7. Douglas Crichton, 'Nero: The Roman Emperor and the Play', lecture transcript, 19 February 1906 (BTC, 28).
8. Percy Macquoid (1852–1925) designed costumes for *Nero* and *Anthony and Cleopatra*
9. Schulz 1995: 19.
10. Ibid.: 36.
11. Ibid.: 110.
12. Ibid.
13. Tree himself had described Nero as 'a creature, a gorgeous butterfly'.
14. See Truman 1984: 31.
15. Ibid.: 39–47.
16. 'Souvenir of Nero', programme for *Nero*, 1906 (BTC).
17. Joseph William Comyns Carr (1849–1916) was Tree's literary adviser and partner at the Haymarket from 1887 to 1893. His wife Alice designed the 'beetle dress' worn by Ellen Terry as Lady Macbeth and in which Sargent painted her. See Beerbohm 1924: 136.
18. Winter 1902: 108.
19. See Blathwayt 1898: 3–4.
20. Arthur Symons said this of the actress Réjane in her role as Sappho, performed in London in 1901; Symons 1909: 30.
21. Shaw 1931: I, 175. See also Cory-Wright 2011.
22. Symons 1903: 27
23. Lewes 1875: 32.
24. Pye 2003.
25. Maud Tree to Felicity and Iris Tree, [1905] (SCW, letter 650).
26. Kendal 1933: 72.
27. Craig, 1932: 157.
28. Auerbach 1982: 63.
29. Craig 1932: 52, 57, 63, 64–66.
30. See Powell 1997: 9–10.
31. Ibid.: 20.
32. Ellen Terry to Maud Tree, 1888 (MBTC 7).
33. Beerbohm 1924: 136.
34. Collier 1929: 176.
35. Tree's portrayal of Nero as a 'degenerate' was audacious: the lily was a symbol of the 'degenerates', the like of which the *Athenaeum* said had 'been seen in the law Court' (January 1906).

CHAPTER 12

Paulina and a Fateful Winter's Tale
1906

In the autumn, Maud was drawn to Tree's next Shakespearean production for two irresistible reasons. Firstly, although Tree directed the play, he was not in it himself, and secondly, their own daughter Viola was, in the role of Perdita. *The Winter's Tale* opened at His Majesty's Theatre on 1 September 1906. With Adolf Schmidt as musical director, the incidental music had been composed by Coleridge Taylor and, in an innovative move, Tree used music (for example, at each of Perdita's appearances) to unify and connect scenes in a stylistic device more conventionally connected with modern cinema.[1] In a rare joint appraisal the *Southampton Times* of 8 September 1906 complimented both husband and wife: 'the spirited rendering of Paulina by Mrs. Tree and stage effects of thunder and darkness [...] make one of those elaborate scenes which Mr. Tree has caused to be identified with his name'. Costumes were once again by Percy Macquoid and Maud's understudy was Honor Wells.

Maud was excited and empowered, after her triumph as Agrippina, to be playing once again at His Majesty's Theatre. She would also have been somewhat gratified to see that a portrait of herself in that role now graced the upper balconies of the theatre, although of the ninety pieces of art displayed a quarter were of Tree alone. The production was to be notable on several counts. The actor Charles Warner (1846–1909), who had played one of the Gourgiran brothers in *Caesar's Wife* opposite Maud, now played Leontes, and Ellen Terry was Hermione, fifty years after she had first appeared as Mamillius at the age of nine in Charles Kean's 1856 production. Tree cut the whole of the second scene of Act v and for the first time since the eighteenth century, the play was reduced to three acts.[2] As Dennis Bartholomeusz notes of Tree's production: 'the art of speech, in all the luxury of scenery and business, became of secondary importance and only Maud Tree's Paulina, Ellen Terry's Hermione and Fisher White [...] achieved any real distinction'.[3] Accompanying it too were the usual sound effects and a pastoral scene featuring a real stream and a donkey. Once again art mirrored nature: in the play, it is Paulina who forces Leontes to look on his child; in real life, May Pinney's third child by Tree was six months old and she was already six months pregnant with her next. Ironically (or because of this) Tree cut any reference to pregnancy or sexual experience, and the line 'Take up the bastard!' (II.3.75), for example, became 'Take up the brat'.

As with Maud's recent Agrippina, the press was enthusiastic about her latest role. It was a performance the *Morning Post* of 3 September 1906 deemed 'flawless', 'superb', and 'gallantly courageous'. The *Sporting Life* and *Daily Chronicle* of the same date said she acted with 'rare feeling' and 'admirable fire and force' respectively. Hers (said the *Daily Chronicle*) was 'the one truly great interpretation — tender yet brave, gentle yet undaunted [...] characteristic of her brilliant acting'. The *Globe*, also of 3 September, described her 'splendid vigour' and her elocution that, as ever, was 'perfect', 'bold and strong'. Comyns Carr's coaching, which had begun with Agrippina, paid off and the *Sphere* praised the 'continuation of her latter and better method'. The *Morning Advertiser* said she gave 'splendid point' to her lines, which were 'decisive, clear-cut', and a performance which was 'ripe, vigorous' and the kind of thing 'we have learned to expect from this talented actress'. The *Stage* of 5 September 1906 elaborated: 'Next to Miss Terry's very beautiful performance we should place the Paulina of Mrs. Tree. Mrs. Tree goes from strength to strength', while *Outlook* of the same date recognized her magnetism: 'The audience surrendered to her instantly'.

The fact that Maud acquitted herself so admirably is worth emphasizing. Ellen Terry was found deficient, her voice pitched so high that it sounded contrived.[4] Shaw, the most exacting critic of all, was scathing of her, saying that she 'passes on to the next length of arid sham-feminine twaddle in blank verse, which she pumps out in little rhythmic strokes in a desperate and all too obvious effort to make music of it'.[5] In contrast, Maud's ability to alternate tones in the space of a scene was noted in *Era* of 8 September 1906:

> Paulina is holding forth in an indignant tirade against the jealous tyrant Leontes, her eyes flash; she stamps with her foot, when Emilia [...] approaches with the infant princess in her arms. At the sight of the babe Paulina's anger evaporates at a breath, the strident note leaves her voice as if by magic, and she coos as softly over it as a dove with a nestling.

If Maud was cryptic about her role — 'I was Paulina' is all she says in her memoir — biographers were equally so concerning the accident that would bring her performance in the play to a shattering end. Madeline Bingham gives it two sentences, Hesketh Pearson three. The teenage, star-struck 'stalker', Olivia Truman, recounted it to her aunt in a letter of 23 October 1906 (but only because she hoped Tree would be widowed).[6] Maud herself didn't refer to it at all at the time, although in her memoir, when describing the ghost of a woman she saw at Walpole House, she wonders if it might not have been as a warning of misfortune to come: the unearthly creature was specific in mourning the loss of her good looks.

The fear of motor smashes was one that was ever-present. A couple of years before, in April 1904, Tree had written from Marienbad:

> It is a good thing that you have your motor again — but please take great care of everybody — for I hear nothing but motor smashes and it is better to go the rate of 20 miles and be alive than to go at the rate of 50 dead — take care there are many terrible accidents. I hear of nothing but motor smashes![7]

Tree was not being over-anxious. In 1902 the *Echo* reported how Maud's car 'had come to grief' while she was out driving with Ellaline Terriss, and in 1905, while acting in the coronation revival of *The Merry Wives of Windsor*, Ellen Terry, Herbert, and Maud had been almost killed when her car skidded into reverse down a hill. 'Talking of violent death,' wrote Maud, 'we very nearly dealt it to the beloved Ellen Terry herself during the sojourn of those two perfect Merry Wives with us'.[8]

It was while Maud was out driving with Lewis Waller between performances of *The Winter's Tale* in October that she was in another, and this time more serious, car accident. She had largely ignored Waller the previous summer and in despair he had written to her:

> I will not bear another year of this. I swear to your hand!
> You <u>should</u> value my love a little more. I mean to school myself not to care where you are or what you are doing or with whom!
> I had counted on visiting you for a happy night tomorrow and now I don't know whether you're alive or <u>dead!</u>

As it happened, Waller did not have to 'bear another year', as he put it. He was unhurt. Maud's jaw was broken, leaving her with what Olivia Truman called 'a foolish looking receding chin' (she also wrote unkindly, 'why could not all our troubles have been ended [...] by something worse than a cut face'), and Sir John Gielgud (Ellen Terry's nephew) remembered as a 'crooked mouth'.[9] She was immediately whisked to Sir Alfred Fripp's nursing home — he had only recently witnessed her Agrippina performance — and her recovery was long and painful. Her friends rallied round with gifts and flowers and letters, but in the beginning the full extent of her injuries was not disclosed. Hamilton Aidé wrote to say he was sorry to hear she was 'hors de combat', and Ellen Terry that she 'was not quite well'. Only Violet's husband, the Duke of Rutland, was aware of her 'fearful' physical pain:

> Just one line, Maud my dear, he wrote, to tell you how deeply I have sympathized with you in all your fearful truth and pain, and to let you know how much your wonderful pluck has impressed us all too. What you have suffered must have been fearful and the way you have borne it, wonderful.

And he concluded his letter with characteristic but well-meaning clumsiness: 'Lily Brayton has had a carriage accident too and her face is cut badly [...] what a time for understudies'.[10]

Waller, of course, was more disconsolate than ever, writing to her on a daily basis:

> Monday night [October 1906]
> My Darling, Darling Baby — I'm so dreadfully sad & sorry you've had such a bad day — I <u>know</u> how bad its [sic] been pet — as I heard first from Alice — then, tonight from Violet & now again at 1.15 from your nurse — & if <u>she</u> says you've had a bad day, it <u>must </u>have been bad![11] I told her, if you were still awake, as I'm afraid you will be, when she next went to you — she was to tell you — <u>I</u> had just asked — they know my voice now — quite well, without asking my name — Does it [sic] matter sweet — I thought & hoped it might cheer you a little presently to know your lover is thinking of you — even although you must really know it always, doesn't [sic] you duck? Still its [sic] nice to know exactly <u>when </u>he was last thinking and asking of you? [...]

> Did they hurt you very much blessed tightening the bandages today, I'm afraid so, & if you knew how it hurts <u>me</u> to think of my Darling <u>girl</u> being hurt & to remember as I always must that it's thro' me — she has to endure all this terrible pain & discomfort & want of food & worst of all, want of sleep & all the while there is nothing in the world I wouldn't do to soothe & pet her & make her well & strong again.[12]

And in one of his daily letters a little later:

> Don't be depressed about the future — you must not give up your will and get well for surely this will not make such a difference and we shall see and love each other as much as before. Isn't it worth getting well to be in my arms?[13]

But the accident of course did make a difference and its psychological impact was considerable. It took Maud almost two years to recover and she would never regain her position as leading lady, or at least not in the way she had known it. Time in Sir Alfred Fripp's nursing home gave her the opportunity to reflect; and when she eventually emerged, she ended her romantic relationship with Waller, restored good feeling with Herbert and endeavoured to show, when possible, no (open) animosity towards May Pinney.

The effects of her injury were no doubt compounded by Maud's background. By her own admission, an education in the Classics had formed her way of thinking and acting and she was equally influenced by the Souls and by their and her great friend Violet Lindsay's aesthetic reverence for classical mythology. Furthermore, the success of an actress was judged above all by her approximation to the then accepted notion of classical beauty, so to lose her looks was to strike at the physical heart of her craft.

The desire and aspiration for beauty permeated theatre journalism and literature alike. In 1893 William Ferrero published the influential article 'Woman's Sphere in Art', declaring that 'Woman is destined to live in the present and to pass away leaving her stamp only among her contemporaries, perhaps only among those who have seen her in the heyday of her beauty'.[14] Actresses may or may not have been able to act but they did have to be beautiful. In her journal Elizabeth Robins recalls to what extent an actress's looks played a part in her success. Lewis Waller once whispered to her, during a performance of *The Sixth Commandment*, that she was 'a goose' for not reconciling herself to 'such a pretty face', while Madge Kendal in her autobiography acknowledges that her acting career was limited by her lack of good looks.[15] The press thought so too. In an article comparing Madge to Maud, one critic wrote in the *Daily Telegraph* of 16 February 1895: 'the latter is very beautiful and Mrs. Kendal is not!' The theatre 'wo-manager' Sarah Thorne told Violet Vanbrugh: 'My dear, I know I can act but I am very plain, and I don't look the parts [*sic*] that is why, I shall never be a leading actress'.[16]

There was, however, one positive outcome to such a hideous event. With the loss of her looks Maud's capability for evoking jealousy in Tree was also neutralized and their relationship changed for the better. From the time of the accident onwards, Tree showed Maud great kindness and respect, and although they did not often live together, they enjoyed a genuine friendship. When he in turn was ill a couple of years later, he wrote to Viola: 'Mother is so sweet and good to me. I don't know what I should do without her, and she is a splendid nurse [...] We do very little except wander along the sea front or into the town'.[17]

Despite visits to the leading specialists of the day and futile promises to get her chin 'eventually back in its right position', Maud never fully regained her looks. Fortunately, however, the timbre and quality of her voice were unaffected. In the two or so years directly following her accident she relied on recitation and public speaking to supplement her income, and it was not until 1908 that she made a significant reappearance, joining Mrs Patrick Campbell to play Clytemnestra in her production of *Electra* at the Garden Theatre in New York. 'This clever actress,' wrote Mrs Campbell of Maud in that production, 'has an odd waggish intelligence that does not fail her'.[18] Moreover, although she was no longer able to compete with younger and more beautiful actresses, she was still famous for her wit,[19] and the beauty and iconic sexual desirability accompanying youth and the 'theatrical rhetoric of statuary' were not a requirement of comedy.[20]

Influenced by the classical ideal, Henry Siddons wrote as early as 1822 that a beautiful actress should not 'disfigure her face by distortions'. This continued to be applicable to the Victorian critique of actresses, where there was still a demarcation between 'stage beauties and funny women'.[21] And in May 1935, over one hundred years after Siddons made his comment, this still held true. In Maxwell Wray's period drama *The Mask of Virtue*, the newcomer Vivien Leigh was cast for her alabaster skin and beautiful face; an ability to act was not obligatory. But, in what proved to be Leigh's first London success and one of Maud's last, her acting had come full circle. In rehearsal with Leigh, Maud broke off and asked for the director. When he appeared from behind the stalls, she asked, 'Do you think you could kindly oblige us with a little more light?' When he asked if there was a problem, Maud replied in the negative, but added, 'I think you don't realize that my comedic effects are purely grimacial'.[22]

Notes to Chapter 12

1. Bartholomeusz 1982: 130.
2. Crosse 1953: 37.
3. Bartholomeusz 1982: 129.
4. Eleonora Tree (1805–1880) was an English actress who married Charles Kean became his leading lady. *Examiner*, 10 November 1823; *Morning Herald*, 12 October 1835.
5. Shaw 1948: 17.
6. Truman 1984: 65.
7. Herbert Tree to Maud Tree, [1904] (MBTC 2).
8. See Beerbohm 1924: 126.
9. Truman 1984: 65–66; Pearson 1988: 2.
10. Henry John Manners, to Maud Tree, 7 November 1906 (MBTC 2).
11. Alice (Maud's maid) and Violet Lindsay.
12. Lewis Waller to Maud Tree, [n.d.] (MBTC 7). Waller was driving and felt he was responsible for the accident.
13. Lewis Waller to Maud Tree, [n.d.] (MBTC 7/RA/420).
14. Ferrero 1893: 554–60.

15. Elizabeth Robins Papers, journal for October 1890 (New York University, Fales Library).
16. Sarah Thorne (1836–1899) was the actress-manager of the Chatham, Worcester, and Margate Theatres. She also founded a school of acting in 1885 and toured successfully throughout the country. See Vanbrugh 1925: 30.
17. Herbert Tree to Viola Tree, 6 February 1908 (BTC); see also Pearson 1988: 151.
18. Campbell 1922: 227.
19. Olivia Truman, Hesketh Pearson, Ivan Moffit, and David Cory-Wright, as well as surviving correspondence, all testify to Maud's sense of humour and wit. See also Collier 1929: 135.
20. Traub 1992: 26.
21. Glenn 2000: 49.
22. Pearson 1988: 'Foreword'.

CHAPTER 13

'Stand and Deliver': Being Lady Tree 1907–13

In December 1907, Maud swapped her real-life stage for a no less dramatic one, disrupting, as Frances Gray has said, 'the tranquil space' of a West End production to announce:

> I have just come from the Court, the Court where the young Robert Wood stood in peril of his life [...]. I was one of those who burst into tears, others burst into cheers which were taken up, echoed and re-echoed by thousands on the streets.[1]

Maud was not exaggerating; millions were 'engulfed in a colossal wave of mass hysteria' enthralled by a case that embodied all 'the excitements of Edwardian theatre'.[2] Theatrical luminaries such as H. B. Irving, George Alexander, and Arthur Pinero packed the galleries to witness a 'crude melodrama' that squeezed 'a farrago of maudlin emotions' from its audience and to see the most famous lawyer of the day, Edward Marshall Hall, for the defence.[3] Elements of this 'well made play' included the well-spoken Bohemian (the accused Robert Wood) and a compromising postcard. It even contained 'whiffs of the social-issue plays of Ibsen' for the victim, like Shaw's Mrs Warren, had chosen prostitution over a life of more conventional domesticity.[4] It took the jury just fifteen minutes to reach a verdict of not guilty.

On the night of 11 September 1907, Emily Elizabeth Dimmock left the Eagle Pub on Royal College Street in Camden and was never seen alive again. She was found with her throat slit in the grubby lodgings in Agar Grove she shared with her common-law-husband Bert Shaw. Bert Shaw often worked nights as a railway man but unbeknown to him Emily had turned to prostitution. Away at the time, he had a watertight alibi; Robert Wood did not. Maud was asked as a 'famous actress' and one 'in whom the dramatic instinct is so highly developed', to witness and comment on his trial at the Old Bailey in a series of articles for the *Weekly Dispatch*. These were entitled: 'A Terrible Cross-Examination', 'Doesn't He Know that He Wrote it?', 'My Blood Ran Cold', 'The Jury's Verdict', and finally 'I Could Not Look Up'.[5]

Four images of Emily Dimmock were also painted in a series later entitled *The Camden Town Murder* by Walter Sickert. One in particular was called *What Shall*

We Do For Rent?. What indeed? Emily was portrayed as a prostitute which was enough to condemn her, Wood was the William Morris protégé, this was enough to exonerate him. In the meantime, wrote Maud:

> The curtain had fallen and I felt that any stage play must seem dull after watching that living drama, how wonderful it seemed to realize that I had been at the court from 10 o'clock in the morning until 8 at night, and yet the time had passed like half an hour.[6]

Nineteen hundred and eight was a leap year and one of the coldest on record with the month of January seeing the heaviest snowfall in the capital to date; in fact, it would continue snowing until April, when the fourth modern-day Olympic Games opened there on the 27th. And on the other side of the globe, bound for the Antarctic, Ernest Shackleton set sail in *Nimrod* from New Zealand. It was a year that would see the first passenger flight in an aeroplane and the sailing of the Cunard-owned *Lusitania* across the Atlantic in only four days and fifteen hours. Maud would make part of that ship's journey home as a guest of Emerald Cunard herself, boarding at Queenstown in Ireland. With no foresight of what was to come, she wrote gleefully to her daughters that 'this great ship in time of war can be turned into a "man-of-war" battle ship'.[7] It was also the year in which her friend Herbert Asquith became Prime Minister.

Despite her anti-suffrage stance, Lena Ashwell invited Maud to join the committee of the Franco-British Women's Exhibition held at White City. One hundred and twenty exhibition pavilions erected for the Olympics were now used to house a 'palace of women's work' where it was hoped the arts would be 'well represented'.[8] A few years later, the case for women's suffrage itself came home to roost in the shape of a suffragette who padlocked herself to a stall in His Majesty's Theatre during the matinee performance of *The Silver King*, in the presence of King George V and Queen Mary. Maud also resumed her public speaking activities: the popular romantic novelist and writer of the supernatural Gertrude Reynolds wrote to her, 'I am very glad that you are going to lecture, for although not a suffragette, I think women should take more part in public effort than they do now'.[9] Names of the other lecturers for the coming season, of which Maud was one, included Professor Mahaffy (who had taught Oscar Wilde at Trinity), George Russell, and the theatre critic A. W. Walkley.[10]

Maud would soon be inundated with requests to appear in or contribute towards such stand-and-deliver engagements when she became Lady Tree. For years she had unsuccessfully canvassed for Tree's knighthood: in 1902 she had approached the Lord Chamberlain and a few years later Violet Lindsay, to no avail. But when Asquith became Prime Minister in April 1908, Tree's name at last appeared in the King's Birthday Honours list in November.

On the eve of the public announcement of his knighthood, Maud was acting in J. M. Barrie's 'New Woman' play *What Every Woman Knows,* in which Maggie's husband eventually realizes he owes his success to her.[11] Yet again, Maud's art seemed to reflect domestic issues. Not only does Maggie write her husband's speeches, but she also supports his platform for women's rights. She is happy to shun the limelight in promoting his career. 'It's nothing unusual I have done, John,' she says, 'Every man who is high up loves to think that he has done it all himself, and the wife smiles, and lets it go at that. It's our joke. Every woman knows that.'[12] A fan writing to Maud from distant La Croix, Trinidad, wrote: 'I don't know the stage version of What Every Woman Knows [...] but being a woman I do know that every woman, whether she be young or old, rich or poor, light or dark, suffers a daily grievance'.[13] With the announcement of her husband's honour, Maud rushed from the Duke of York's Theatre to lead her husband triumphantly onto the stage at His Majesty's. Barrie had turned down the same honour, preferring to remain 'Mister Barrie'.

If Maud had always followed her instinct in choosing 'new' plays, she could now afford to indulge herself completely. Later that year she played Madame X in Strindberg's one-character, one-act play *The Stronger Woman,* and wrote to Strindberg's translator Maurice Magnus with the suggestion his plays should be taken on tour in America. She then toyed with a curious proposition put to her by the stage designer Percy Anderson and Arthur Quiller-Couch.[14] As time went on, however, it became more mysterious with every twist. On 4 July 'Q', as he was widely known, wrote to insist that Maud act the Regent in a play 'suggested' to him by the actor Charles Thursby. Q went on to say that he was probably better known to Maud 'as a writer of novels' but that if the part would 'tempt' her 'or Sir Herbert to produce the play', he would be extremely proud. The following day she received a letter from Percy Anderson to say the play (which she had already received) was on its way.[15] After that there was silence, probably because, unbeknown to Maud, Q had written an almost identical letter to Ellen Terry.[16] A few weeks later Percy Anderson wrote again. This time he owned to actually having co-written the play himself with this aforementioned Charles Thursby, who had, however, wished his name to be withheld.

Bombarded with invitations to luncheons and dinners that never materialized, Maud began to lose patience. After a few more weeks when the project did not appear to be progressing any further, she turned the part down, as did Ellen Terry. However, there is an interesting footnote to this episode. The play, a drama in one act, was dedicated to 'Charles Thursby, the onlie Begetter'. It may be remembered that Quiller-Couch edited the *Oxford Book of Verse 1250–1918* and that Shakespeare obliquely dedicated Sonnet 55 to 'W. H.', 'the onlie begetter'. A few years later, in 1912, the Lord Chancellor and H. G. Wells condemned a suffragette play called *The Coronation*. It was written by Mr Christopher St John and Mr Charles Thursby, described by the *New York Times* of 26 January 1912 as 'two *women* with masculine pennames'.

It would seem that Q and Anderson were not the only ones to be attracted by Maud's newly elevated status. At least Anderson had written 'My Dear Lady Tree', whereas Lewis Waller, with no hint of any shared intimacy, addressed Maud as 'Lady Tree' when proposing she play another regent in a play he was planning to produce, his own version of *Sir Walter Raleigh*. As he would be away on tour, he asked for an answer at her 'earliest convenience'. The days when he wrote 'and I didn't adore you then as I adore you now', the times of romance and roses were clearly long gone. It was not so for Tree. As Maud once said the trouble with Herbert's compliments is that 'they end in confinements'. On 18 May 1910 Maud's officious private detective, J. G. Littlechild, once again 'begged to report' another certificate of birth. Herbert's newest child by May Pinney was a little girl called Juliet.

But that was still a few months away. In January there was also a new play in the offing, based on Arthur Scott Craven's tragic tale *The Sirocco*. Maud agreed to star in the play (staged in Liverpool) to please Oswald Stoll, manager of the London Coliseum and founder of the Stoll Film Company. (He would later prove to be a very useful contact when Maud acted in the first silent films produced by his company). She had also agreed with the Lord Mayor of Liverpool that out of her £350-a-week salary, £100 would go to a charity of his choice. She had already played a twenty-eight-year-old when she was forty-four, and now at the age of fifty-two she was the Arab girl Biskra, with whom Fulmard, a French army officer, falls in love and because of her has deserted his regiment. Guilt-ridden, and for the love of this good woman, Fulmard eventually shoots himself. Her reviews were good, *The Stage* of 14 February 1910 attesting that 'Lady Tree is none the less tense, thrilling and determined in her interpretation of her art'. But she was also tired, which led to some unintentional farce, as she described to her daughters:

> Dear Loves
> [...] I had rather fun dressing myself up + acting the little play <u>twice</u> last night. — I don't know how I look — but I ought to look weirdly beautiful.
> [...]
> I was very glad of all letters. Yesterday was an odd day for me, for I had to do the little play <u>three</u> times & by the 2nd I was so dazed that I began doing Mrs. Mackenzie in Colonel Newcome instead![17] But that was because I discarded the black wig & wore a red one instead. I looked like a rather old, very ugly Mediaeval witch — so that the audience shouted with one voice 'Which is witch?'[18]

And then in September she acted in a play that once again resonated uncannily with events in her personal life. Elizabeth Robins understudied for Maud, who played Grace in Somerset Maugham's *Grace or Landed Gentry*. She was paid a salary of £40 a week for six performances, full salary for the seventh and half salary for the eighth.[19] J. T. Grein, in the *Sunday Times* of 16 October 1910, summarized the plot as being 'a tale of two women, their fault and their atonement', one that suited Maud perfectly, and described her role as 'an old dame' (albeit one played with distinction) whose 'portraiture by the author recalls [...] Chippendale and Delft'. Maugham wrote more graciously, 'You should be a duchess in your own right, for you are gracious and witty and the eyes of those men rest on you with pleasure'.[20]

When the run of the play ended, Maud set about finding other country houses to escape to when the theatre season closed. She took a house in Brancaster (where her daughter Viola met her future husband Alan Parsons) and another, The Wharf, at Sutton Courtenay. Only in Oxfordshire for a short time, however, she then moved to Glottenham House ('Glotters') at Robertsbridge in Sussex, to which her sisters Harrie and Bertha became frequent visitors; she described it and them as 'the old wives tale'.

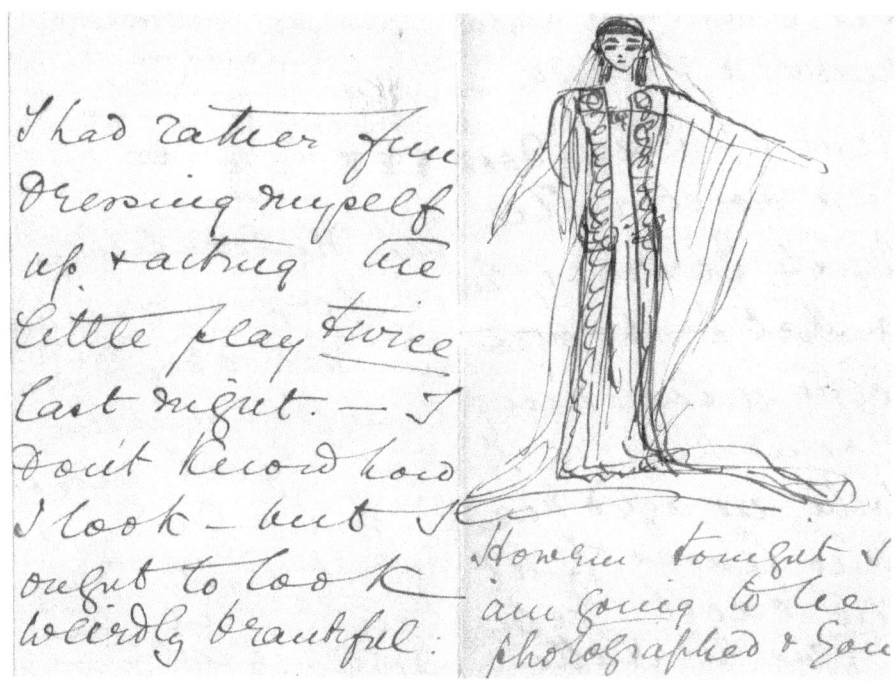

FIG. 13.1. Letter from Maud Tree to her daughters, 15 February 1910 (SCW, letter 103)

But generally Maud felt that rekindling friendships with playwrights and producers had paid off, and from Sutton Courtenay she wrote to Tree hoping 'to get the play' for him. She resumed her networking, giving George Tyler supper so as to introduce him to Somerset Maugham. The former, she wrote to Herbert, 'tells me that Louis Parker's Disraeli is a big fine play, exactly suited to you. Also he thinks Per [sic] Grimm of Belasco a very good idea'. The latter had also translated Molière's *Le Bourgeois Gentilhomme* as *The Perfect Gentleman* and Tree would produce this a couple of years later. For her own part, Maud was delighted when she was engaged by Arthur Collins to play the character of Lady Franklin at a command performance of *Money* at Drury Lane on 17 May 1911, when Kaiser Wilhem II was in England to celebrate the coronation of George V. Collins was certain, he wrote to Maud, 'that the inclusion of your name in the cast will give great satisfaction in court circles'.

This, however, proved by no means the first time an actress — not least Lady Tree — had been passed over for another actor's favourite, or in this case, his wife. The very next day Collins wrote to inform Maud of 'a difficulty' that had arisen, the essence of which was that her part had now gone to Miss Emery.[21] Mr Cyril Maude (the actor-manager of the Theatre Royal, Haymarket, from 1896 to 1905) had spoken to Sir Herbert only the day before, assuring him that Maud had 'generously suggested' the part be offered first to Miss Emery, who was Cyril Maude's wife. But this was far from the case and the after-sting was still evident in a speech Maud made at the twenty-first Annual Meeting of the Rehearsal Club in which she deftly alluded to the incident, as reported in the *Era* of 3 May 1913:

> The New Theatre and Wyndham's Theatre take the place of mysterious meanderings. 'Ready Money' and 'Diplomacy' (those opposites attract) are brought face to face by the nightly crowds round their doors, though I might suggest that where there is 'Ready Money' ready there is no need for 'Diplomacy'.

'Nothing comes off in life except buttons,' Maud is quoted as saying, and in the ensuing months there followed a series of disappointments.[22] In the end, the part did go to Miss Emery who was described as being 'something more than excellent' in her role as Lady Franklin. It was a spectacular event, with five horse-drawn carriages, complete with footmen, transporting members of the royal household. Arthur Collins accompanied the Kaiser, his wife, and King George and Queen Mary to their seats, while Sir Squire Bancroft attended to the Prince of Wales and Princess Victoria Louise. Lewis Waller made all the announcements and Lyn Harding poured sherry. The Strand was lined with thousands of people when the carriages departed.[23]

Towards the end of the year, and having hardly spent any time at all in it, Maud was persuaded to sell The Wharf to Margot Asquith for £1,300. The Prime Minister's wife had long coveted the place and reluctantly Maud agreed to part with it, but the sale, as she wrote in her memoir, caused 'a temporary black-out' in their friendship. Maud now moved to 1 All Souls Place, behind All Souls Church, a funny wedge-shaped building that no one in the family liked, least of all Viola, who after a row with Felicity used this excuse to leave England for Italy. The press was careful to stress that up until now, as *Home Notes* of 6 January 1912 put it, 'Miss Viola has been kept away from the stage as much as possible'. Emphasis was placed on her social activities and the fact that she had been presented at court. Nonetheless, now at the age of twenty-six, the 'unusually tall' daughter of the 'poplar trees' was branching out on her own (*Candid Friend*, 12 April 1912).[24]

The entire family supported Viola's decision, but her parents, and Maud in particular, seem to have been under no illusion that a singing career would come easily. From a distance Maud proffered advice as Viola made preparations to make her debut: remembering meetings with Oscar Wilde so many years ago she now suggested that Viola sing Salome in the opera by Richard Strauss based on Wilde's play. There had been huge controversy surrounding the opera when it was first sung in 1905; it was banned in Vienna until 1918 and by the London censor until Thomas Beecham conducted it at Covent Garden in 1910, and its heady and provocative combination of biblical and erotic scenes still managed to shock most spectators. The Dance of the Seven Veils, in particular, shocked even its performers, with some singers insisting dancers stand in for them. This did not seem to be the case for Viola, however, who was photographed scantily dressed in 1912 by Varischi and Artico.

Even so, Maud instinctively doubted Viola would make her debut at all. Perhaps in her heart she realized that the role of Salome, which requires a Wagnerian voice, that is, the stamina and power of a truly dramatic soprano, was probably unsuited to Viola's sweet 'warble'. Besides which, she appeared to be suffering from endless throat infections and was chronically nervous like her father.[25] Behind the scenes both Trees did what they could, as Herbert prepared to travel to Genoa, ostensibly to see what was happening in the 'too futuristic Vienna' but in reality to be with his daughter. He still relied on Maud's professional input and wrote while on his travels that she might 'consult with Beecham'. He also wanted her to see Carl Meyers and Ernest Cassel to tactfully 'push things' his way, but he ended his letter expressing empathy for Viola, saying it would be a terrible 'setback' to her career if she were to return to London 'without laurels'.[26] Recently, Iris had been dispatched to keep Viola company and they seemed to subsist on macaroons. A visit to see Richard Strauss at his home in Munich had been anything but reassuring. As Viola would later recount in her autobiography, Strauss told her that she sang 'like a good actress — not like a singer' and that 'for London' he wanted 'a voice that is ready, not a growing, uncertain voice' like hers.[27]

In the event the end of her dream to become a singer was played out in the increasingly frantic telegrams and letters that bounced between Viola and her family. Ultimately, the strain and throat infection proved too much; her debut was cancelled and she returned home to England and to her fiancé Alan Parsons. In July 1912 they were married amid great pomp, the bride wearing a dress modelled on the one worn by the Empress Marie-Louise when she married Napoleon. *The Times* devoted several columns to listing the wedding gifts, and with his letter Asquith enclosed a poem by the suffragette Alice Meynell — somewhat ironic given his opposition to women's suffrage — that begins 'I must not think of thee'. Three thousand people lined the streets to see the bride and her father approach St Martin-in-the-Fields and in Trafalgar Square the traffic had to be stopped because of the crowds. Tree then famously asked his daughter, 'Do you *like* Alan, dear?' Viola's was unquestionably a grand wedding, but in marrying Alan Parsons she had embarked on a life of what Maud called 'radiant poverty'.

There was no lull, however, in the anxieties occasioned by her remaining, unmarried daughters. Maud had no sooner recovered from the excitement of Viola's wedding than her attention was once more diverted to Felicity, who like her older sister had a lovely voice. She was also hot-headed and her waywardness had caused Tree to write from his usual summer holiday in Marienbad that 'they [Felicity and her friends] are at a very delicate age and will be mixed up in a sort of semi-bohemian artistic society to which Iris leans already, with thoughts of independence'.[28] The semi-bohemian society to which he referred was of course 'the Coterie', or 'corrupt Coterie' as it came quickly to be known, made up of the children of the Souls. Within it Iris, Nancy Cunard, and Diana Manners were a formidable threesome, but Felicity was also making her mark. It was agreed that there 'was a great deal too much freedom' — especially when she was 'on the river'.[29]

Rivers, it would seem, were to be approached with caution. Iris and Nancy Cunard had been charged once already by police for swimming in the Serpentine, having been pulled dripping out of the water in sequins and feathers. But in 1914 there would be another far more alarming, indeed tragic, incident involving some of the

Coterie and Count Constantine Benckendorff, the son of the Russian ambassador. Benckendorff and Edward Horner had arranged a boat on the Thames to which Raymond and Katharine Asquith were invited, and included in the party were Duff Cooper and his sister Sybil, Denis Anson, Diana Manners, Nancy Cunard, and Iris Tree. Raymond Asquith bet Diana £10 to see if she could get Anson to go into the water. It is unclear what happened next, but within minutes of diving into the water Anson was swept away by the force of the current. Benckendorff and a bandsman jumped in after him, but in the event only Benckendorff, who was an exceptionally strong swimmer, survived.

The press predictably had a field day as the young people's parents rallied to their defence. Violet Lindsay intervened to ensure her daughter Diana was not called as a witness, while Thomas Beecham (whose lover Emerald was Nancy Cunard's mother) had a difficult job preventing his Covent Garden orchestra from speaking to the tabloids. Raymond's part in the tragedy was not disclosed, nor did he make an appearance, but a deliberately imposing Herbert Tree arrived at the inquest a few days later, with Viola on one arm and Iris on the other. The coroner was somewhat surprised to find himself in the presence of the greatest legal guns of the day. F. E. Smith, later Lord Chancellor, Ernest Pollock, later Master of the Rolls, and Hugh Fraser, a future High Court Judge, were engaged to represent the various interests of their clients. The verdict was, unsurprisingly, that of death by misadventure.

Maud may have been able to call in favours from men at the top of their game to defend her daughter's reputation, but behind the scenes she was sorely vexed. As a consequence of all this it was decided that Felicity should not spend too much time in London, and once the initial risk of cholera in Milan had abated, Iris and Felicity were duly dispatched thither, where Felicity in particular was to 'work hard at' her 'languages + singing'.[30] Maud advised her daughter to: 'Read the life of Jenny Lind! I should not wonder if you have a great career before you + in that case all else sinks to insignificance'. Viola's vocal experience had been sobering, and Maud continued to press home her point: 'Sing lots — if not _now_ then when?' Bernard Shaw once advised Viola that if singing was the great passion she claimed it was, then she should sing on street corners if she must. 'Do you remember how Viola saved up her voice when she was young?' Maud reminded Felicity, 'we _never_ heard it. Now we never _shall_.'[31]

The education of her daughters preoccupied Maud most when she was away on tour and unable to oversee matters. Correspondence documents the tireless suggestions of books (Trollope was always a mainstay, and Wilkie Collins for lighter reading) but as Maud counselled Felicity, 'I would rather you bought 6d editions of the Classics — though you will not have 6d — & alas! Nor have I!' It was soon evident, however, that Felicity did not have Viola's resolve. 'Darling,' wrote Maud, 'I had a lovely long letter [...] But I was rather sad that your singing seems less to you than the idea of hunts + balls'.[32] If Maud wanted her daughters to look to their careers, there was just as much emphasis placed on 'looking after' their 'manners'. The following autumn, Felicity was invited to Venice, under the very loose chaperonage of the wealthy, eligible bachelor Lord Vernon. Almost all the daily letters written during September 1913 detail clothes: 'Darling — I will send you silk of that ilk. Is the coat the coat or the dress — is the dress the dress of the coat?', Maud wrote in haste and in between rehearsals. They also implore Felicity to 'be modest, dignified, courteous'. The initial envy and the directive to 'drink it up — don't let a single half-hour of delight escape' were rapidly replaced by concern:

> Darling, I am terribly exercised about your staying on especially as all the really grown ups are going — Remember that in any case I should not think Sybil a sufficient chaperone [...] about being dignified and careful — no amount of present fun will make up for the neglect of one's high held head — ask Lord Vernon himself. He would understand. What is right for Irene and her mother is not right for you.[33]

The exuberance with which Maud began her next communication — 'oh to be in Venice now that all are there' — was met with silence. Increasingly exasperated, Maud wrote testily: 'I am thinking you are unkind + unreasonable not to send me a telegram or a Post Card — Remember I do not even know whether you have arrived or no!'[34] Maud's patience was well tried by the time Iris returned home after cutting off her Rheingold tresses and leaving them on a train. Iris was not sent back to Italy but closer to home, to Glottenham, to stay with a 'sad married cousin' and cool off. Later Iris would be photographed by Man Ray, painted by Vanessa Bell, Dora Carrington, and Augustus John and sculpted by Epstein. One day, she would play herself in Fellini's *La Dolce Vita* and have a small part in *Moby Dick*. But that was all in the future. For the moment she contented herself with writing poetry, and Maud, recognizing her talent, endeavoured to get her work published, if not read. Tapping once again into her extensive network, Maud duly organized a reading in the presence of the Sitwells, Edward Marsh, and Siegfried Sassoon. Herbert Asquith too valued her originality and in a letter to Viola once complained, 'You have forgotten to send me the irises'.[35]

In the meantime Maud resumed her punishing workload. As Montpellier Chambers wrote to her in 1912, he was only too aware that obtaining 'her patronage' was 'essential to ensuring financial success'.[36] In 1913 alone, together with her professional engagements, Maud had become associated with a 'Theatrical Garden Party' for which 14,000 tickets were sold in just two hours and which 947 members of the theatrical profession attended, including Gladys Cooper (who took over from Maud in *Diplomacy*), Mrs Kendal and the ballet dancer Anna Pavlova. On 31 May, the *Evening News*, in an article called 'Fun and Frolic', paid tribute both to a suffragette skit it featured, entitled 'Votes for Men', and to a programme that consisted of one John Harwood's 'Murderous Melodramas', *The Black Torture*, *The Wildest Worst Menagerie*, and *Eightpence a Smile*, in which Herbert Tree played Louis Goodrich. As well as being involved in the organization of what the *Daily News* of 7 June 1913, called this 'Great Bohemian Fête', for which an entire theatre was erected in Chelsea, Maud also arranged a 'Stage Skating Party' in Holland Park for the Actors Benevolent Fund. Rallying fellow actors Mrs Patrick Campbell, Ellen Terry, Irene Vanbrugh (the Duke of Rutland's current paramour), Maxine Elliot (his ex-paramour), and Gladys Cooper, Maud gave a speech in which she made the point:

> Actors and actresses are gay, debonair and bejewelled behind the footlights and the public is apt to forget that these adornments are 'properties.' So a skating party in which all the services and organizations are given gratuitously is extremely welcome to us.[37]

During the same month, Maud performed in the matinee which supported the Duke of Westminster's 'Olympic Fund' at the London Opera House and, as the *Stage* reported on 18 December 1913, proposed the toast in the presence of 300 guests at the Actors Association dinner. She made one speech at the Hotel Cecil — in which she addressed Herbert as her 'lord and master' — for a debate on Sunday openings and another at the Rehearsal Club, where she joined colleagues Lena Ashwell and Lillian Braithwaite. But the lassitude of recent months, having to go on to yet another 'disgusting dirty platform', impelled Maud to write to her daughters:

> Everything seems very remote as it is so long since London and I can't get hold of it again. One stagnates so on tour. One gets into a groove apart [...] From the time I get home there is one continuous round of Charity matinées, bazaars and charity fancy balls and I shy like a wild horse from the dreary prospect.[38]

As was so often the case with Maud, however, a period of despondency was succeeded by enthusiasm as she once more sought new challenges. Two quickly presented themselves. One was in the form of a new house, this time in France and on the banks of the Seine (or 'Insane' as Tree dubbed it);[39] the other, in February 1913, was the role of Lady Henry Fairfax in Gerald du Maurier's revival of the popular *Fedora* under its new title, *Diplomacy*, adapted by Clement Scott and B. C. Stephenson. Maud was to be paid £50 a week for seven performances, £30 of which she promptly spent on food and servants entertaining Gerald for a weekend. It was an expense she instantly regretted, for keeping up with the du Mauriers came at a price. Gerald himself was notoriously extravagant: new Slazengers were provided for every set in tennis matches and he had a passion for brand new Rolls Royce cars.[40]

Rehearsals were soon under way, but they were not without tension: Gerald du Maurier could be exacting, and after a particularly strict rehearsal he was forced to apologize. 'Maud dearest,' he wrote, 'Forgive my rudeness on parade, but personages, wives, children, fathers and mothers, sweethearts, do not exist at rehearsal'.[41] Maud had no small infatuation with Gerald, and her emotions were somewhat complex as a result. She had a tried and tested strategy when it came to networking and one that generally worked. If her intended target was a woman, she would send small gifts (as in the case of Alice Comyns Carr and the Duchess of Portland); were it a man, she generally sent out books (as in the case of Winston Churchill and Noel Coward) or complimentary tickets to her shows.

Gerald du Maurier was already, of course, well known to Maud and the links between their two families would entwine far into the future. Gerald, it will be remembered, was the son of George (Kicky) du Maurier, from whom Tree had purchased the rights to *Trilby*. His sister was Sylvia Llewelyn Davies, upon whose family J. M. Barrie based his play *Peter Pan* (which Tree famously declined to produce), and Gerald and Maud had already acted together on several occasions. To compound things further, Maud's daughter Viola would later enter into her own semi-romantic relationship with Gerald, a relationship that Viola claimed restored the 'games and tricks of a palpitant heart'. In 1919 Viola was to play 'a social butterfly' to du Maurier's much older 'superman businessman' in a new play by Alfred Sutro ominously called *The Choice*. Meanwhile the *Graphic* helped things along by displaying the twenty-one-year-old scantily clad Viola lovingly draped over a stern du Maurier. Two years later Viola was the co-author of the play *The Dancers* that appeared under the pen name Hubert Parsons, a combination of Gerald's second name and Viola's married name.

Now, in response to Gerald's contrite letter, Maud initiated a campaign of gifts, tickets, and tokens, not only to Gerald but to his wife. At first perhaps flattered, he in turn made her a gift of a leather tooled box, in which to keep 'tomorrow's script'. The accompanying card read 'Dearest Lady Tree', and a few days later he wrote: 'Maud dearest, I admire you and your humour and wit so much'.[42] But ultimately her infatuation remained unreciprocated. By the end of the play's rehearsals Gerald had written: 'Maud Darling, I know how deeply you feel for me, and what a tender heart you have towards me and mine. I am utterly grateful and value your dear friendship very much indeed'.[43] But friendship was all it was, and by the time the play opened Maud was once again the formal 'Lady Tree'.

Gerald's revival of *Fedora* (in which Maud had played the title role eighteen years previously) opened as *Diplomacy* on 26 March 1913 at Wyndham's Theatre. It ran for 455 performances and was yet another play Tree later regretted not having 'seized the opportunity' to produce. As early as 1877, Squire Bancroft had purchased the rights to the original Sardou play, *Dora*, for £1,500 and now, diplomatically, du Maurier asked George Pleydell Bancroft (Squire Bancroft's son) to adapt the text for a 'modern' audience. In the process the original play was cut from five acts to four and a completely new character invented in the guise of the Hon. Algernon Fairfax, while Lady Henry Fairfax (Maud) was substituted for Sardou's Princess Bariatine.

These were changes that Sardou himself approved. When he came to revive his original play under the new title of *L'Espionne* at the Théâtre de la Renaissance, he incorporated all the changes made in *Diplomacy*, an example, commented George Rowell, 'of the English Theatre repaying its debt to the French, and *Diplomacy* should be remembered as the one Sardou play which was conspicuously more successful in English than French'.[44] Following on from provincial tours and recitations, this role regained for Maud some of her former acting kudos.[45] One fan wrote to Maud to say that she must be the 'most delightful creature' and how she longed to hide in her 'muff'.[46] Socially, too, the play placed her back in the forefront of theatrical gossip, with the *New York Times* of 24 January 1914 reporting that, together with Norman Forbes-Robertson, Marie Doro, and Ellis Jeffrey, Lady Tree travelled to Windsor to perform the play for the King and Queen, with 180 guests gathered in the Waterloo Chamber of the castle, where 'everybody applauded and even smiled'.

FIG. 13.2. Cast of *Diplomacy* (Rotary Photo postcard 6914; author's own)

With a coincidental prefiguration of war this latest adaptation of *Dora* had also transformed the two male lead characters from French officials into English diplomats working at the embassy in Paris. Thus Maud flitted from the onstage 'France' in London during the week to the real-life France, across the Channel, at the weekend. Exhaustingly, she would travel through Saturday night in order to spend Sunday decorating her new house and be back at Wyndham's for Monday performances. With a view to occupying Iris, Maud left her in charge to look after friends who rented the house in her absence. 'Now Darling,' she wrote to Iris, in anticipation of Sybil Hart-Davis (Duff Cooper's sister) coming to stay:

> The game is in your hands — just see how good a 'little hostess' you can be. Pray see that their coffee & rolls are excellent & abundant. Butter 'sans reproche' — meals on the sun boats & motors & expeditions. Pray make them happy & make them stay a long time.[47]

Iris had other ideas She wrote to her closest friend, Maud Nelkie, begging her to come and 'drink flame-coloured cider and eat wild strawberries and cream-cheese'. It really was 'such a lovely uncomfortable house,' she told her, but as recompense there was 'such a long river to bathe in; such willows to entangle one'.[48]

That September, while Iris dangled her toes in the river, Maud was on the lookout for inspiration for when her role in *Diplomacy* came to an end. Herbert was enjoying a certain success with *Joseph and His Brethren*, which opened at His Majesty's on 2 September. The play was, as Maud described to Iris, 'such an angel on the doorstep, such a fiend on the stage'.[49] It was also the first West End production of a biblical subject to be granted a licence — hitherto there had been a ban on the dramatization of Bible stories — but it was nonetheless, according to Maud, being met with 'delirious success'. A reluctant Maxine Elliot who had been persuaded by Maud to play Zuleika, Potiphar's wife, was not so thrilled, as the success of the play meant that it continued for a further 154 performances. Herding camels, sheep, and goats through nearby Charles Street was also proving something of a challenge, especially as on the first night the sheep trained to follow Joseph got stage fright and bolted, causing pandemonium.

Four days later Maud witnessed a different sort of commotion, however, when Barrie was booed on the opening night of *his* new play, which opened at the Duke of York's Theatre on 6 September. Mrs Patrick Campbell starred as Leonora, a woman who pushes a man out of her train carriage when he refuses to shut the window. It was seemingly more than the audience could cope with; Barrie was catcalled and the play closed. He later revised the play, cutting it from three acts to two and re-staging it as *The Legend of Leonora*. In New York, where it was later produced by Charles Frohman, it starred Maude Adams (who had played the original Peter Pan) and who was much closer to Barrie's description of his heroine as being 'an unspeakable darling'. It was a great success, running at the Empire Theatre for 136 performances, and the Americans blamed Mrs Patrick Campbell for not having interpreted the role sympathetically and the British for lacking a sense of humour.

While Maud had enjoyed both *The Legend of Leonora* and *Joseph*, she was positively enthralled by a play from which daughter Viola had already reenacted the characters. Shaw's *Androcles and the Lion*, a fable play with prologue and two acts, opened at the St James's Theatre on 1 September 1913, starring Edward Silward as the Lion and Lillah McCarthy as Lavinia. But while Maud was captivated, her critic and friend 'E. A. B', in the *Daily News* of 2 September 1913, was less so:

> Up and down the fable was strewn with many clever lines and amusing ideas but the fable is one of Mr. Bernard Shaw's mistakes, and it was not surprising that such very heavy fooling mixed with serious ideas did not receive very enthusiastic applause.

Despite Maud being so determined to procure the play and produce it for Christmas matinees, it was one of the rare occasions when her flare for backing a winner let her down. The play was withdrawn after fifty-two performances.

Within the next six months, Maud's performance as the 'wonderful Lady Henry' in *Diplomacy* also came to an end after what her co-actor Norman Forbes-Robertson claimed had been one of the happiest engagements he had known on the London stage for forty years. For Maud it had been that and more. Significantly, as a result of seeing her performance, the playwrights Charles Hawtrey, Douglas Murray, and Sir Thomas Henry Hall (author of *The Eternal City* performed at His Majesty's in 1902) all now wrote to Maud with dramas they hoped might appeal. She was therefore in cheerful mood when she made her journey to France to chaperone Iris. The weather was already hot and she knew Iris had spent more time bathing than looking after her guests. She anticipated a long holiday and 'a white muslin summer', a summer that would be, although she could not know it then, the last summer of peace.[50]

Notes to Chapter 13

1. See Gray 2003: 1, and Hogarth 1936: 41.
2. Hogarth 1936: 41, and Gray 2003: 1.
3. Hogarth 1936: 42.
4. Ibid.
5. Maud also wrote in 'Herbert and I' that she had never before attended a 'criminal court'. This was not strictly true. In 1890 she was invited by Sir Edward Clarke himself to sit in at the trial of Sir William Gordon-Cumming in what was known as the Royal Baccarat Scandal. See Beerbohm 1924: 60–61.
6. Ibid.: 61.
7. Maud Tree to Viola Tree and Felicity Tree, [n.d.] (MBTC 7).
8. Lena Ashwell to Maud Tree, 7 February 1908 (MBTC 3).
9. Maud gave an anti-suffragette speech for the Tuesday Society at the Hans Crescent Hotel, London.
10. As early as 1899, Maud gave a speech entitled 'How I Became a Public Speaker', published in the *Daily Telegraph* of 16 April 1899.
11. *What Every Woman Knows* opened on 3 September 1908 at the Duke of York's Theatre, London, before transferring to the Hicks Theatre on 21 December. John Shand was played by Gerald du Maurier, Lady Sybil by Lillah McCarthy, Mr Venables by Norman Forbes-Robertson, and the Comtesse de la Brière by Maud.
12. Barrie 1926: 89.
13. Gwendoline Williams to Maud Tree, [n.d.] (MBTC 6).
14. Percy Anderson (1851–1935) was a stage designer and costume designer for the D'Oyly Carte and Her Majesty's Theatre. He designed the costume and sets for Tree's *A Midsummer Night's Dream* (1900) and *Chu Chin Chow* (1916).
15. Percy Anderson to Maud Tree, 6 July 1909 (MBTC 2).
16. Arthur Quiller-Couch to Ellen Terry, 6 May 1909 (British Library, ET IN, PQ, ET-Z1, 371), encloses the play written in blank verse by Thursby, asking her to be Quiller-Couch's 'regent'.
17. *Colonel Newcome* was produced in 1906, adapted from Thackeray's novel *The Newcomes*. In the 1906 production, Maud played Mrs Mackenzie to Herbert's Colonel Newcome.
18. Maud Tree to daughters Viola, Felicity and Iris Tree, 15 February 1910 (SCW, letter 103).
19. W. Lestocq to Maud Tree, 28 September 1910 (MBTC 2).
20. Somerset Maugham to Maud Tree, October 1910 (MBTC 6).
21. Arthur Collins to Lady Tree, 10 March 1911 (MBTC 2).
22. See Aria 1906: 243.
23. See Rowell 1972: 112.
24. George Bernard Shaw had coined this nickname for the family.
25. Maud Tree to Felicity Tree, 3 November 1912 (SCW, letter 103).
26. Herbert Tree to Maud Tree, 5 November 1912 (HBT).
27. See Tree 1926: 114.
28. Herbert Tree to Maud Tree, [n.d.] (HBT/RA/420).
29. Ibid.
30. Maud Tree to Felicity Tree, 5 August 1911 (SCW, letter 163).
31. Maud Tree to Felicity Tree, 2 September 1912 (SCW, letter 289). George Bernard Shaw to Viola Tree, 29 November 1912, as quoted in Tree 1926: 115–17.
32. Maud Tree to Felicity Tree, [n.d.] (SCW, letter 210).
33. Maud Tree to Felicity Tree, 5 September 1913 (SCW, letter 154).
34. Maud Tree to Felicity Tree, 8 September 1913 (SCW, letter 368).
35. As quoted in Fielding 1974: 39.
36. Montpellier Chambers to Maud Tree, 16 October 1912 (MBTC 6).
37. As reported in the *Evening Standard* of 1 November 1913.
38. Maud Tree to her daughters, [n.d.] (SCW, letter 43).
39. The name of the new house in France was 'Maison du Canal', at Pont de l'Arche, south of Rouen.

40. See Dudgeon 2009: 223; Maud Tree to Felicity Tree, [n.d.] (SCW, letter 183).
41. Gerald du Maurier to Maud Tree, [1913] (MBTC).
42. Gerald du Maurier to Maud Tree, [1913] (MBTC 6).
43. Gerald du Maurier to Maud Tree, [n.d.] (MBTC 6).
44. Rowell 2009: 38.
45. Forbes-Robertson, du Maurier, and Maud had all acted in Barrie's 1908 play, *What Every Woman Knows*.
46. Maud's costume in the play included a fur muff.
47. Maud Tree to Iris Tree, [n.d.] (SCW, letter 153).
48. See Fielding 1974: 48.
49. Maud Tree to Iris Tree, [n.d.] (SCW, letter 154).
50. See Beerbohm 1924: 155.

CHAPTER 14

❖

Sir Herbert and Lady Tree
1914–16

On Sunday, 2 August 1914 Maud wrote to Felicity (in a letter headed 'day of Mobilization general in France') that 'the sleepy village woke to an eager people at four o'clock with the great word 'guerre'. She implored her daughter to keep all newspapers and pictures and confessed to being terribly 'moved + excited + exalté'.[1] To Violet Lindsay, who was at Stanton Woodhouse, the Rutlands' family home in Derbyshire, she described a scene where there was no means of communication with the outside world, yet within an hour everything had changed from peace to war. Maud recounted sobbing 'with sobbing peasants' and 'no carriages — no taxis because no one to drive them — oh what a lesson to Suffragettes!'[2] In her memoir Maud recalls how in the pandemonium — she travelled with four English servants, her daughters Viola and Iris, and Viola's husband Alan Parsons, who up to the last moment was critically ill in bed with asthma — she was left alone on the quay at Dieppe, but that she rejoiced at the delay because of the 'divine welcome' Herbert gave her when he met her at Victoria station.

Within hours of war being declared the British public demanded that the hero of Omdurman, Lord Kitchener, take charge of the army. (Margot Asquith famously quipped that he might not be a great man, but he made a great poster.) Within a week, 30,000 men a day of all classes rushed to enlist at his side. The theatrical world for its part, although 'fairly panic stricken', responded in kind and Tree kept his head, immediately opening his theatre (theatres were normally closed during August) to produce the most patriotic plays he could muster: L. N. Parker's *Drake*, followed swiftly by Shakespeare's *Henry V*. In this way, a large number of people were instantly employed and profits were given to war charities.

However, while Herbert made rousing speeches to galvanize the men and women of his audience, Maud felt equally impelled to speak for posterity and to her younger daughters Felicity and Iris, who were still living at home. On 12 August, too moved by her own rhetoric to speak, Maud wrote to them instead:

> I mean dear darlings, that this war has come to change us <u>all</u> — not to make us less cheerful or less glad of any pleasure but to make us think so much more seriously about everything — This is not panic on my part, children dear — it is a mere inevitable outcome of the situation — A new spirit does infect every man, woman + child in this country in all countries — + not one of us, not even "young Iris" can afford to shut her eyes to its presence —

> Therefore darlings, rack your brains, each of you to think how you can help + remember you can help spiritually as well as bodily — If nothing better, every stitch of needlework is of help for the present — + every act of self denial in the way of luxuries is a help for example's sake.
>
> Force yourself to believe that the power of multitudes' intercessions strengthens the <u>will</u> of the universe — I write this as though I were writing to heathens — instead of to two children who, in their heart believe in + love God.
>
> I am not asking you to pray against our enemy — but to pray for the poor, poor soldiers in their suffering + anxiety — the pain + hunger + terror that they have to face.[3]

When her poetic words fell on deaf ears, Maud sent more practical instructions to Felicity:

> I have sent you garments to make — do them <u>very</u> nicely [...] If you have kept all the Daily Mails you will see on the back of <u>each</u>, directions as <u>how</u> to make each. I am starving myself & the 2 servants to pay for flannel and wool. The darling Polytechnic gives the stuff all ready cut out: so different from the Grand Ladies who make one pay for <u>all</u> materials.[4]

By the end of September, Maud had sent a hundred pairs of socks and a hundred belts as gifts to the troops. The constant anxiety over money — she was overdrawn at the bank by £20 that month — added to the self-imposed physical discomforts of having cold baths, no wine ('you know what that means to me', she told her daughters) and little light. Not because she was panicking, as she again stressed, but as 'a poor attempt at Discipline and disgust to luxuries while our darling soldiers are enduring such hardships'.[5]

Excitement, however, in those feverish days gave way to brutal reality as Maud discovered less than three weeks later, when Lady Randolph, a guest in her box at the theatre, 'whispered' to her of the fall of Brussels. The unsuspecting Belgian people, unaware that they were to be invaded, now found their pathetic attempts at barricading an open city quite useless. By the autumn Maud's close friend the actress Maxine Elliot had come up with a scheme for taking £1,000 worth of food a month in a barge along the canals to give to the starving Belgians. In a request to support one of Maud's own causes, Maxine replied:

> Maud dearest,
> Of course I will give you 100 shillings. I only wish I could make it ten thousand times more but I have given away every penny I can beg, borrow and steal! I stress how grateful these poor broken men are for anything one does for them in their unimaginable sufferings. To think that creatures of civilization can lead us to a horror like this. Why is God hiding his face?[6]

London buzzed with the news as Elliot's contemporaries and friends eagerly volunteered to do their bit. Like Maud, Lady Desborough set up a working party at her Taplow home, sending some 955 garments to soldiers abroad. The majority of Maud's aristocratic lady friends had taken up nursing: the Duchess of Sutherland ran a hospital under the auspices of the Red Cross, and over the course of the war a military canteen opened by Lady Forbes fed 4.5 million people. For many young ladies it was a legitimate excuse to escape the tedium of home, but there was also selflessness in performing tasks hitherto carried out only by servants.[7]

The high spirits that had inspired Lady Diana Manners and Felicity to escort Herbert Asquith dressed as a doge around Venice now propelled them to rebellion of a different kind. Diana Cooper volunteered as part of the Voluntary Aid Detachment (VAD), not at the front (her mother Violet Lindsay was convinced she would be raped) but at Guy's Hospital in the East End of London. She describes her mother literally 'writhing' at the sight of her shapeless uniform, while Felicity, having spent time putting war flags in a map 'very accurately', had her work undone by a cat that came to sit on the map, effectively obliterating the German army. It was not long before Felicity followed Diana into nursing, although unlike Diana she chose to go abroad. Maud recounted that 'The Allies' and she (Felicity) departed in a 'blaze of taxis' for France. But if Felicity had given her parents headaches being unchaperoned in Venice, it was nothing to what she now did to them by the thought of her being unchaperoned as a nurse 'auxiliaire' in Paris.[8] Various Beerbohm aunts made vague attempts to encourage her to pursue her singing, anxious that the 'fatigue of nursing' might spoil her 'heavenly voice', but music was the last thing on Felicity's mind. Herbert wrote from His Majesty's Theatre that he was 'glad' she was doing such a fine thing. He continued:

> I suppose it is something to be in the midst of all the terror — that is brave and right — but I cannot bear to think that you a delicate creature should have to bear so much suffering in looking at it. Now you must not go to the front without consulting us at home first.[9]

Four days later, not trusting her daughter not to do just that, Maud made it her business to 'find out something about Serbia', having received a telegram from Felicity in the midst of a work party. What she found out sent her into a tailspin: Felicity had volunteered to join the now famous Lipton Expedition. Sir Thomas Lipton, creator of Lipton's tea and dedicated yachtsman, had put his yachts at the disposal of the Red Cross during 1914–15, when typhus killed thousands of civilians and soldiers in Serbia. Lipton himself took his boat *Erin* to Serbia to rescue medical staff who had fallen ill there, as reported in a *New York Times* headline of 30 June 1915: 'Lipton Rescues Nurses'. To her relief, however, after contacting Lady Paget, who had set up a hospital in Skopje (and who would herself contract typhus), Maud was reassured that no one under the age of thirty was being allowed to travel to the region, as the very young were more susceptible to infection. Typhus was also rampant in Vichy, where according to Maud's sister-in-law Constance Beerbohm there were a hundred new cases a day; the French nurses, fearful of contracting the disease themselves, had all fled. In the meantime Violet Lindsay, prepared to go to any lengths to prevent Diana from following Felicity, turned her Arlington Street residence into a hospital — a very small hospital for very select officers — not for philanthropic reasons, she hastened to reassure her husband, but as a means of keeping their daughter safe.[10] Maud ended her own letter to Felicity: 'Don't get thin or Bacilli will do deadly work with you'.[11]

Mobilizing 'young Iris' was more of a challenge, and she was no longer so young;

after all, boys of the same age were volunteering to fight and dying. Iris's presence at Lady Ottoline Morrell's Thursday gatherings, organized to provide comfort not for English but German soldiers, evoked disgust from the Beerbohm aunts and dismay from Maud. Moreover, unseemly reports were trickling through to Maud of debauched parties held by Iris and Nancy Cunard at 8 Fitzroy Square, the flat the girls had leased, unbeknown to their parents, to get away from home. Parties, hastily arranged for officer friends on leave from the front, turned into something else entirely. In her own memoir, Diana Manners famously called those evenings 'dances of death', where the young women present lived on a 'high wire of tension', awaiting the news of a loved one's death.[12] Alarmed, Maud attempted a different tack. 'Try and wean yourself back to the most childlike form of your once religious feelings,' she wrote to her daughter, 'Form a habit of prayer & trust in god & reverence & worship & it will come back.'[13]

But with Felicity momentarily out of harm's way and Iris at least still in London, Maud could concentrate once more on garnering the talents that would be of most use in raising funds for the war effort. Solo performance in particular, which was inexpensive to give and quickly assembled, enjoyed renewed popularity as charities struggled to invent imaginative means of raising money and entertaining the wounded. If the blueprint among philanthropic societies could be also be used to galvanize women into action, it was one with which Maud was exceedingly familiar. Together with speeches, recitation was once again rapidly reincorporated into the main body of her war work. She had always been associated with numerous charities but she was now invited to head the Entertainment Committee of the League of Mercy and War Emergency Entertainment and the King George Hospital.[14] Women's organizations, regardless of political affiliation, joined forces to raise funds for the war effort. The Actresses' Franchise League was not the only suffrage party to show its patriotism under the umbrella of the Women's Emergency Corps, on whose committee Viola Tree joined Lena Ashwell, Elizabeth Asquith, and Gladys Cooper. Maud, despite her anti-suffrage stance before the war, now gave her support to the Woman's Theatre, another affiliate of the AFL.

But despite practice in public speaking, solo performance could still provoke stage fright, as she confessed to Felicity at the end of January 1915:

> I have just come from Chelsea Barracks where I recited for Bimbo's soldiers. Terrified at first but better when I got into their stride. They couldn't bear George Washington, loved and adored 'If' and Forward Grenadiers. I am very sad at my hospital, as a dear little pneumonia boy has died after fighting for 10 days — a Grenadier drummer.[15]

Correspondence corroborates the tireless search for new material for performance. Popular pieces such as 'George Washington' were often requested, although, as can be seen from the above extract, they were not always well received. The condition was that it should be 'a good stirring recitation or a cheery one'.[16] Further correspondence indicates that, as ever, upholding this balance of acting and charity work was a carefully constructed network of aristocratic friends and acquaintances. Names were now shamelessly exploited to promote the war effort. Maud, as Lady

Tree, was inundated with requests for a performance that was easily transported yet had immediate 'drawing power', and both Trees now collaborated in a series of high profile benefit performances and events. Before the war the press carefully recorded their formidable, if separate, agendas of engagements. With the war, their names began to appear on billboards together as they united in joint ventures. For example, the Théâtre Français listed 'Sir Herbert and Lady Tree' as joint patrons.

If Maud's association with the aristocracy in philanthropic benefits of the late 1880s and 1890s was a means of enhancing her reputation as an actress, now in the war effort her presence was a positive money-spinner.[17] Engagement diaries for the period 1914–16 contain notes on days crammed with concerts and recitations. She also attends fellow actresses' concerts, not only to support the war effort but to glean ideas for her own. Lists of musical instruments and singers accompany annotations such as, for example, Philip Ritte ('lovely tenor') or Mr D'arcy Wollen ('excellent'). And as ever, Maud's networking pays off when she is able to command an army of celebrities and aristocrats to support both Trees. For the first night of a war-time revival of *The Merchant of Venice,* for example, she mustered a party that included Elizabeth Robins, Lady Lewis, the Duke of Rutland, J. M. Barrie, the Prime Minster, the Baden-Powells, and her daughter Viola.

As Lady Tree, Maud gave additional lustre and her own patronage to select charities. The most popular at the time were those ennobled by the Princess Royal and Princess Christian Schlesweig, as aristocratic ladies and actresses now competed on an intense scale to contribute to the war effort. The urgent pace at which the public and the theatrical profession were encouraged to participate, volunteer, and work towards supporting the war effort was measured on an almost weekly basis. One-off extravaganzas for charity were no longer enough; a continuous fundraising programme was necessary to ensure patriotism. At first, the press praised the opening of theatres during wartime, but then began to question the actors' position. Articles began to appear entitled 'Artists under Arms', 'United Arts Force', 'Theatrical Distress' and 'Actors Fighting'. The *Sporting Life* ran a series under the general title of 'The Use of the Theatre', and in a separate column J. Henly wrote a piece entitled 'Patriotism and the Playhouse' (7 August 1914), in which he argued that the objective of theatre just now 'is to offer a relaxation, a little rest from the more present things of life. The dust of war is heard without its grim reality. We do not need its counterfeit in the theatre'.

Following Tree's example of putting on additional matinees during wartime, the Drury Lane Theatre, for one, began to offer extended matinee performances. For their part, the Trees now organized two huge back-to-back wartime benefits that would have been spectacular even without the background of exhausting administration involved in their domestic arrangements. Not only was Maud still commuting to her house at Pont de l'Arche but she was also travelling to Paris, while she still could, to visit Felicity, and overseeing the country house in England at Glottenham and that at All Souls Place in London. However, it was also a time of renewed intimacy with Herbert, in that he spent much time at 'Glotters' completing his *Thoughts and Afterthoughts,* and correspondence reflects the extent to which they were mutually dependent. Although Herbert was established in the Dome of His Majesty's Theatre when in London, Maud continued to oversee his laundry and clothing requirements. Within the theatre world and society at large they presented a united front as never before.

On 26 January 1915 the Trees starred in and organized 'a remarkable cast' for a production of *The School for Scandal*. Tickets were sold out in two and a half hours and prices for the 120 boxes ranged from two and a half to ten guineas for the larger pit and grand tier respectively. Orchestra stalls were 11 shillings, with seats in the balcony at 15 shillings. The *Court Journal* of 2 February 1915 reported that Covent Garden had been 'lent by Mr. Frank Rendl' for a 'host of stars'. The excitement surrounding the event, according to the *Daily Sketch* of 22 February, had rarely 'been seen even with Melba and Caruso'. In coverage reminiscent of pre-war days the press also concentrated on Lady Tree's 'flaming gown full of wide golden stripes as Mrs. Candour', while the *Daily Chronicle* of 22 February 1915 called it 'a deliciously sunny buoyant performance', in which Lena Ashwell played Lady Sneerwell and Herbert Tree Sir Peter Teazle. A total of £2,050 was raised for the Actors Benevolent Fund and the Royal party was said to be 'tickled by the merry wit' (the *Evening Standard* and *Daily Mirror* of 22 February 1915).

Less than three weeks later, along with having 'concerts afternoon and evening', weekends at Walmer with the Asquiths, and continuing to fret about her speeches to the soldiers, Maud embarked on what would the press would soon dub the 'Entente Matinée'.[18] Both Trees now combined forces to do what they did best, in a spectacular effort to aid French and Belgian artists. On 9 February 1915, Tree explained the reason for the 'Entente's inception to the *Western Gazette*:

> The English stage has been placed in a position to cope with any distress that may arise in the near future [...] But while the London theatres are mostly open, the theatres of Paris, of France and of Belgium are rigidly closed. Not more than 11% of those usually employed in the theatre are able to gain their bread by following their vocation.

The Trees now fell back on a life of organizing large scale philanthropic events to constitute an Anglo-French programme to be attended by, and with the participation of, a stellar cast. If the Charing Cross Bazaar of the previous century was spectacular, this Matinée extravaganza, in collaboration with French and Belgian theatres and organized in wartime, was no less memorable. Remarkably, it would be the first time in forty-four years that the Comédie-Française had visited England and the first theatrical performance the King and Queen would attend since the outbreak of war. The *Daily Telegraph* of 11 February 1915 compared it to the 'famous banquet held at the Crystal Palace some 44 years ago', while the *Era* of 27 January 1915 said it 'recalled the famous company's visit during the Franco-Prussian war of 1871', when 'la grande Sarah' was a 'very young woman'. As André Charlot, the French manager of the Alhambra, stressed, in peacetime it would have been impossible for so many actors to leave the French stage. Press coverage delighted in relaying every detail of the event, with generous acknowledgement of the allied effort involved. The Gare du Nord, for example, and South Eastern and

Chatham Railway Companies were reported as offering free travel for the French artists who were to be met at Boulogne, as reported by the *Daily Chronicle* on 3 February 1915.

In advance the press also ran features on the artists who were due to visit, namely Mme Marguerite Carré (Prima Donna of the Opéra Comique), M. de Ferandy of the Comédie Française, Madame Andrée Megard, Mlle Lifrand, Albert Lambert *fils*, and M. Leconte, who would recite and perform with other actors from the Théâtres Antoine and Sarah Bernhardt. Their programme would consist of a selection from their best-known authors and composers, including Musset's 'La Nuit d'Octobre' and 'Le Rhin allemand', *Le Coeur a ses raisons* (scene 4), and music by Bizet and Fauré. Elgar would compose and play for the English selection, which would also incorporate the quarrel scene from the recently performed *The School for Scandal*, Henry Airly singing the patriotic *Chantons Belges, Chantons,* and Max Beerbohm's one-act *A Social Success* — which, its artistic content aside, it clearly was.

Maud headed the organization and welcome committee, once more drawing on her network of friends and connections. The *Observer* of 14 February 1915 reported 'the velvet and furs' worn by Lady Cunard, the Duchess of Rutland, and Mrs Keppel while the welcoming committee itself consisted of Maud recruits such as the actresses Violet Vanbrugh and Mrs Madge Kendal and the actors Gerald du Maurier, Sir Squire Bancroft, and Sir John Hare. After luncheon on 28 January 1915, *Reynolds News* reported that King George V and Queen Mary attended the 2.15 pm performance of the Entente Matinée. Also in attendance were Prime Minister Asquith, two Portuguese Queens — the dowager Amelia and Victoria Augusta, consort of King Manuel — the duc d'Orleans and the ambassadors of Japan, France, Russia, and representatives of Serbia and Belgium. The programme itself was decorated with facsimile signatures of Asquith and the French, Russian, Japanese, Belgian, and Serbian delegates. M. Albert Carré, director of the Opéra Comique in Paris, represented the French government. This 'Constantinople of the Stage' moved Tree to declare: 'We are living in a great and inspiring time — this hour, it seems to me, is the very centre of gravity of the world's history'.[19]

Once more the Entente demonstrated what could be achieved by artists who were far from 'shirking' their duty. The *New Witness* of 11 February 1915 wrote that 'it was fine to think that we allies are joining hands in the field of art as well as in the field of battle'. The obvious support and 'generous practical sympathy with the misfortune of the vanquished' led M. Donnay of the Académie française to cry to the audience that they were being taken 'vers la victoire, amis, vers la victoire!' An event that the *Manchester Dispatch* called 'unique in the annals of the English stage', raised £5,000 and also acknowledged the hitherto unacknowledged debt some English playwrights owed French artists as a source of inspiration. Tree affirmed this in a further speech he gave, begging his audience 'to salute the Actors of France' who 'in art' had 'long been allies'. He stressed how Sarah Bernhardt, Réjane and Yvette Gilbert had 'long been household names'. In emotive rhetoric he went on to say:

> We are fighting under one banner, for the colours of our flags are the same —

red for war, blue for hope and white for peace. But let us not forget that over all the countries of the world floats the flag of the Red Cross, reminding us that Christ's message of love is stronger than the Kaiser's hymn of hate.[20]

The Entente Matinée was a social, professional, and public relations success and reinstated Maud at the centre of His Majesty's Theatre. It was a formula repeated by the remarkable Lady Paget who, recovering from typhus, organized her own fundraiser. The *Lady's Pictorial* of 20 January 1915 and *Pall Mall Gazette* of 27 April 1915 reported on this wealthy American woman's phenomenal success — the *Daily Express* also in April, claimed she enjoyed a 'more soothing climate' here in England — with a pageant which incorporated a masque 'of war and peace' especially written for it by Tree's very own Louis N. Parker, with music composed by James Glover. In aid of the American Women's War Hospital, boxes were being touted at a hundred guineas: not only was it a novel way of raising money but it was being heralded as another 'elite' event. It had the predictable support of Princess Christian and the Princess Royal and was attended by Queen Mary. Subsequent London press coverage reported Viola Tree as enacting the 'voice of the wind' and Lady Tree in the cameo role of 'Nature'.[21]

The fun involved in setting up the Entente, however, belied the gravity of the reasons for doing so. Soon Maud was to lose friends on and off the battlefield. In June 1915 while Maud was preoccupied with auditions for a stage version of *The Woman in White* to be staged at His Majesty's, Lewis Waller appeared at Wyndham's as John Leighton in May Martindale's *Gamblers All,* with co-stars Gerald du Maurier and Madge Titheradge, whose dresses were made by the famous *Lucile* of Paris in what the *Manchester Guardian* (of 2 November 1915) considered 'a personal triumph'. Only the programme for the play indicated this was anything other than a normal theatre season. 'To the Men of London: Good Opportunity for smart men to "do their bit",' reads an advertisement, 'Join Now! Age 19 to 38 — uniform supplied within 12 hours'. The success of the play guaranteed an autumn tour, but it would be Waller's last. While in Nottingham, he caught pneumonia and died there on 1 November, a few days before his fifty-fifth birthday. There is no record of either Tree commenting at the time. It is worth noting, however, that Maud did not destroy his letters, which were kept in turn after her death by her daughter Viola. It is poignant that the tone of Waller's early letters however, should be replaced by a formal one later, shortly before he died. In these Maud is no longer 'pet' or 'Maudie', but simply 'Lady Tree'. To my mind, it is more poignant still, that among a box of uncatalogued letters, tucked away amid the receipts of theatre paraphernalia, is a leather bound sepia photograph of a young man. The portrait could be of anyone — it is unlikely to have aroused suspicion or even a second glance. It is unlikely that Viola's son David or anyone else would easily identify the dashing Lewis Waller.

When Felicity married Geoffrey Cory-Wright during a weekend's leave, on 11 November 1915 (ten days after Waller's death) Maud's words that 'only the very young could ever know real happiness again after the outbreak of the War' would be more than prophetic. By the end of the first year no family would be unaffected, with some 5,233 officers dying. Of the Coterie, only Alan Parsons (Viola's husband, who had chronic asthma) and Duff Cooper (Diana Manners's future husband working for the Foreign Office) were not enlisted, but Charles Lister (Margot Asquith's nephew), Percy Wyndham, George Cecil, and George Bernard Shaw's nephew (another Bernard Shaw) were all dead, as would be most of the young men who had spent so many short breaks at 'Glotters' or Brancaster during what the Trees had called 'children's weekends'. Lord Brabourne (Felicity's then fiancé), Patrick Shaw-Stewart, Billy Grenfell (Letty Manners' husband), Edward Horner, Edward Wyndham Tennant (Margot Tennant's nephew), and the Prime Minister's own son Raymond were all subsequently killed. Anecdotes within the family abounded, the most poignant being that of the Trees' family friend Pamela Fitzgerald, who was trying on her wedding dress at the very moment her fiancé was shot.

Meanwhile, Maud's Violet Lindsay was almost hysterical with fear that her remaining son would be killed. 'I look to Russia,' she later wrote to Maud, 'with terrifying eyes [...] like any desperate woman waiting for help.' It was a constant, ever-present fear. 'I thought myself safe but no — how lovely it must be to have had no sons ever!' But there were plenty of her friends' sons (including her own son-in-law) who did perish, and not least the pleasure-loving, spoilt, and immensely wealthy little Lord Vernon, that darling of the Coterie whose Venice escapade so vexed Maud, and who had appeared at her Shakespeare ball dressed as Henry VIII, who was to die rather ignobly of dysentery at Gallipoli. And Rupert Brooke would recall happier times not only in poetry but also in an earlier letter to Edward Marsh:

> You at home, have no conception how you're getting a sanctity and halo about you in my mind [...] Would God I were eating plover's eggs and drinking champagne with the Bernard Shaws [...] Eddie, six or seven Asquiths and Felicity Tree in Downing Street again.[22]

Notes to Chapter 14

1. Maud Tree to Felicity Tree, 2 August 1914 (SCW, letter 907).
2. Maud Tree to Violet Lindsay, 13 August 1914 (by kind permission of His Grace the Duke of Rutland).
3. Maud Tree to Felicity Tree and Iris Tree, 12 August 1914 (SCW, letter 549).
4. Maud Tree to Felicity Tree, [n.d.] (SCW, letter 72).
5. Maud Tree to Felicity Tree and Iris Tree, 17 September 1914 (SCW, letter 78).
6. Maxine Elliot to Maud Tree, [n.d.] (MBTC 2). Elliot (1868–1940), American stage actress and leading lady at Her Majesty's, whose fiancé, the tennis champion Tony Wilding (1863–1915), taught the Tree girls tennis. Viola wrote to Felicity on a postcard: 'Maxine is going up the dykes in barges as hospitals which sounds both helpless and insanitary but she says it's very good and has advised Diana (Cooper) to do the same'. See Cooper 1958: 117–18. After the war, Belgium awarded Elliot the Order of the Crown for her humanitarian work.
7. See Lambert 1984: 179.
8. Voluntary Aid Detachments had been established in 1909 and by 1914, of the 74,000 volunteers, two thirds were women and girls.
9. Herbert Tree to Felicity Tree, 18 January 1915 (SCW, letter 345).
10. See Bailey 2012: 350–51.
11. Maud Tree to Felicity Tree, 13 January 1915 (SCW, letter 125).

12. Cooper 1958: 142–50; Ziegler 1982: 54.
13. Maud Tree to Felicity Tree, 1914 (SCW, letter 72).
14. Maud also worked for the Ealing Hospital, Royal Waterloo Hospital, Blinded Soldiers' Association, and the Rehearsal Club, to name but a few.
15. Maud Tree to Felicity Tree, [January 1915] (SCW, letter 123). Edward Wyndham Tennant ('Bim', 'Bimbo') 1897–1916, was the elder son of Lord Glenconner and nephew of Margot Asquith. He died at the Battle of the Somme, a few days after his cousin, Raymond Asquith.
16. Victoria Adelaide, Duchess of Albany, to Maud Tree, 17 April 1916 (MBTC 7).
17. See, for example, *Encore* for 23 April 1914.
18. Maud Tree to Felicity Tree, [n.d.] (SCW, letter 565). Walmer Castle, Kent was the official residence for the Lord Warden of the Cinque Ports but had been lent to the Prime Minister as a wartime weekend retreat.
19. Tree 1915b.
20. Herbert Tree, untitled speech at Montague House, 7 July 1915, Montague House, scrapbook, 1915 (BTC).
21. See, for example, the *Lady's Pictorial* of 20 January 1915, and *Pall Mall Gazette* and *Daily Sketch* of 27 April 1915.
22. Rupert Brooke to Edward Marsh, 29 June 1913, written from the Montreal Express train; quoted in Marsh 2009.

CHAPTER 15

Still Waters 1916

In just one breathless week in May 1916 Maud attended events like the Lord Mayor's Ball, Daly's Theatre Concert, the Music Hall Ladies Guild, the Daily Express Concert, the Navy League (a lecture given on airships by a Mr Mallet), Miss Irene Vanbrugh's Concert, the Australian War Contingent Concert, a meeting at the Actors' Church Union, the Australian Red Cross Ball; she gave speeches at Mansion House and the War Emergency Entertainments Concert, and a recitation at the Palladium, organized 'Lady Tree's Four Hundred Ragtime Band', rehearsed with Lena Ashwell, and read for Edy Craig (Ellen Terry's daughter) at a Palace matinee. Tree's *David Copperfield*, starring Owen Nares, was playing at His Majesty's Theatre and, by coincidence, earlier in the year, she had attended a concert by the granddaughter of Charles Dickens.

Maud, at fifty-eight, found that her roles were exceptionally diverse. As ever, she continued to seek new material for performance, and as her correspondence testifies she was pivotal in having that material performed. But once again her own professional achievements were overshadowed by the much-documented reports of Tree's Hollywood odyssey. Earlier in the year Herbert, accompanied by Iris had set sail for America. Keeping Iris occupied during the war had preoccupied Maud — 'What is young Iris dong?' she had written to Felicity, '*Can* she work?'[1] Waiting for them was Claude Beerbohm, Herbert's son by May Pinney. Herbert had intended to reveal to Iris that Claude was her half-brother but losing his nerve and much to Iris's surprise, Herbert introduced him as a 'cousin'. While Herbert was filming *Macbeth* in America, billboards for the three-year old Empire Picture Hall, Watford ('Where the Best Pictures Are') announced 'Lady Tree's Film Début in *Still Waters Run Deep*'.[2] The Empire Picture Hall was a typical early picture house with an orchestra pit but no stage, while the film itself had been adapted from Tom Taylor's 1855 play of that name, which was itself a translation and adaptation of Charles de Bernard's novelette *Le Gendre* [the son-in-law]. Ellen Terry nicknamed Taylor 'Tom the Adapter' in recognition of all the pieces, 'which some openly, some deviously', he brought to the English stage.[3] His anglicized renditions of French plays such as *The Ticket-of-Leave Man* (originally *Le Retour de Melun*) were characteristic of the Olympic Theatre so beloved of Maud's sisters many years before. In fact, the plays produced there whose 'cleverly devised narratives' that were 'neither over-melodramatic nor overtly literary in nature', became known as 'Olympic Drama'.[4]

Still Waters Run Deep was a far cry from Taylor's *Masks and Faces*, which had

Fig. 15.1. The Empire Picture Hall advertising Maud in the film *Still Waters Run Deep*, 1916 (Edwards 1992: Figure 125, [n.p.])

formed part of Maud's repertoire, and the role she played was no longer that of a 'delightfully pretty and innocent' Mabel Vane, although the 'quiet humour' running through the play and demanded by the role of Mrs Sternhold was very much the kind of part in which Maud excelled. The plot, in which the mild-tempered businessman John Mildmay entraps a swindler who has wormed his way into the family's confidence and in so doing reasserts his authority over a household ruled hitherto by his wife and her domineering aunt, had a 'tenacious hold on public favour'.[5] Advertised as an 'original comedy', the play nevertheless borrowed shamelessly from Bernard's text: entire sections of dialogue were translated and 'lifted' from the original, albeit with the sexual innuendoes of the French version — where mother and daughter compete for the swindler Hawksley's affections — attributed to aunt and niece in the English. The settings are also English and the names anglicized accordingly. If the idea of infidelity and of the woman scorned had been symptomatic of the type of role in which Maud had excelled, the part of Mrs Sternhold reflects a leaning towards more financially-centred themes for which Maud could also draw on personal experience. (Her financial worries showed little sign of abating even now, as like Ellen Terry she was working to support an extended family.) In the play Hawksley is interested less in the seduction of Mrs Sternhold and her niece, 'whose love-code has been learnt in the hot south where passion excuses boldness', than in trying to persuade the niece's father to invest £1,000 in the Galvanic Navigation Company, while Mrs Sternhold herself tries to persuade her brother to invest even more of his capital with Hawksley.

When the film opened in Watford in 1916, silent films had already been in existence for some time, with Tree's first film of *King John* dating from 1899 and *A Man's Shadow* from 1913, but what Maud's performance did, with her name advertised on billboards, was to enhance the popularity of this medium. Five years later, the 1918 film by D. W. Griffith, *The Great Love*, starring Lillian Gish and Lily Elsie, was most popular with the aristocracy for featuring a cameo role with Lady Diana Manners and celebrity 'walk-ons' such as Baroness Rothschild, Lady Paget DBE (of Serbia fame), Violet Keppel, the Princess of Monaco, and even the Dowager Queen Alexandra.[6]

A month later Maud was once again involved with theatre, and this time in a patriotic Shakespearean display of which Tree would have been proud. Entitled 'A Shakespeare Pageant', with Arthur Collins as director, the extravaganza opened on 2 May at the Theatre Royal, Drury Lane. For this tercentenary of the playwright's death, Maud collaborated with the actor-manager George Alexander, appointed the actors, and arranged scenes from *The Merry Wives*, with Anne Page played by Viola Tree and Mistress Quickly by Lottie Venne. Norman Forbes-Robertson (who had performed with her in *Diplomacy*) played Slender and Maud Mistress Ford. Elgar composed the incidental music.

Maud's decision to support such English projects was not entirely altruistic. At the outbreak of war Tree's German name elicited commentary in the press, *The Times* claiming that 'his brother does not seem to mind being regarded as a German' and taking great delight in reproducing Tree's entry from *Who's Who*, underlining the fact that he had been educated in Germany and currently held (amongst other honours) the Order of the Prussian Crown (3rd class). There was general anti-German sentiment expressed not only towards persons but to things as well, the Bechstein Hall, for example, being seized as 'enemy property' before reopening in 1917 as the Wigmore Hall. In this respect, the recurring, niggling question over Tree's nationality renewed the vulnerability of their public position. Maud was careful to record and report Tree's American speeches in support of the allies and was in frequent contact with the Prime Minister. Never before had Asquith's support (and subsequently Lloyd George's) and that of Maud's more aristocratic patrons been so important.

But the press would not let the question of Tree's nationality rest. It now went further, accusing Tree once more of being not only German, but also Jewish. There were rumblings of anti-Semitic prejudice akin to those that had triggered Zola's *J'Accuse*, particularly in the proclamation in the *Stage* of 21 December 1916 that began, 'We assert that he [Tree] is of German extraction, that if he is not a Jew he misled us by not contradicting the statement we made in 1915'. That year the question of his race had surfaced when he produced the controversial *Marie Odile* by Edward Knoblock, an American who had 'the honour of becoming a naturalized Britisher'. Less interested in the so-called morality of the play — a Catholic nun miraculously conceives a child through having taken an enemy solider to be Saint Michael — than by the nationality of its author, the *Statement* of 13 September 1916 insisted that Tree was a Jew who had changed his German name to accept honours and become a loyal 'Britisher'. In a spiteful article it went on to say that a number of his compatriots had become naturalized for their own purposes and for their own profit. With regard to the performance, it commented that it did not rate Tree as an actor and that given that he was a 'German Jew' was not surprised that he should so 'utterly and absolutely misunderstand the Catholic point of view'.

Tree countered all of this by reaffirming the fact that his mother was an English Anglican and his father, though born German, was naturalized before Tree was born. 'You are more English than the King,' Maud reassured him, but encouraged him to come home to England to 'share her last throes and anxieties <u>before</u> the dawning of her joy'. And she added, 'don't leave it until her times are over'.[7]

But if Tree was denying being a Jew himself to the press in England, now in America he defended the very character of the Jew as portrayed by Shakespeare. The Council of Jews, unhappy with the way Shylock is portrayed in *The Merchant of Venice*, considered banning the play from schools. Addressing the American Easter Council of Reform Rabbis, Tree insisted that to banish Shylock from the stage 'would be to banish one of the most important creatures of Shakespeare's genius'.[8]

At the start of his visit to America Maud had received letters at regular intervals, sometimes twice a week if Tree was feeling unwell or lonely. In fact their correspondence reveals a renewed intimacy as husband and wife faced the terrible world events and the prospect of old age together. Tree's letters to Maud also reveal a touching, increasing reliance on her and an appreciation of their shared history. They are optimistic that the war will soon end and there is a desire to put his affairs in order. Hers to him reveal a woman in control of her destiny and at peace with herself. But now she needed him home; moreover, by staying away he gave credence to the rumours that questioned his nationality.

The threat of scandal, however, did not pertain only to Tree's German parentage but to parentage in general. Maud and May Pinney were both being blackmailed. The latter was not at all happy with this latest twist, but Maud, perhaps well used to it, wrote to Tree that the 'anonymous letters and postcards' did not 'annoy' her. She was, notwithstanding, mildly curious, as their author must be 'someone from the old days who knows us because they always refer to you as "Herby"'.[9] What both wife and mistress were unaware of at the time of writing was that Tree was seeing one Muriel Ridley in New York and that she was already pregnant with what would be his tenth and last child. (His daughter Felicity was pregnant with her first and Viola with her third, while May's youngest two children were only four and five-years old.) Tree still vigorously denied any extramarital activity. In a letter to the star-struck Olivia Truman he did once confess that it was 'difficult to fulfil one's duties in every relationship', but to the charge of 'three establishments' he claimed he had a London home and theatre but knew of 'no others'.[10]

Endless matinee performances for the war effort and the organization of yet another patriotic pageant at Covent Garden had kept Maud busy. Despite writing that she imagined charity benefits would let up, there was no immediate indication that this would be the case. The offer of a part in *The Show Shop* at the Globe in April 1916 was taken on only as a favour to Marie Lohr (who had played the pregnant nun in Tree's *Marie Odile* and was married to Val Prinsep) and for the £40 it promised. Not enough, as it turned out, for a few months later in writing

FIG. 15.2. 'France's Day in Aid of the French Red Cross', originally published by the London Committee of the French Red Cross, 1916 (Imperial War Museum Posters)

to Herbert, Maud complained of being short despite having spent none of her *Show Shop* earnings on herself. Tree's solicitor, Mr Lambert, she told her husband, was 'rabid' at her for requiring more money, though it was only for the 'absolutely necessary dresses' required for the play.[11] She was certainly very short of money when she wrote again to Herbert in December of that same year. Tree's solicitor had lent her £100, just as she was down to her 'last shilling' but she had had to give his pearl studs as security.[12]

Maud did not enjoy her engagement at the Globe and was preoccupied besides with other issues, the least being an invitation to participate in 'France's Day', organized by the French Red Cross, the greatest being the withdrawal of Tree's film of *Macbeth* from His Majesty's. It was to have had a ten-week exclusive run but closed after only one week. He had insisted (at great expense) on miming the whole part, and the result was nothing short of disastrous, proving a failure on both sides of the Atlantic, and the entire American project of 'Tree in Shakespeare' was abandoned. According to his co-star Constance Collier, he did not understand the method of film-making and had 'long arguments with the director as to whether the whole of Shakespeare should be spoken or not'.[13] For the moment, not even Maud's close relationship with J. M. Barrie could stave off his spoof, which did nothing to promote the film's credibility. Barrie's version of *Macbeth*, called *The Real Thing at Last*, had a cast of 'four murderers, two murdered, one willing to be murdered, one afterwards murdered, one nearly murdered, one not worth murdering but murdered and three murder specialists'. Its captions included: 'If Burnham Wood moves, it's a cinch!' and 'Mac visits his wife surreptitiously'.[14]

However, following on the heels of the embarrassment of *Macbeth* came the unexpectedly popular musical *Chu Chin Chow*, which premiered at His Majesty's on 3 August of the same year. On the strength of Maud's recommendation, but without having seen the script himself, Tree had invested an initial £2,000 in the production. The Australian actor Oscar Asche (1871–1936) not only wrote this wartime hit but also directed and starred in it. Coincidentally it was the 'Arabian Nights' adaptation *Kismet*, a 1911 play by Edward Knoblock, that inspired Asche to create *Chu Chin Chow*, in which he played Abu Hasan (leader of the forty thieves) and which co-starred his wife Lily Brayton (who had also been injured in a road accident at the same time as Maud). Part pantomime, part musical, it ran for five years with some 2,238 performances and a total of 2,800,000 people seeing the show, a British record that survived until the success of *Salad Days* in 1945. At the time it cost a colossal £5,300, with over a dozen scene changes and featuring a donkey and snakes, fabulous dance routines, and exotic costumes. It was the scantily-dressed slave girls who proved such a success with soldiers on leave from the Western front and tickets were hotly in demand. Maud was involved with choreography, though it was everything that Tree disliked. Moreover, it seemed to have reopened the whole music hall versus theatre debate begun almost twenty years earlier when Maud recited 'The Absent-Minded Beggar', though Tree reportedly commented cheerily enough that the show's actresses were more 'navel than millinery'.[15]

Meanwhile Tree, in America, had very different plans for his London theatre, the theatre in which he would never act again. But this time the ever-faithful Dana was vehemently opposed not only to Tree coming home but to his latest proposition, as against it as Tree was for it. The more pessimistic Dana became (his son was also wounded in action at this time), the more Maud was bombarded with correspondence to the contrary. Tree had hit upon a new play called *The Great Lover* by Leo Ditrichstein, which he was intent on producing at His Majesty's on his return. The hero of the play was a certain Jean Paurel, 'a vain, fêted, pampered, philandering favourite' of a metropolitan opera house whose waning baritone voice sends him to seek out the love of a young girl while the ghost of an old flame comes between them. The similarities between Tree and this fictitious hero were obvious to Maud and Dana but evidently not to Tree. Reluctantly, Dana eventually paid £5 for scripts and contracts were agreed. According to the contract lodged at Langton & Passmore Solicitors, the production was to be staged within 'one year of Peace being declared in the city of London'.[16]

That autumn, there was no let-up in Maud's work schedule. Not only was she absorbed with her two married daughters and their children (and the juggling of domestic arrangements made necessary by all three women working) but with securing her own employment. There were a further two plays in the offing — *Madame Ghika* and Robert Hichens's *Black Magic*.[17] Hichens had co-written the successful *Becky Sharp* and Maud hoped to replicate that success by producing his new play at the Coliseum. Elisabeth Marbury, the Trees' theatrical agent, was duly appointed to negotiate terms, and a weekly royalty of £25 was agreed. Maud had also paid $250 for the rights to *The Blind Man's Eyes* by the American novelist Edwin Balmer, which she also planned to dramatize. As well as all this she was in the process of negotiating terms with Curtis Brown for the American publication of Tree's *Nothing Matters*, the profits from which were to go towards a fund for actors disabled in the war.

In November, some six months after Maud's film debut and that frantic week in May, Tree wrote to her from Chicago to say that he had not heard from her lately. He expressed sadness at the state of Romania — by the end of the year Germany would occupy two thirds of the country, including Bucharest — and a sense of depression generally; he longed to be home. Tree also seems to have been envious of Maud's contacts with Westminster: 'How interesting,' he wrote to her, 'to have been with the prime minister in this tremendous time'. The battle of Jutland had taken place at the end of May and both Maud and Viola had been frequent visitors to Walmer Castle or Downing Street. Tree saved his bombshell till last, however: it transpired that Iris, who up until then had done nothing but write poetry and ride, 'was practically engaged' to a young man called Curtis Moffat.[18]

Maud only received Tree's letter some eighteen days later, on 16 December, and was suitably astounded, although the news came as a welcome distraction from her war work. Most days, Maud could be found at the King George Hospital, if not reciting for the Rutland Officers or wooing Hichens with dinners at her flat. However, she was not at all reassured by the fact that the family's close friend, the Irish novelist George Moore, had given her daughter's engagement his blessing.

'Married, you say, at Christmas!' Maud wrote by return and then bemoaned the lack of time, and money (she was down to her last shilling) required to get Iris the lovely things she might need for her wedding. To Felicity she put on a brave face, writing that none of that mattered: the important thing was that Iris should be happy, 'have lovely children, be rich + marry a good man. — When, how + where doesn't matter'.[19] Herbert's next letter enclosed clippings of the wedding that took place in New York, the mayor himself having given them a reception, although he took care to omit those that listed the presence of Claude Beerbohm.

Five months later, in May 1917, Herbert finally returned (without Iris who was honeymooning in the Bahamas) via Madrid, as King's Messenger. His efforts for an alliance had been much publicized and he received a hero's welcome. When America had entered the war in April, both Lloyd George and Arthur Balfour wrote to acknowledge his contribution, and on the eve of his departure for England he met with President Wilson. With that the voices of dissent had been silenced once and for all and no one could question Herbert's patriotism. And it was this same patriotism that prompted him to suggest that his newborn granddaughter be called Colombia or Virginia: Viola chose Virginia.

Having arrived at Dover, Herbert went straight down to his old home The Wharf, Sutton Courtenay, where Maud was staying with the Asquiths. For once it seemed that Herbert did not mind the countryside and he was exuberant company. It would also seem that past tensions and misunderstandings, the squabbles and jostling for position between husband and wife, were no longer so important. But then he made no mention of the fact that the actress Muriel Ridley had given birth to their son Paul in December; nor presumably did he tell May Pinney. Instead he told Olivia Truman that he hoped May would return with him to America. It would appear that even at the grand old age of sixty-five Herbert was still juggling his women. For the moment, he delighted in being home in England, and in the weeks that followed he and Maud caught up with old friends. They went to the theatre to see George Alexander's *The Aristocrat* and, though terminally ill, Alexander insisted on acting that night because he knew Herbert would be in the audience.[20] In July Herbert went alone to his one-time leading lady Constance Collier's tiny cottage in Kent. It was a primitive place where water had to be drawn from a well, and inside a rickety staircase was sorely in need of mending, but it was where Herbert had often gone to write and get away from London, returning in time for an evening's performance.

That same month Maud gathered in Herbert's laundry, ordered him new nightshirts, and wrote to Felicity that 'Daddy' had hurt his knee falling down Constance's staircase; a planned weekend in the country would have to be postponed. He was operated on by Sir Alfred Fripp and appeared to be recovering well. The operation had been minor and he was given nothing but gas and oxygen. He had also had many visitors and was very cheerful, reading and re-reading *The Great Lover*, which he was more determined than ever to produce.

In her letter Maud enclosed a detailed illustration of Herbert's knee: 'it is not the Patella but the chain leading to the Patella — therefore less serious,' she reassured

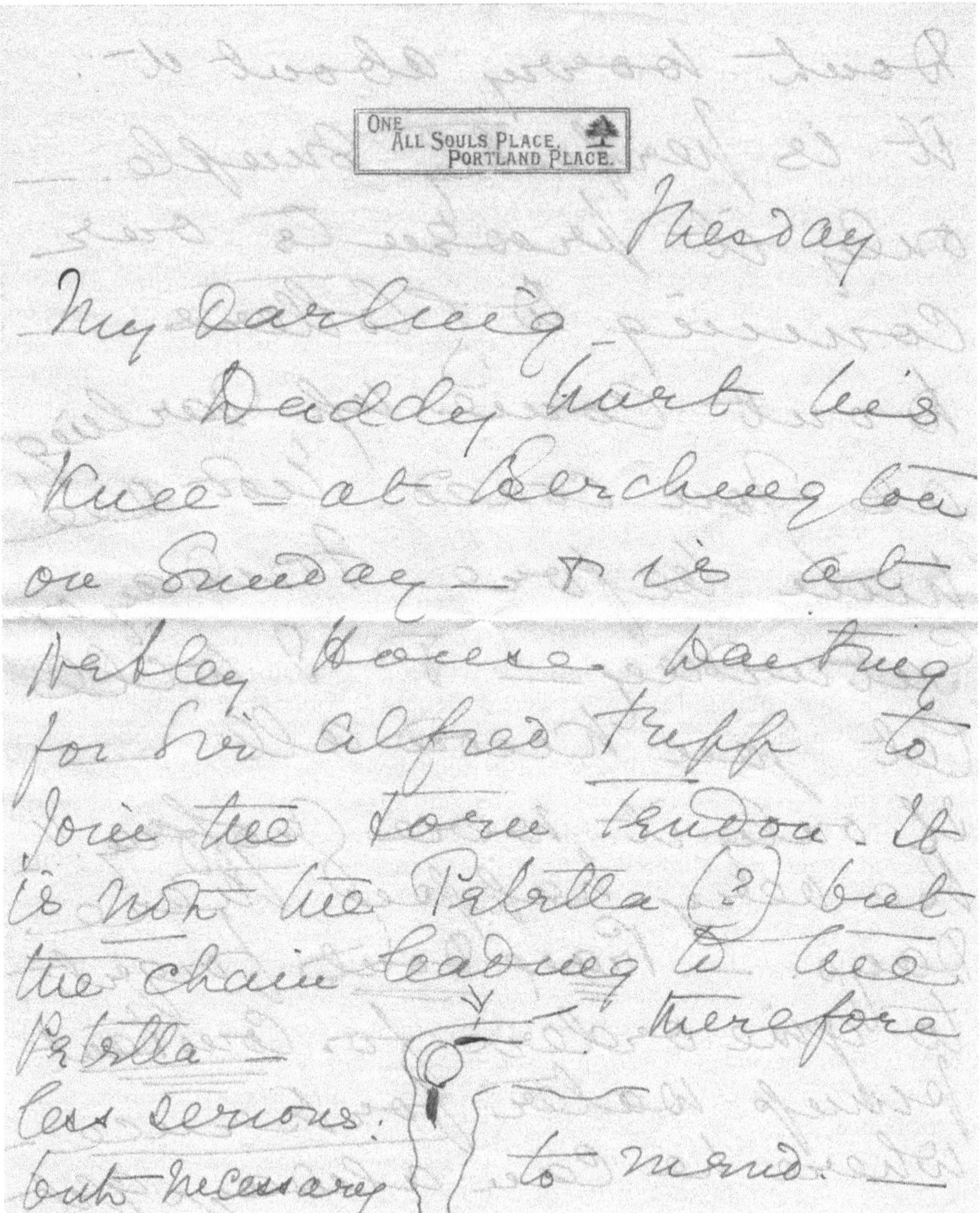

> ONE
> ALL SOULS PLACE,
> PORTLAND PLACE.
>
> Tuesday
>
> My Darling —
>
> Daddy hurt his knee at Berchurg [?] on Sunday — & is at Netley House. Darling for Sir Alfred Fripp to join the torn tendon. It is not the Patella (?) but the chain leading to the Patella — therefore less serious. but necessary to mend.

FIG. 15.3. Letter from Maud Tree to Felicity Tree, 20 June 1917 (SCW, letter 164)

her daughter.[21] But what she could not see, still less draw, was the blood clot that was slowly forming. Ironically, feeling perfectly well, Herbert had wanted to get up and visit his theatre, but Sir Alfred Fripp had prevented him from doing so. On Monday, 2 July at 6pm, Maud wrote again to Felicity from the King George Hospital to say that she had had functions to attend all week and was seeing to Herbert in between. The dining room at 'Glotters' was being converted into a bedroom for him, as he was coming home in a few days. At almost exactly the moment that Maud scribbled her note, and shortly after May Pinney had been to visit, Tree was sitting up in bed after finishing his supper. It was a balmy summer's evening and while his nurse pared him a peach he asked her to open the window. When she turned back to the bed he was dead.

Notes to Chapter 15

1. Maud Tree to Felicity Tree, [1915] (SCW, letter 130).
2. See photograph 125 in Edwards 1992.
3. Terry 1908: 114; and Coleman 1888: II, 118.
4. Tolles 1940: 187. The Olympic Theatre, erected on the site of the former Drury House, is reported to have been built with timber from the French warship *Ville de Paris*. Maud had played Thordisa in Herman Merivale's poem 'The White Pilgrim' at the Olympic in 1885.
5. Tolles 1940: 138.
6. The films no longer exist, but to view a still of *The Great Love*, see <https://i.pinimg.com/736x/78/85/65/78856564213712251d18a9a1de9d0dfbac--lily-elsie-strange-photos.jpg> [accessed 15 November 2017].
7. Maud Tree to Herbert Tree, 17 July 1916 (HBT/RA/267).
8. Herbert Tree, *Vogue* (June 1916).
9. Maud Tree to Herbert Tree, 18 January 1916 (TFA). My own belief is that Olivia Truman, who began writing to Herbert when she was a twelve-year-old child, was behind these anonymous letters. In the past she had sent anonymous photographs of Herbert to the press and she was obsessed with him until her death.
10. Herbert Tree to Olivia Truman, 18 September 1906; see Truman 1984: 63.
11. Maud Tree to Herbert Tree, 18 December 1916 (TFA).
12. Ibid.
13. Collier 1929: 245.
14. See Morley 2006: 27–28. See also *Cinema News* for 6 April 1916, and Collier 1929: 245.
15. See Pearson 1940.
16. There was to be a £1,500 straight bonus and £200 paid in advance in respect of royalties. However, by 1920 both Langton (Tree's executor) and Tree himself were dead. Correspondence from Alice Kauser (the dramatist's agent) to Maud Tree in 1921 indicates, in response to a query regarding motion picture rights, that they had already been sold.
17. *Madame Ghika* was an adaptation of Sir Max Pemberton's *The Mystery of the Green Hat*, based on the real-life woman of the title, the wife of the former secretary to the Rumanian legation in London. Robert Smythe Hichens (1864–1950) was an English playwright and journalist, who had replaced George Bernard Shaw as music critic on the *World*. He published *The Green Carnation* (1894), a satire of Oscar Wilde and Lord Alfred Douglas, but it was withdrawn from publication a year later. His *Garden of Allah* (1904) was made into a film three times. The play in question here has not been identified.
18. Herbert Tree to Maud Tree, 30 November 1916 (HBT). Curtis Moffat (1887–1949) was a photographer and Modernist interior designer. He created dynamic abstract photography and was a pioneer of experimental developing techniques. There is a permanent exhibition of his work at the V&A Museum in London.

19. Maud Tree to Felicity Tree, 2 December 1916 (SCW, letter 598).
20. Beerbohm 1924: 169.
21. Maud Tree to Felicity Tree, 20 June 1917 (SCW, letter 164).

CHAPTER 16

Herbert and I...
1917–20

Herbert's funeral procession, which took place some days later, encompassed the kind of dramatic moments of which he would have been proud. On the way to the crematorium in Golders Green a daylight air raid lit up the sky with the crackling of anti-aircraft guns and bursting bombs. Maud, dressed in histrionic black widow's weeds, mourned noisily; at one point, she flung herself over the coffin, remaining sprawled across it for some time. Maud's appearance at Herbert's funeral was as staged as any theatrical performance with just as much attention to detail. There might be other mothers of his children, other loves and lovers in the congregation, but there would only ever be one Lady Tree. In the days that followed she received visitors wrapped in Herbert's funeral pall, but there were times, especially 'divine summer evenings' when she confessed to being 'under Daddy's quilt, in vino veronal'.[1]

In his address at Tree's memorial service the Bishop of Birmingham praised Tree's 'strong national feeling' and the fact that while in America until a short time before he died he had been a strong exponent of Britain's position, 'an unofficial but influential ambassador of right'. Two days later Maud began tackling replies to the 843 letters of condolence she had received, the very act of writing helping, she said, to thaw her 'freezing heart'. The tributes had come pouring in from people from all walks of life. Herbert was remembered for his love of the theatre, his sometimes controversial but always exuberant interpretation of Shakespeare. But for those who really knew him he was mourned for the boyish quality that delighted in everything new, that made the world seem, to use his favourite expression, 'radiant'. Viola remembered him 'less as a man' and more as 'a mood, a gesture towards fancy'. Maud, however, had no intention of allowing Herbert to be remembered in any way less extravagantly than he deserved. In the next few days she set about feverishly planting out his grave with violas. His magnificent, upstanding monument was to be no less 'impressive + historic than David Garrick's in the lovely Chiswick Churchyard'.[2] However, it was not perhaps quite as Herbert might have wished. On 25 November 1917 the *Referee*, and then on 14 December the *Brighton Star*, and other press outlets, published the following statement, lodged with Messrs Anderson and Anderson, Solicitors:

> Dear Sirs, In the event of my not reaching home please ask Mr Langton [another of Tree's solicitors] to send my love to all my family and friends and my gratitude to the English public for their unfailing kindness and loyalty to me. I would like my obsequies to be entirely unostentatious and private, especially considering the time and the mourning, which this war inflicts upon all. I have done my best to help our cause in America and am thus consoled for my long absence from home.

But twelve days after he died Maud was forced to come out of mourning. The private grief she might feel along with that of her family was compounded by the very public discussion of their finances. Although there was no mention of Tree's other family — 'the stranger within his gates', as Maud referred to May Pinney — articles had begun to appear in the press suggesting that he had not provided for his first, legitimate family. Maud's instinctive flair for self-preservation, and the PR adroitness with which she had shaped the couple's public persona, was immediately triggered. She retaliated swiftly by writing to her solicitor and to the editor of the *Daily Mail* to assure him that Tree had died 'radiantly happy', and especially so about her settlement, which was fixed and secured twenty years before. This was of course not the case, but Maud's pride had been stung: galvanized into action, she had sprung to defend Herbert's reputation, for as she wrote to Felicity:

> There is nothing at all to mourn or grieve about or be ashamed of. I mourn more & more terribly that Darling Daddy had no good angel at his side to make him leave Viola £1,000 by name to help her worries. Otherwise I do want us to realize that poor Daddy has done everything that is most honourable and just.[3]

Herbert, 'by name', had bequeathed to Maud: two hairbrushes, three small books (*Macbeth*, *Timon of Athens*, *Richard II*), one 'small *Hamlet*', one 'small Shakespeare', and his own bound book of cuttings of his knighthood.[4]

The sixteen months or so that remained of the war brought Maud no change in that they continued to be crammed with the juggling of work and family, her 'exhilarating visitors' consisting primarily of her elderly sister Harrie (who now complained vocally that she was 'just the no account poor relation') and a Miss Barnes. The grief of losing Herbert had not diminished and there were still times when both Maud and Viola cried 'too much' as they faced 'the immense time ahead'. But the absolute need to work, if an initial shock, also gave them focus. The 'unspeakable alternative of ruin + disgrace of Bankruptcy', as Maud wrote to Viola, spurred her on.[5] In theory, her daughters were to receive £200 per year, although this might be increased if they invested in war loans at five per cent. The reality proved otherwise, and given that the annual rent for Maud's London residence at 1, All Souls Place, was £160, there was not much left over. Her solution was to continue to rent the London house with her daughters. Felicity (whose husband was away fighting) would contribute to expenses together with Viola (whose husband was all but an invalid). Maud would pay the rates, taxes, and a man to clean the windows, and would provide furniture. She would also contribute £5 a week to the household and live half at Robertsbridge (when required with the grandchildren) and half at a friend's flat when she was not on tour, which at present was nearly always the case.

Ultimately, she was still forced to be responsible for all her daughters, even though they were now married. Viola's husband Alan Parsons was often ill and unable to work, and as a result they were so poor that at one time they were living in a one-bedroom flat, leaving their three children to Maud's care, who was less than amused at her son-in-law's inability properly to support his family. The £40 she had earned as an actress when she was younger, she told Viola, was spent not only on the toilette and dress essential to the work of an actress but as principal breadwinner for travel and living. What remained went on 'unnecessary luxuries, furniture + china and the chateau at Pont de l'Arche + lovely clothes for you children + extra hams + asparagus'. But Maud always had money for her London rent even when *not* acting. She wrote to Viola:

> I am so unsympathetic about your apparently paying everything because one fortnight out of work + bang goes all your contributions whereas the fixed yearly income of a journalist [a reference to Viola's husband] can withstand even a month cessation under the plea of ill health.[6]

Nothing changed. Iris, expecting her own baby, would in due course leave her infant son Ivan with Maud, while Felicity was also on her own with a young child, as her husband was away fighting. Maud also continued to lend money to her brother Horace and support her older sisters. As with Ellen Terry, who was forced to work well past her retirement age in order to support her family, there was to be little respite for Maud. At one point she was looking after six young children when their parents could not, a mean feat for any working actor but even more so when that person was in her sixties. In addition, there was the constant hiring and firing of staff as grandchildren were shuffled from one household to the next. As a result, there were moments when Maud felt utterly depressed by it all, and a recent aerial torpedo in Piccadilly Circus had terrified her 'beyond endurance'. Nor did she always refrain from expressing her feelings, as she did to Felicity (nicknamed 'Fit') in the following note: 'Fit dear, I have just got back from Scarborough — dead + starving after 8 hours journey to find my telephone broken — which enrages me — because I wanted to hear if you are back and what has happened'. And when there was no reply, she wrote in frustration:

> It really is terrible to get no news of any of you [...] I don't think it right considering that I am away working for us all that you should not telephone me a telegram — I have been in agony since Saturday afternoon — but always in the train — & not knowing how or when to telephone. I don't mind a bit if it means you are all well & safe [...] I have had no sort of sleep for two nights [...] Forgive if I scold. I will send money tomorrow.[7]

By the end of 1918 the war was over and His Majesty's Theatre finally sold for £105,000 (£35,000 more than Tree had paid for it) to Messrs George Grossmith and Edward Laurillard. As a result, Tree left property valued at £44,085 (£39,515 net). Half of the estate went to May Pinney for her use absolutely, £1,000 to be immediately available. The other half was to be held in trust for Maud, whose financial situation remained critical: she was to receive £700 per annum from her share and would receive a further twentieth of the profits from *Chu Chin Chow* when the production came to an end, but this would not be enough for her to live on, she assured Tree's executor, Mr Webb.⁸ She also owed premiums on His Majesty's for Burglary and Employer's Liability and, having supported her daughters since Tree died, she owed a straight £350 to the bank. Moreover, she had taken on another country house which was intended to be more (but was proving far less) economical than Robertsbridge. Since leasing it, Maud declared, she had not known 'one happy hour' at Binfield Priory. But her grievance was against the damaging articles appearing in the press implying that she was wealthy, for which she took the journalist Max Pemberton personally to task: she would be 'a far richer woman', she wrote to him crustily, '<u>with </u>a theatrical engagement than without'.⁹

But as ever Maud found great comfort in her friendship with Violet Lindsay. At the time of Tree's death the two women had already been friends for half a century, and in that time had shared similar, if not overlapping experiences. The war had drawn them even closer together, united once again in their mutual grief. Most of the young men they had known as children, indeed the sons of their closest friends and family, had been killed. Both women had experienced great loss and survived, but their place in a world in which the natural order of things had been so drastically displaced, was no longer assured. It was Violet's turn to comfort Maud: 'We must not,' she told her friend, 'get old in ways & thoughts whatever our poor faces get to'.¹⁰

The reality was that they had to struggle to regain a foothold in a fast-changing world, unfamiliar to them. After the accelerated pace of the war years the reality of loss hit home. On account of the war, coupled with Tree's death, Maud's old way of life was gone forever, with the whole nexus of His Majesty's Theatre dismantled. Iris had stayed a long time away, first in the Bahamas, then in Cuba. For Tree's daughters the magic had vanished: 'everyone was poorer and disillusioned after the blaze and havoc of war, with its loves and deaths', Iris wrote nostalgically:

> For us no Glottenham or Brancaster, no Shakespeare [...] I wonder what Daddy would have done? Would his genius have survived the slump and change, found plays? Or would he have gone touring as he meant to — to Australia and have become uprooted? I don't think the grand romantic would have prospered, nor the classic, nor any revivals then. I long for Mother and Daddy young again and everything fresh like daffodils.¹¹

Maud, however, could not afford to be sentimental. Rage at her financial struggles — 'I can't go on bearing this anxiety and misery,' she railed to Viola — only drove her on.¹² By March 1918, the same month in which Herbert's stepmother old Mrs Beerbohm died, Maud had set to work with renewed energy to 'rid herself' of Binfield Priory, now referred to as that 'cruel Binfield', and had started on an altogether different project. In the midst of limping from one financial crisis to the next, psychological support came from an unexpected quarter. Max Beerbohm, who had 'retired' to Italy in 1910 to compose *Zuleika Dobson*, returned to England soon after the outbreak of war. In April 1917 he came to London for his sister

Aggie's marriage, and again when Herbert died in July. As the only surviving male Beerbohm, he had taken uncharacteristically energetic control of family affairs: not only had he helped to organize Herbert's funeral but afterwards saw to the disposal of his papers and posters. He (and Maud) completed a task that Herbert had begun in America: the destruction of anything considered by them to be indiscreet.

But Max's initial objective had been twofold, the more important being the writing of a memoir. He now offered Maud an emotional lifeline, proposing a compilation of chapters detailing Herbert's achievements, for which he needed her collaboration. In fact, when the work was finished Maud's would be the longest chapter by far, extending to over 170 pages (more than half the book's total) and its first, under the title of 'Herbert and I'. By August, with typical diligence Maud turned to her widespread network of friends for advice. Burne-Jones's widow, Georgiana, wrote to her by return with the practical suggestion of simply procuring a thick, ruled notebook and keeping the 'subject of the memoir always predominant'.[13] Within the year Maud had a draft ready and sent it for an initial reading to the playwright Stuart Ogilvie, but the latter was too devastated by the death of his eldest son to offer any critical advice: 'Things are sadly altered since we met — it seems years ago,' he concluded.[14] Shaw's response was hardly more positive. 'It was too late,' he wrote [of his association with Tree], 'for us to work together: we were both past being made use of to carry out other people's ideas.' And he was hardly encouraging:

> Dare you write a real sketch of him? I suppose no widow can. But it is a pity that we have nothing but tomfool collections of spoilt anecdotes or insincere sentimentalities to remember him by when his contemporaries are gone.[15]

In the meantime, Maud had fulfilled one solitary engagement, in February 1919, when she played the Queen Mother at St Martin's Theatre in *A Certain Liveliness* by Basil Macdonald Hastings, which also starred Vera Neville. By September she had retreated to Glottenham with Max — the same month in which a national railway strike was declared — to finalize work on the book. She now had a project, but was still uncertain. Max encouraged her not to be afraid of 'any trivial detail or mentioning any small faults', and he dispelled any self-doubt: 'Assurance I offer it,' he wrote, 'Proceed!'[16] With this final flourish Max returned to Italy, leaving Maud to negotiate all contracts with publishers, agents, and the American rights. She was given an understanding by Hutchinson & Co. a year later that there was £390 available for distribution and that 1,500 copies had been sold to an American publisher (Dutton as it happened). Shaw, having recanted on his decision not to contribute to the book, now not only wrote his own chapter but also offered practical help as well. 'I am in arrogant and overwhelming command of the situation, which means that you may sleep peacefully,' he wrote to Maud, though at the same time he managed to instil terror into Curtis Brown, who in turn wrote to Maud that Shaw would 'eat them alive if they published a minute before he gave them authority to do so'.[17]

A year later, the book finally appeared under the title *Herbert Beerbohm Tree — Some Memories of Him and of His Art Collected by Max Beerbohm*. There were contributions from Viola, Iris, and Max, and the writing fraternity was represented by Louis N. Parker, Haddon Chambers, and of course Shaw, who concluded by saying that 'happily no bones were broken' in his encounters with Tree.

Such was the book's success that Maud immediately set about seeking a publisher for a separate biography of Tree. Thornton Butterworth was initially enthusiastic, offering £100 on the signing of a contract and £200 on receipt of a manuscript. A further £300 would be paid on the publication of a book that should be of roughly 80,000 words, the length, he told her, not of a 'Compton Mackenzie novel' but an ordinary one.[18] Writing it, however, became problematic, as in attempting to create a memoir of Herbert's childhood, she invariably began with her own. Entitled 'Our Little Life', the book never expanded beyond draft form, and despite the success of Max Beerbohm's compilation Maud's agent was unsuccessful in finding a publisher for hers. But the warm response with which the Beerbohm book was received gave her immense satisfaction. Members of the old Souls gang came forward to praise her labour of love. Ettie Desborough in particular now wrote to say that she had been unable to put the book down. What Maud had achieved, she said, was 'so infinitely more rare and triumphant than the black and white literature of pain'; in her opinion 'the literature of joy is so far more difficult'.[19] Ettie spoke with feeling: her well documented refusal to admit to the reality of death when her own son was dying, and her insistence that the experience was anything less than joyful had turned him into an apotheosis of a lost generation.

Queen Alexandra, Princess Helena, and the Prime Minister were just a few of the many dignitaries who also wrote to congratulate Maud. But while the writing of the book had been therapeutic and its publicity had placed her firmly back in society after a period of mourning, neither the advance nor subsequent sales meant that she could afford to give up her acting engagements. Financially, Maud and her daughters were struggling as never before, and since the sale of His Majesty's Theatre austerity was felt at every level. Gone were the days when she could send out little gifts of complimentary tickets to her own or Herbert's performances: she was informed of this in no uncertain terms by the new theatre's management when a request for a £4 box at His Majesty's was emphatically rebuffed. Just keeping afloat was proving to be a Herculean challenge, to say nothing of the £200 (which represented four per cent of the whole) needed for debentures in the Academy of Dramatic Art, founded in 1909 by Herbert and in which Maud remained active.

All Maud's efforts had now to be channelled into finding new work, and there was no hiding the disappointment she experienced when she failed to get a part. 'Of course,' she wrote to her daughter Felicity, 'I <u>couldn't hope</u> or pray for poor Lottie Venne to be ill: but that adventure + its anticlimax really broke my heart. I can't recover my equilibrium.'[20] On this occasion, however, Violet Lindsay stepped in unexpectedly with the lavish gift of £600, not, she hastened to add, that it was her doing but rather her husband Henry's, as he knew how devastated she had been when her 'play didn't come off'. Even Maud's censorial older sister, Harrie (who usually wrote about the pernicious air of the theatre) in a rare moment of solidarity conveyed her dismay that Irene Vanbrugh, for one, was getting all Maud's parts and that she wished she (Irene) would 'settle into her widowhood for a bit'.[21] As a very last resort and not, as she stressed to her daughters, that she was forced to do so out of poverty, Maud hired out her clothes as costume: she was paid £20 for the loan of her clothes in the revival of Barrie's *The Admirable Crichton*.

As the year came to an end she was finding it difficult to recover her equilibrium. Her financial worries seemed to be ever increasing just as there appeared to be no let-up in the constant battle to juggle childcare and houses. Her eldest daughter Viola, always loving and appreciative, wrote to say how 'wretched' she was not to be with her. Viola's own struggle to make ends meet was just as acute as Maud's, and this further forged the already strong bond between them. For as she wrote to her mother, Felicity was 'sort of stuck and Iris a happy creature but a butterfly'. Always in tune with her mother's feelings, she added 'Please darling Mother, don't grieve [...] life I have discovered is for the young — One cannot actually be happy [...] when one is older one can enjoy natural things, food, flowers, soft shirts, sun'.[22] If she could indeed have afforded any of those things, Maud's life might well have seemed less uncomfortable. Although she looked forward to Christmas with Violet, her friend too was looking to economize, and the Arlington Street mansion was on the market. After the war the Duke of Rutland had been forced to sell 28,000 acres, half his Belvoir estate. Increasingly, Violet told her, she wore one set of clothes and lived on Bath biscuits. Harrie, Maud's older sister, with characteristic restraint, wrote that she thought a new role for her would be just 'fine', and she hoped too the next year would be rather better for Maud than the last.

Notes to Chapter 16

1. Maud Tree to Felicity Tree, 22 August 1917 (SCW, letter 390), and 3 September 1917 (SCW, letter 167).
2. Maud Tree to Viola Tree, [September 1917] (SCW, letter 423).
3. Maud Tree to Felicity Tree, 14 July 1917 (SCW, letter 373).
4. See BTC/HBT/F/000060.
5. Maud Tree to Viola Tree, [October 1917] (SCW, letter 98).
6. Maud Tree to Viola Tree, [n.d.] (MBTC 6).
7. Maud Tree to Felicity Tree, 22 October 1917 (SCW, letter 896).
8. See the production papers and business journals for *Chu Chin Chow* (BTC/HBT/F/000057).
9. Maud Tree to Max Pemberton and Charles Russell, 18 November 1917 (MBTC 7).
10. Violet Lindsay to Maud Tree, [n.d.] (MBTC 6).
11. Iris Tree to Viola Tree, see Fielding 1974: 105.
12. Maud Tree to Viola Tree, [n.d.] (SCW, letter 98).
13. Georgiana Burne-Jones to Maud Tree, 2 August 1917 (MBTC 6).
14. Stuart Ogilvie to Maud Tree, 8 March 1919 (MBTC 6).
15. George Bernard Shaw to Maud Tree, 28 September 1919 (TFA).
16. Max Beerbohm to Maud Tree, [September 1919] (MBTC 6).
17. George Bernard Shaw to Maud Tree, 18 June 1920 (MBTC); Albert Curtis Brown to Maud Tree, 15 September 1920 (MBTC 2). See also Walter Hutchinson to Maud Tree, 30 September 1920 (MBTC 6).
18. Thornton Butterworth to Maud Tree, 22 February 1921 (MBTC 6).
19. Ettie Desborough to Maud Tree, [n.d.] (MBTC 6).
20. Maud Tree to Felicity Tree, 13 September 1920 (SCW, letter 183).
21. Harriet (Harrie) Holt to Maud Tree, [n.d.] (MBTC 6).
22. Viola Tree to Maud Tree, [n.d.] (MBTC 7).

CHAPTER 17

Maud Helen Louise, Lady Tree OBE
1920–29

1920 did indeed prove to be a better year. In fact the next decade would be the busiest and most fulfilling of Maud's career, as she created many of the character roles for which she would later be known. To begin with, on 1 January 1920, 'Maud Helen Louise, Lady Tree', was awarded the OBE in recognition of her tireless work for charity.[1] And tireless it was; it would seem that no request had been too much. Along with her regular theatre work Maud was involved with organizing balls, concerts, and recitals at Lincoln's Inn, St James's Palace, her own alma mater Queen's College, and for the Red Cross. She was on the board of the Children's Jewel Fund, the King's Fund, the Association for Promoting the General Welfare of the Blind, Queen Victoria's Jubilee Institute for Nurses, the Daughters of the Empire, the Hospitals of London, and the Dickens Operatic and Dramatics Society, to list some but by no means all.

It was, however, in recognition of Maud's charity work and for the League of Mercy in particular that her award was conferred. The League was founded in 1899 by the then Prince of Wales with the clear object of enabling all classes to donate funds to London hospitals on a voluntary basis, and in the twenty-three years of its existence it had raised £324,000 for this purpose. It was stressed that 'every farthing' of the subscriptions collected was directed to the hospitals and all those collecting were doing so without remuneration. By November of the same year, Maud had to be reminded that she had not as yet claimed her insignia.

Throughout her life she had been known by many names. Born Hellen Maud Holt, her stage name for a while had been Helen Maude before marrying Herbert and becoming Mrs Beerbohm Tree. Later she became Lady Beerbohm Tree and until recently had been known simply as Lady Tree. With the addition of OBE to her name, Maud Helen Louise was now a woman of substance, with a clearly defined public persona. Her ability to attract the grand ladies of the aristocracy was soon further enhanced when she performed a month later for a matinee in aid of the Middlesex Hospital. In Gertrude Jennings's *The Young Person in Pink* she played Lady Tonbridge opposite Leslie Howard, who was said by the *Daily Mail* of 11 February 1920 to have been 'a trifle nervous among so many clever women'. In the audience were no fewer than six duchesses, three marchionesses, six countesses, twenty-odd mere 'ladies', and H.R.H. Princess Alice, Queen Victoria's granddaughter.

Six months later, however, on 9 August 1920, she appeared in a play that could not have contrasted more strongly with Jennings's romantic comedy and was all the more challenging as a result. Of her three daughters, Viola was the one whose artistic temperament most resembled her own and over the years she and Viola appeared in several plays together, but in 1919 Viola had taken over the management of the Aldwych Theatre, where she now produced *The Unknown*, a play in three acts by Somerset Maugham, who also dedicated his latest work to Viola. Maud starred as Mrs Wharton with Basil Rathbone playing her son John. If at one time Max Beerbohm had criticized Somerset Maugham for asserting that serious ideas were out of place in the theatre, that notion was certainly belied in a work in which disquiet about the war is expressed as a loss of religious faith and in which characters discuss the possibility of a good God in a world of suffering. 'Either,' as one character says, 'God can't stop the war even if he wants to, or wants to but won't.' The press responded by initiating a quasi-philosophical debate: 'Who Will Forgive God?', ran *The Times* headline, while another theatre critic in the *Stage* of 5 August 1920 dubbed the play a treatise on 'Belief and Unbelief', where the characters 'discuss God for 3 acts'.

Slipping from her own country house drawing-room to the stage set of a manor house in Kent, Maud made the transition appear effortless. Even the opening lines of the play, with their discussion of the local butcher and gardens, might have been lifted directly from Maud's correspondence at the time. But no longer acting in plays that uncannily appeared to mimic real-life scandal, she now appeared in one that more soberly took on the semblance of a chronicle of a death (or deaths) foretold. Two of Maud's grandsons, Felicity's boys, would be killed in the Second World War, another incarcerated in the notorious Changi prisoner of war camp, while Viola's son David Parsons would abandon his own acting career for a time after being maimed. When Violet Lindsay wrote to Maud that she prayed Felicity (after giving birth to twin boys) would never know the loss of sons in war, she could not have known that by the time they were eighteen the world would once again be in conflict. Moreover, *The Unknown*, starring the 'great bohemian Lady Tree' and directed by Viola, seemed very much a family affair, with the programme even carrying the Beerbohm logo of a tree, though there is no mention in the *Stage* review of 5 August 1920 that the role of Kate was played by Gwendolyn Floyd, Viola's cousin and Maud's niece.

The hostility of the critics, however, undermined the profound nature of the questions raised in the play, while the characters themselves reflected the socio-cultural view held by the British upper classes at the time that proportionately more of their sons had died than those from other classes but that war was glorious and just.[2] The reaction of aristocratic women such as Ettie Desborough (and indeed Maud, who wrote of Herbert's nephew, killed in 1917, as dying 'magnificently') only succeeded in underpinning this further.[3] Equally, the ontological debate initiated by the character of Mrs Littlewood and her refusal to accept the sacrifice of not one but two sons, which is met with such incomprehension by the other characters, was glossed over by theatre critics. The modern-day reader would see the play in terms of the nature of twentieth-century warfare in general.

Prophetically too, the play mirrored Maud's own sometimes conflicting beliefs. If the play takes the broadly existential view of life (intrinsically meaningless but given meaning by human action) this was a view that Maud shared, although at times it could seem at odds with her religiosity. Despite the war and personal loss, her faith never wavered and correspondence to her daughters indicates that she encouraged them to nurture theirs. She might also have identified with Mrs Littlewood who, when criticized for seeking distraction in the wake of her great loss, says: 'You're surprised that I should go to the theatre? To me it's no more unreal a spectacle than life. Life does seem just like a play now'. At all events, whatever the moral question, the reality was that Maud was once again in the public domain and much in demand as a character actress. 'Every note rang true', Lewis Arthur wrote to her after seeing her as Mrs Wharton, 'with the exquisite simplicity of your rendering'.[4]

But if life seemed like a play to some, the play in which Maud appeared three months later could not have seemed more like real life. In one of what Shaw termed his 'plays pleasant', Maud was the progressive Mrs Clarendon in *You Never Can Tell*. In summary, the plot hinges on a single mother returning to England, after an absence of eighteen years, with the three children who have never known their father. In what is essentially a comedy of errors, the play nonetheless proclaims the difficulty of family reconciliations, together with a woman's loss of autonomy. These were painful questions for Maud: in a perverse reversal of the play, Maud had experienced a son returning home having known his father but not his stepmother. A few years earlier in 1918, Maud had received a disturbing letter from her good friend Edith Lyttelton (on behalf of the Victoria League) asking her about the personal character of a certain private in the Canadian Army, who claimed to be Herbert Tree's nephew and who wished to head an Entertainments Committee for the League. 'I am so sorry to bother you about such a matter,' she wrote, 'but you know how people claim relationship with anyone so prominent as Sir Herbert was and no one on the committee but myself knew you well enough to ask this question.'[5]

The person in question was Claude Beerbohm, Herbert's son by May Pinney, not his nephew. (Iris, of course had met Claude on her arrival in America in 1916.) But in March 1920, the *New York Times* advertised not only the fact that Claude was to produce a farce called *The Bonehead* at the Fulton Theatre but also quite openly that Claude was the late Sir Herbert's son. The cat was, as they say, out of the proverbial bag. There was more: Claude Beerbohm now planned to produce his own *Chu Chin Chow*. In the event, he proved not to have his father's panache and neither project amounted to much, but Maud was suitably unsettled. Correspondence flowed between Maud and Viola and between Viola and her aunts, who advised not seeing Claude. The situation was much debated, the distress once felt by Maud rekindled. But once again in a moment of crisis she was comforted by old friends such as Philip Burne-Jones, who now wrote to her 'to remind her' and lift her spirits:

> For brilliant wit and repartee
> Commend me please to Lady Tree
> If you're in need she fails you never
> For she's as kind as she is clever.[6]

Supported by so much good will, Maud again threw herself into her charitable and professional activities with gusto, leaving Claude to his dreams of greatness. (By contrast Sir Carol Reed, Claude's younger brother, never referred to his parentage during *his* lifetime.) Maud now proceeded to unveil plaques, to chair debates — one on behalf of the Rheims Committee, a follow-up to war work carried out on behalf of the 'Entente Matinée', and another discussing the licences of London theatres — and she gave a speech on Warriors Day for which Lord Haig thanked her personally. She judged elocution competitions, wrote book reviews, a series of articles entitled *The Wife a Man Wants*, *Our Rosebud Garden of Debutantes*, *Keep the Chaperones*, and an evaluation of the Souls. She attended receptions for Sarah Bernhardt, received complimentary gifts of stockings, and continued to endorse Ponds Extract. She also negotiated contracts for acting jobs of £100 (£120 if travel was required) and made appeals for her various charities. She even wrote to May Pinney on the death of her mother, enclosing 'a little poem'. Maurice (known as Mumbles) Baring, for whom she had played Mrs James in his *The Grey Stocking* in 1908, now wrote to her from the Berg Theatre in Vienna entreating her to lecture on behalf of the British Legion. She visited Paris, was received at Buckingham Palace, and negotiated the film rights to an old Tree play called *Business is Business* with the Jamaican-born screenwriter Rudolph de Cordova.

But that was not all. In 1920 the Progress Film Company, based at the Shoreham Beach Studio complex in West Sussex and in its way a mini-Hollywood with its studios, darkroom facilities, preview theatre, and accommodation for cast and crew, produced *Little Dorrit* in which Maud played Mrs Clennam. Directed by Sydney Morgan and starring his daughter Joan as Amy, the film won such plaudits that Joan Morgan was offered a five-year Hollywood contract. Made on 35 mm. film and intended for general release, it ran for sixty-eight minutes and exemplified the film style that dominated the latter half of the silent cinema era. Dickens, with his melodramatic narratives, proved a popular choice for filmmakers, and *Little Dorrit* with its lavish sets, costumes, and a distinguished cast, was just the sort of thing that Maud would relish.

The film also attracted fan mail the like of which Maud had not seen since her early days on the stage. Friends who last wrote to her requesting boxes or complimentary theatre tickets now contacted Maud for entirely different purposes. Ethel Brilliana was one of them. Better known by her married name of Mrs Alec Tweedie, Ethel was a pioneer in travel journalism and one of the first professional travel writers. She wrote some twenty books, travelled 50,000 miles in two years and survived being cast adrift in Newfoundland, an earthquake in Japan, and a rail crash in Siberia. Previously, Ethel had greatly enjoyed Maud's stage performances, writing to her after seeing her in *What Every Woman Knows* that she was 'quite excellent' and that when she lifted her finger and 'admonished folk' she was reminded of the days at Queen's College when Ethel 'dithered' before her.[7] However, now the motive behind enclosing her impressive CV was that Ethel needed Maud's influence to get her into film.

By dint of perseverance and stoic resolve Maud was beginning to carve a niche for herself in the portrayal of older (sometimes ugly) grandes dames of the screen.

But her next role took her back to the theatre as the Countess of Crewkerne in a lavish 1921 production of J. C. Snaith and Dorothy Brandon's *Araminta Arrives* at the Comedy Theatre. Maud was to be paid £50 and with the proviso that no actor would be billed above her. Concurrently, the *Graphic* published numerous photographs of scenes from the play showing Maud in a fetching lace cap lying on a canopied bed; she looks both wan and wide-eyed. Leon M. Lion, its producer, was not so captivated. He was, rather, as he wrote to her, 'full of anxiety' about her interpretation of what she was supposed to be, and behaving like 'an old lady of 70 (without her wig)'. To be specific, he thought she was far too slow and there was 'too much lying down in the pillows'. In fact, he expostulated:

> The essential quality of the play is 'exuberance,' just as the essential characteristic of Lady Crewkerne is a <u>short</u>, <u>sharp</u> dogmatic manner. When this is dropped (as was done last night in <u>far too many places</u>) the character loses conviction.
>
> <u>PPS</u> Will you remember to have your grey wig changed. It must be nearly bald because of course with your golden curls & the rouge pot you are reduced to under sixty.[8]

When Viola was a child she famously commented that it took her mother far longer to make herself beautiful than it did her father to make himself ugly.[9] Maud had no intention of making herself appear any uglier than necessary and certainly no intention of replacing her wig — if that indeed is what she was wearing — even for the sake of this production. Publicity photographs show a neatly groomed Maud, with thick, curly hair and not 'nearly bald' as advised. In this instance she was absolutely not suffering for her art; indeed she was being uncharacteristically coquettish, or at least in contrast to her demeanour of recent years. The explanation for this sudden vanity was that she was engaged in a pleasant flirtation with Sir Philip Bourchier-Wrey CBE. Sir Philip had been Governor of Northern Rhodesia and a respected political figure in the region, known to have pressed the British government to disclose its intention with regard to that country and whether or not Rhodesia was to join the Union of South Africa or become a self-governing colony. His prose was rather more poetic when he wrote to Maud: 'For there never could never <u>will</u> be another true & loyal as an oak as full of life as an Aspen as beautiful and rich as Copper Beech!'[10] He said her name was written across his heart and that if he could see her once a week he would be 'oh so so happy'. But although he came to see her in her plays and waited for her at her dressing-room door, the flirtation on Maud's part was short-lived. Bourchier-Wrey continued to write loving, longing letters and they remained friends; years later her admirer was still trying to persuade her to live in a cottage with him by the sea, now that, as he cheerfully pointed out, most of their contemporaries were dead.

By March 1922 Maud was back in rehearsal, directed once again by Gerald du Maurier (who also starred), in a J. M. Barrie play. Together with old friends such as Stella Patrick Campbell, Norman Forbes-Robertson, and Irene Vanbrugh (and old rival Marie Lohr), Maud joined newcomers John Gielgud and Sybil Thorndike, as well as old stager Cyril Maude, in what Barrie himself said was the first act of an unfinished mystery.[11] In the presence of the Prince of Wales, *Shall We Join the*

Fig. 17.1. Maud Tree as the Countess of Crewkerne in *Araminta Arrives* at the Comedy Theatre (*Graphic*, 29 October 1921)

Fig. 17.2. Maud Tree in the film *Mayfair to Montmartre* (still from British Pathe Film, Id, 994.21, 27 April 1922)

Ladies? opened at the theatre of RADA in Gower Street on 27 May. The play, a precursor for Agatha Christie's *Murder on the Orient Express,* concerns twelve people gathered together for a dinner party in Monte Carlo, all of whom are somehow connected with the death of the host's brother seven years before. One by one the guests are forced to drop their masks as their host reveals the murderer. Despite its air of incompletion and being, as the *Stage* of 8 June considered it, a 'study in the grim and the grotesque', it was a success. Later on Broadway, Leslie Howard would play Mr Preen in a 1925 adaptation.

Some eleven months later Maud was cast in a very different role, appearing at the New Oxford Theatre alongside Alice Delysia, the former Moulin Rouge dancer-turned-superstar, as the pipe-smoking French 'hag' Gabrielle in C. B. Cochran's Babylonian extravaganza *Mayfair and Montmartre*.[12] The press announced the appearance of 'the fabulous Delysia and Lady Tree' and stills from the silent Pathé film version screamed the caption 'Lady Tree's Remarkable Makeup'. A few months later, in February 1923, she was a more authentic harridan, a genuinely horrific mother, La Fronchard, in an adaptation of a French play at the Lyceum, Adolphe d'Ennery and Eugène Moar's *Les Deux Orphelines*, itself a 'take' on *Babes in the Wood*. With its backdrop of Saint Sulpice and French Revolution intrigue, *The Two Orphans* had mass appeal and was later filmed as *Orphans of the Storm* with Lillian Gish.

In the following months Maud's professional life filled with rich and varied theatre engagements, and with the advent of radio — the BBC began broadcasting in Britain in 1922 — roles in this medium too. As a result of her long theatrical career she was also perfectly poised not only to appear in the new silent films, but to write about film as well. Celebrating their tenth birthday, Paramount Films asked Maud for a contribution, while *Theatre News* engaged her to write a series of articles evaluating the effect film was having on the theatre and vice versa (see 13 December 1926). The *Evening News* paid her 500 guineas for six to ten articles, and on radio *Popular Science Siftings* asked for her participation in a programme by 'Distinguished Theatrical Personages'.[13]

In the meantime, Maud performed in a series of revivals. In May 1923 she was the Comtesse de la Brière in Barrie's *What Every Woman Knows* and less than a year later she was Lady Fairfax once more in *Diplomacy*, before taking on another Barrie play, *A Kiss for Cinderella*, in April. Barrie and Maud had enjoyed a long friendship, far smoother than Barrie's had been with Tree. Herbert initially backed Barrie's membership of the Garrick Club, but they began sparring after Tree turned down the opportunity of producing *Peter Pan,* and perhaps in retaliation Barrie had famously lampooned Tree's *Macbeth*. Maud, on the other hand, did not allow this to colour her relationship with Barrie and encouraged both Violet Lindsay and Herbert Asquith to include the writer in their weekend house parties. She admired Barrie's work, starred in and collaborated with him on his plays, plays that furnished her with some of her most notable successes, which in turn encouraged him to mount revivals.

Barrie's other favourite actor was Gerald du Maurier, and it was specifically for du Maurier that he had originally written this play. The latter's engagement in the revival run in 1924 of *A Kiss for Cinderella,* a 'fancy in 3 acts', was no doubt one of the reasons Maud agreed to play the 'comic queen', that and the fact that it was initially written, according to the *Graphic* (15 April 1916), 'to keep the nation sweet' after the 'horrors' of those times. The characters included a 'Miss Thing' as the heroine, 'a romantic policeman', and a 'patriotic baby' singing 'Ye Mariners of England', but the play proved less than challenging and even the excitement of acting again with Gerald had palled by the time it opened. Maud admitted that she could no longer 'stoop to it'.[14] James Agate of the *Sunday Times* put it rather more delicately: 'Lady Tree is as always too adorable, and too perfectly wonderful, as they would say in The Vortex [...] I do very exactly adore Lady Tree, and wonder how she can make so much out of so small a part'.[15]

The rest of the decade was a period of continuing economic prosperity and social dynamism, while the huge advances made in technology were reflected in popular culture, the visual arts, architecture, and intellectual movements. At the same time, the global map as Maud knew it was changing irrevocably. The USSR was created in 1922, and in the same year Mussolini formed the world's first ever fascist government, while in 1924, the year that also saw the Paris Olympic Games, Ramsay Macdonald became Britain's first Labour Prime Minister. There was change too in accelerated consumer demand and in the aspirations of people from every stratum of society, a change reflected not only in the symbolic bobbing of Iris's hair and the raising of hemlines but in the way society conducted itself as a whole. Maud was informed that she could now be admitted to the Royal Enclosure at Ascot, the edict banning members of the theatrical profession from entering this enclosure having been lifted in 1921.

Inevitably, there was change too in how the theatre was perceived. Once again members of the aristocracy were flocking to the theatre, now not only to see themselves represented on stage, although this was still often the case, nor to be moved as they had once been by talent for talent's sake, but also motivated by a desire to experience interesting work there. Violet Lindsay had long overcome her distaste at seeing her daughter Diana in uniform and she now willingly travelled to America to witness her and Iris Tree shrouded in nuns' habits in the Austrian theatre director Max Reinhardt's play *The Miracle* set in the twelfth century. The production, first staged at London's Olympia and revived at New York's Century Theatre in 1924, was a resounding success, making stars of both Iris and Diana. The latter might have been a duke's daughter but she had married a civil servant on £900 a year and considered her *Miracle* money to be indispensable. The very members of the Souls who had questioned the Trees' inclusion in their select club were now forced to revise their views on the theatrical profession in general, as they chose to seek work there for their children. Most importantly, Maud as Lady Tree OBE had proved in a career spanning forty years that acting was not incompatible with maintaining a reputable position in society. The Countess of Lytton wrote urgently to Maud directly from the Governor's camp in Bengal to request acting parts for her daughters Hermione and Davina.[16] As a result, Hermione appeared in a silent movie scripted by Barrie in 1923 called *The Yellow Week at Stanway: A Record of Fair Women and Brainy Men*.

Against this backdrop of social change and mobility, therefore, within an entertainment sector almost unrecognizable from the one she had known at the outset of her career, Maud was once again perfectly poised to play the dowager countesses, grandmothers, and misplaced wives demanded by both stage and screen. Capitalizing on her wide experience, she reinvented herself yet again to play witty cameo roles with bite. It was not blithe praise that led the actor-producer Leslie Henson (who would appear with her in *The Girl from Maxim's*) to hail Maud as the 'the only humorist left in England'.[17] Humour had always been Maud's forte, and as her grandson Ivan observed, his grandmother had once 'not only been beautiful but funny'. However, he concluded, having come to live with her, now she was only funny.[18]

In 1925, Maud was Lady Maria in *The Last of Mrs Cheyney* by Frederick Lonsdale, a comedy in three acts about a jewel thief who passes herself off as a society lady. Highlighting the plight of the upwardly mobile and coated in a frothy exterior, it opened in September at St James's Theatre and ran for 514 performances. A year later Maud was praised for her role as the Grand Duchess Emilie of Zinger in Noel Coward's new comedy, the title of which was taken from a well-known nursery rhyme. *The Queen Was In the Parlour* was said to be one of 'the lightest quality, which means that it is never very far from tears'. The *Stage* of 26 August 1926 also remarked that the keynote of Coward's play 'is a sentence spoken by a wise old Grand Duchess in the middle act. She is a princess of the royal line', a description that could not have summed Maud up better at the time. 'To persons in our walk of life,' says the Duchess, 'self-sacrifice has become the rule.' Elsewhere the author was commended for having a heart and 'not being afraid to show it', while the audience was reminded that 'Lady Tree, in an all too brief appearance [...] can still "dowager" it over anyone'.

For the rest of the decade and beyond, this very humour and 'dowager' quality would be used to greatest effect in her frequent appeals on behalf of the League of Mercy on the BBC. By the late twenties she had overcome the fear deriving from her very first broadcast when she wondered 'in agony' how many people might be listening. By December 1927, Maud was well aware of the impact of her appeals and that over one million people now regularly tuned in to the wireless to hear her voice. She exploited this for all it was worth: 'I beg to announce,' she said, 'that the next song will be a dance. I am going to perform the dance of handing round the hat — a large hat & I want it filled to the brim'. Soon there was no curtailing her broadcasts that combined anecdotes (some blatantly made up) with brashness. She recounted the tale of one listener who had written to her to say that she could give Maud 'nothing', but had Ivor Novello been speaking in Maud's stead, she would have donated twice as much. Novello possessed, said the female listener, 'such speaking eyes'. Another had said she was sending the League best wishes as she was after 'a little peace' herself.[19] Maud grew bolder. During another broadcast she declared: 'Gracie Fields is going to sing for you & Charles Laughton is going to lift up *his* voice for you. I want £1,000'. And no less persuasive:

> You are always very lovely to me when I can see you. I want you to be just as lovely to me tonight, when you can only hear me; and instead of clapping your hands, clap your hands into your pockets.

Maud's appeals were predictably dramatic but they produced the desired effect. After an evening's transmission she would receive two to three thousand letters, all including a donation. Not everyone, however, was as responsive: Rudyard Kipling, ever jittery about copyright, refused Maud's request in May 1928 to broadcast one of his stories from *The Jungle Book* because, as he told her bluntly, he did not like the BBC.[20] This did nothing to deter her from being a 'shark of a Shylock', however, in her next and most successful broadcast as President of the League's Westminster District. She grew bolder still:

> This time, you must give me what I want without being acted to, or ruffled to, humbugged by beautiful young ladies into buying things you don't want for three times what you could buy them for at the nearest shop.
> My hat will hold pennies & postage stamps as well as cheques for hundreds of pounds [...] Miss Gertrude Lawrence was to play Portia and Ivor Novello Bassanio. Alas no [...] It is to test the quality of your mercy that we are here — mercy which is another word for charity.

The following morning she was inundated with letters. An anonymous listener sent two shillings, 'For your hat, Lady Tree as a result of your wireless appeal', while 'two old Bristol Listeners' thought her speech 'wonderful'. As did, evidently, the Prince of Wales, for he mentioned Maud personally in his address to the League on 11 December 1929:

> Lady Tree has added still more to the debt of gratitude which the League owes [...] During the past fortnight, by the kindness of the British Broadcasting Company and with the generous assistance of Mr. Ainley, Mr. Harry Dearth and Mr. Leslie Henson, she broadcast an appeal which has met with the splendid response of practically £700.[21]

If once Maud could boast of having 'drawn the crowd' with her rendition of 'The Absent-Minded Beggar', she could be equally proud of her no less mean contribution to the League. But now it was time for her to get back to the business of theatre.

Notes to Chapter 17

1. Maud's name at birth was registered Hellen Maud Holt, with no mention of 'Louise'.
2. This is no fanciful claim: junior officers typically came from the public school and university-educated sector, sons of the aristocracy, and landed gentry Not only their orders but their upbringing put them in the line of fire, where they consciously took the greatest risks. These men were also fitter than their working-class counterparts. Over one million men examined in 1917–18 alone were found to be unfit for combat. The total of Oxford and Cambridge graduates killed came to 4,933.
3. 'So he died magnificently commanding his Battery'; see Beerbohm 1924: 88.
4. Lewis Arthur to Maud Tree, 7 August 1920 (MBTC 6).
5. Edith, Lady Lyttelton to Maud Tree, 1 January 1918 (MBTC).
6. Philip Burne-Jones to Maud Tree, [n.d.] (MBTC 6).
7. Mrs Alec Tweedie to Maud Tree, 1 November 1920 (MBTC 2).
8. Leon M. Lion to Maud Tree, 30 October 1921 (MBTC 6).
9. See Bingham 1979: 77.
10. Sir Philip Bourchier-Wrey to Maud Tree, 6 June 1919 and 29 January 1922 (MBTC 2).
11. John Gielgud was not unknown to Maud, being the son of her good friend Kate Terry.
12. Born Alice Lapize, Delysia was discovered by C. B. Cochran in 1914. Within five years she had reached superstar status when she was transferred to the New York stage for £2,500 (the equivalent of £800,000 today). Delysia had performed with Viola Tree at the Pan Ball at Covent Garden on 15 January 1920.
13. Maud also wrote several articles for the *Sketch* entitled: 'In Defence of Baby Faces' (2 December 1923); 'Christians and the Stage' (11 June 1926); 'The Wife a Man Wants'; and 'Keep the Chaperones' (1933) (MBTC).
14. Maud Tree to Felicity Tree, [n.d.] (SCW, letter 1567).
15. Agate 1924.
16. Pamela, Countess of Lytton (née Chichele-Plowden) was Winston Churchill's first great love. She married Lord Edward Robert Bulwer-Lytton, son of the novelist Edward Bulwer-Lytton, who became Acting Viceroy of India.
17. Leslie Henson to Maud Tree, 20 July 1936 (SCW, letter 954).
18. See Moffat 2004: 61.
19. Anon. to Maud Tree, [n.d.] (MBTC 6).
20. Rudyard Kipling to Maud Tree, 21 May 1928 (MBTC 6).
21. Anonymous letter entitled 'Two Listeners', 27 November 1929 (MBTC 6). £700 would have amounted to an equivalent income value of approximately £200,000 today.

CHAPTER 18

The Man Who Could Work Miracles
1931–37

Towards the end of the 1920s Maud acted in a couple of plays indicative of the kind of theatrical fare that would soon be adapted for films. *Alibi,* which premiered at the Prince of Wales Theatre on 15 May 1928, running for 255 performances, was the first ever staging of an Agatha Christie novel; in fact it was the first adaptation of a Christie work in any medium.[1] Directed once again by Maud's favourite Gerald du Maurier, and based on the novel *The Murder of Roger Ackroyd*, the stage version was dramatized by Michael Morton who was known to Maud for having written *Colonel Newcome* especially for Herbert Tree over twenty years earlier. *Alibi* was to become just as much a winner starring Charles Laughton as Hercule Poirot. The link with the past was not lost on the critic who, in the *Stage* of 11 July 1929, praised Laughton for revealing 'under his skin [...] the old Tree quality of subtlety', while Maud as Mrs Ackroyd, was thought to have created 'an uncanny atmosphere'.

The other production, a year later, was *Beauty,* again starring Charles Laughton and once again adapted by Michael Morton from Jacques Deval's original *Beauté*, with Maud playing Honoria Sopite. (In a neat reversal, Deval would subsequently translate *Alibi* into French.)[2] But in amongst the crime and comedy came a stream of innovative plays featuring families and family life during the inter-war years. They once again appeared perfectly to reflect Maud's personal life and she was ideally placed to act in them, as if all that was required was to step out of her own domestic drama to appear in a fictitious counterpart. These new women's dramas featured matriarchal, maternal figures as the resolvers of family conflict and the maintainers of order within the family unit. Moving away from the Ibsenesque model, plays such as Dodie Smith's *Call It a Day* or Gertrude Jennings's *Our Own Lives,* (which appeared simultaneously at the Globe and Ambassador Theatres respectively), continued to foreground questions of heredity, matrilinearity, femininity, gender, economic power, and division of power, but unlike Ibsen's all-suffering Nora, the matriarchs in these plays offered two principal models: the wisely tender (with lace and bustle) and the strongly dictatorial (with ebony stick).[3] Maud could be either but in this instance chose to play the Duchess of Stroud in *Our Own Lives*.

And then in the 1930s came the major transition from silent to sound film. But while these new 'talkies' were exciting and innovative, technical difficulties multiplied and production costs soared as a consequence. Furthermore, many of the hitherto idols of the silent screen were unable to adjust their work to the new sound technology. European film-makers were further hindered by the huge costs they were forced to meet if they wished to use a sound system for which only Hollywood owned the patents. The 1927 Cinematography Film Act was designed to counter this problem by artificially inflating the market and stimulating a failing British film industry. In practical terms this meant that cinemas were required to show a quota of British films, the defining criteria for which were that the film had to be made by a British or British-controlled company, that studio scenes must be photographed within a film studio in the British Empire or Commonwealth, that the author of the original work or screenplay must be a British subject and that at least seventy-five per cent of the salaries must be paid to British subjects — though with the additional proviso that a British film could engage an international star, producer, or director and still be considered British.

The consequence of all this was twofold. On the one hand, the Act was said to be responsible for the speculative, boom-or-bust investment in the lavish productions emerging from Korda's London Films studios which could never hope to recoup their production costs. On the other hand, it generated a rise in the so-called 'quota quickies', low-cost, poor-quality films commissioned by American distributors operating in Britain solely to satisfy the quota requirements. Over the next few years Maud acted in several Korda films that fell into one or other of these categories. In 1930 she played the granny (of the ebony-stick variety) in *Such is the Law*, a British-made film directed by the Hon. Pamela Boscawen and Sinclair Hill, and starring C. Aubrey Smith. It was about a mother who attempts to save her daughter's marriage, a subject somewhat close to the bone for Maud at the time, as daughter Iris had only recently declined to return home to England (or to her husband and child), having abandoned the play *The Miracle* (and Diana Cooper) and preferring to stay on in America with a man she had fallen in love with. Off stage, the complexity of Maud's domestic arrangements would only intensify as a result, but on stage (or rather screen) she was considered 'splendid', the film, according to E. A. Baughan in the *Weekly Dispatch* in November 1930, a 'box office certainty, first from the big list of star performers and secondly from the fine combination of silent and "talkie"'.

Maud's next engagement, dressed in lace and bustle and following swiftly on the heels of the Boscawen/Hill film, was as Lady Stokeshire in *Wedding Rehearsal*, the first picture to be directed by Alexander Korda for London Film Productions in 1932. Publicity for the film said it was 'joyous, witty and sparkling [...] likened to champagne of the highest vintage', and it starred Merle Oberon and Roland Young, who had travelled from Hollywood specially to appear in it.[4] Another 'quota quickie' a year later was *Her Imaginary Lover,* based on a play by A. E. W. Mason called *Green Stockings* and directed by George King for Warner Brothers. Maud was 'splendid as the grandmother' (*Embassy* of 4 May 1933) in a romantic tale about a New York socialite who invents an aristocratic English fiancé to deflect her other suitors, only to find of course, that the imaginary romance becomes real.

Maud's theatre engagements now began to compete with her film appearances as her need for work intensified. In January 1933 Viola's husband Alan Parsons died at the age of only forty-three and Viola was forced more or less to give up the stage to look after their children. Iris, pregnant with her second child whom she was secretly planning to have adopted by Diana Cooper, had formally left her firstborn to Maud, and with the birth of Felicity's fifth son Maud's grandchildren now totalled ten. On 4 May of the same year, Maud made her 'rentrée', as the critic for the *Embassy* called it, as a 'weather-beaten' (if not exhausted) 'old she-dragon' in a revival at the Ambassadors Theatre of Sheridan's *The Rivals*. The critic continued:

> To utter with point and consummate ease all the long series of nice derangement of epitaphs delivered con amore [...] making a hit of the evening. It was delightful to see and hear Sir Herbert's widow again gracing the boards [...] As already indicated [...] the main successes of this ably carried out Sheridan revival were those made by Lady Tree and Mr. Holloway.

But Maud was soon back again on screen, and between August and November she acted in a further two Korda films. Korda had quickly come to replace du Maurier in Maud's affections; she would refer to him coyly as 'he who shall remain nameless'.[5] She played the King's nurse, in *The Private Life of Henry VIII*, a film starring Charles Laughton (with whom she had last acted in *Alibi*), his real-life wife Elsa Lanchester, Robert Donat, Wendy Barrie, and Merle Oberon. Both Barrie and Oberon had also played in *Wedding Rehearsal,* and Oberon would soon marry Korda, appearing in many of his subsequent films. It was a lavish commercial creation and proved Oberon's springboard to stardom as well as a huge success, in fact the twelfth most successful film at the US box office, taking a colossal £500,000 on its initial release. It gained Laughton an Academy Award for his part as Henry and was the first British production to be nominated for an Academy Award for Best Picture. At ninety-seven minutes in duration, it was also as far removed from any Shakespeare play Maud had ever experienced, reminiscent rather of J. M. Barrie's *Macbeth* spoof. Catherine of Aragon (who was in fact written out of the story completely) was referred to as 'a respectable lady', and the film carried the tagline:

> He gave his wives a pain in the neck
> And did his necking with an axe...
> Every woman got it in the neck — Eventually.[6]

As with her next film, released a month later, there was a strong link with the past, but any similarity with the Feydeau plays that Maud had known was dispelled in *The Girl from Maxim's,* in which she played Gabrielle Petypon. Uniting a brilliant team, Harry Graham's screenplay was based on the original 1899 Feydeau farce, *La Dame de Chez Maxim,* which Maud alone was old enough to remember seeing at first hand. As if acknowledging the debt to the many years of plagiarism and liberal adaptation from the French, to which the English stage owed so much, Korda made a French-language version at the same time. A sort of *Pygmalion* story, the film starred Stanley Holloway (who had last acted with Maud in *The Rivals*) and George Grossmith in a 'hilarious' comedy about a doctor who is forced to pass off a singer as his wife. Grossmith, speaking to *The Times* (20 June 1933) said that 'Lady Tree added magnificently to the brilliant comedy of the picture [...] and the lavish settings are some of the most magnificent ever seen'.

Maud's next film role was somewhat more adventurous, if not entirely politic, for in the same month that Hitler was appointed Chancellor of Germany and Hindenburg dissolved the Reichstag, Maud travelled to Berlin to play Frau Seidelblast in a British-German film called *Early to Bed*. Between 1920 and 1969 Ludwig Berger directed thirty-six films, including the recent *The Vagabond King*, which had been produced entirely in two-colour Technicolor, the ultimate in state-of-the-art technology at the time. Now, in 1933, Berger's latest film was equally innovative, a multiple-language production with three separate versions modelled on the German original *Ich bei Tag und du bei Nacht* [I By Day and You By Night]. Created at the Babelsberg Studio along with its French and German counterparts, it ran for eighty-three minutes and premiered on the 27 November, the month in which the Nazi party won ninety-two per cent of votes cast in an election. Berger wrote to Maud that 'after seeing yesterday's rushes' he just wanted to thank her 'for the sincere way' her art had 'impressed' him.[7]

Between January 1935 and 1936 Maud appeared in revivals, new plays, and films that both encapsulated the range of her work and neatly brought it full circle. In January, she played Mrs Candour in *The School for Scandal*, once again reprising a role that had brought her such acclaim on other occasions. From February to May she was then again at His Majesty's Theatre performing, as was fitting, Shakespeare. Giving up any pretence to vanity, Maud was wimpled and virtually shapeless in a vast skirt and apron as Mistress Quickly in *Henry IV, Part 1*. Produced by Robert Atkins, the play starred John Drinkwater as King Henry IV and George Robey as Falstaff, the role once made so flamboyantly his own by Herbert Tree. Extracts from the show were then heard on the BBC on 15 March in what formed part of the *London Theatre Series*, produced by Val Gielgud (Sir John's elder brother), head of productions at the BBC at the time.

But no sooner had *Henry IV, Part I*, come to an end than *The Mask of Virtue* opened at the Ambassadors later that same month. Set in 1760 Paris, this adaptation from Carl Sternheim's original *La Marquise d'Arcis*, formed the ideal backdrop not for Maud but for the beautiful Vivien Leigh, who would make a triumphant debut. Nevertheless, the *Morning Post* of 25 May 1935 said that 'Lady Tree gives a perfect display of costume, character and manners', while Leigh described her as 'dear Lady Tree who has spent so many wonderful years doing triumphantly what I am just trying to do with all my inexperience, my want of knowledge'.[8]

But age could still come before beauty in what would be Maud's last ever play, *Our Own Lives*, which opened at the same theatre six months later. In fact, the author of an article entitled 'The People and the Play' for the *Catholic Herald* in 1935 wrote that he was left with the 'melancholy thought that very few of our younger actresses, admirable in other ways, look like achieving a quarter of her finesse. Lady Tree is riotously funny in the sort of part that Pinero wrote when he was young'. Like Dodie Smith (alias C. L. Anthony) Gertrude Jennings had written 'a woman's play that men will enjoy'. But the moral at the heart of her *Our Own Lives,* which transports the action of a modern-day *Le Weekend* to Venice, is the necessity of doing precisely that. Its conclusion — that 'the decree nisi is perilously near, but the curtain drops in time to save the play's respectability' — is part of what the

FIG. 18.1. Maud Tree as Mistress Quickly in *King Henry IV, Part I* at His Majesty's Theatre, 29 April 1935 (photograph by Leadlay-Dallison)

The Duchess and the Tripper. Duchess of Stroud (Lady Tree) and George Bunting (Lewis Stringer).

FIG. 18.2. Maud Tree as the Duchess of Stroud in
Our Own Lives at the Ambassadors Theatre (*Play Pictorial*, 67: 404)

article calls the 'destructive idealism' begun with Ibsen. However, as the December edition of the *Play Pictorial* surmised, 'beautiful studies from Lady Tree and Stanley Lathbury', as the knitting duchess and a dry-as-dust bookworm, alone made the play 'worth the price of one's ticket'.[9]

For the previous few months, however, Maud had been unwell. Years of financial and domestic juggling coupled with sheer hard work had at last taken their toll. Nonetheless, there were still moments of humour to be enjoyed on the home front with the toing and froing of grandchildren and the chaos generated by the nannies and governesses required to look after them. When a grandchild's pet rabbit died Maud deliberated for days as to how best the news might be broken and whether the truth — the pet had died of kindness (or at any rate some nougat stuck in the throat) — would do more harm than good. And too old and too tired to be much bothered with minor considerations, Maud dispatched her grandson Ivan to his new boarding school dressed not in the habitual tweed jacket but a green silk blouse embroidered with an enormous scarlet dragon. He recounts many other amusing anecdotes to do with her attempts at maintaining their unravelling status quo in his autobiographical 'file'.[10]

But professionally, it was somehow fitting that in rounding off her extensive career Maud's final screen appearance should be in a whimsical film based on a work by H. G. Wells, when one of her first roles had also been in one of the same author's adaptations. In 1881 Maud had played Olivia Primrose, a woman possessing 'that luxuriance of beauty with which painters generally draw Hebe' in a play Wells based on Oliver Goldsmith's one and only novel, *The Vicar of Wakefield*.[11] Now, over half a century later, she was an old woman working as one Mr Grigsby's housekeeper. First published in 1898 as a short story in *The Illustrated London News*, *The Man Who Could Work Miracles* starred Roland Young as the ordinary 'little' man who is elevated to unimaginable greatness. As a film it displayed innovative, state-of-the-art special effects and made stars of the actors Michael Rennie and George Sanders. Directed by Lothar Mendes and produced once again by Korda, it was said by Frank S. Nugent in the *New York Times* of 22 February 1937 to strike a 'sound balance between the jocund and the profound'. Released on 8 February 1936, it would be adapted for radio on New Year's Day 1959, starring Tony Hancock; in 2003 it would also be the inspiration for the American comedy film *Bruce Almighty*, directed by Tom Shadyac and starring Jim Carrey. But now however, the film's opening, in which a trio of gods discuss the worthiness of Earth, must have given Maud cause to reflect on a life that was quietly coming to an end; only now there would be no miracle to right her world. In the days that followed she quipped that she supposed her lawyer had come to teach her her 'death duties'.[12] She did not act again and after undergoing treatment at University College London hospital, she died there following an operation on 7 August 1937. Her three daughters, Viola, Felicity, and Iris were all with her at the end.

Maud's coffin was covered with a grey velvet cloth and a cross composed of lilies. Her ten grandchildren sent a wreath and there were numerous floral tributes representing members of the theatre world and the various charities with which she had been associated. A few days later, on 12 August, her body was cremated in a far quieter ceremony than Herbert's had been, her ashes buried with his and alongside their son-in-law Alan Parsons. Written tributes poured in from friends and colleagues. Frank Benson wrote in the *Sunday Times* of 8 August 1937 that 'the theatre had lost a brilliant, witty actress and society a leading figure. There is so much I would care to say but I am overcome'. In the *Daily Telegraph* of 9 August 1937 Sybil Thorndike remembered Maud for her 'overwhelming kindness, particularly to the young'. Queen Mary, who wrote to Maud's daughters, recalled the fun times they had enjoyed together. Violet Lindsay was bereft. Maud's obituary, appearing in papers across the country was given over to analysis of her many stage roles. After a life straddling two centuries, the *Sunday Pictorial* of 8 August 1937 called her 'the Stage's Grand Old Lady'.

By the end of her life, Maud was indeed grand and an old hand at her craft. In the days after her death she was remembered for her tremendous wit, the laughter that consumed her household, her devotion to her family. She had seen three monarchs come to the throne, the First World War, and advances in virtually every field of transport and technology. She had been with the Prime Minister when he planned the Battle of Jutland, visited Balmoral, Buckingham Palace, and the White House as guests of the respective heads of state. She was a close friend of some of the greatest artists, writers, and musicians of the age. In her profession specifically, she had further developed the music hall versus theatre debate, aligned herself with the experimental theatre of the continent to promote the work of Ibsen and Strindberg, and not only witnessed the advent of, but taken part in silent films and talkies. More importantly, she had seen at first hand the ascent of the actress from something little more than a harlot to attain the celebrity status she enjoys today.

Throughout her life, Maud appeared in many roles to many people: assuming a mask, and in particular one of humour, was second nature to her. But she had always, through action and example, demonstrated an unflinching sense of duty to family and to her profession. Likewise, the free, romantic spirit that compelled her to cancel her grandchildren's lessons when she heard the first cuckoo in spring remained with her to the end. Nonetheless, in a letter that Maud wrote to Viola she gives a portrait of herself in which she is first and foremost an actress. In this she is stripped of family, of social status, and is simply a woman revelling in her craft. The portrait presented is as Maud saw herself, and it is an image that endures:

> Think of me at midnight, tonight darling and write me my beauty back —
> Try + see before you a woman no longer in her first youth but with that indescribable air of mystery + wonder which only <u>time</u> can prime upon delicate features — features at no time remarkable for their regularity but now fantastic, whimsical. I had almost said exaggerated in their placid imperfection — think of me a tall, pliant figure swathed rather than clothed in radiant yellow fabric, trailing, unconventional with an enormous bunch of Neapolitan violets almost concealing the rounded curves of the somewhat attenuated bosom — think of my misty brown hair, clasped, confined, almost nailed to a small head by a heavy richly pearled medieval bandeau whither the small white hands wander restlessly from moment to moment.[13]

Notes to Chapter 18

1. *Alibi* was made into a film in 1931 and presented as a radio play by the BBC in 1944.
2. Jacques Boularan (1890–1972) known as Jacques Deval, French playwright married to the actress Claude Godard.
3. *Our Own Lives* was staged in December 1935.
4. Brochure for the Gaumont-British Picture Corporation, Ltd.
5. Fielding 1974: 112.
6. See Ball 2013: 223–25.
7. Ludwig Berger to Maud Tree, 14 August 1933 (MBTC 3).
8. Vivien Leigh, in the *Theatre Illustrated Quarterly* (Summer 1935).
9. *Play Pictorial*, 67 (1935), 404.
10. Maud Tree to Ivan Moffat, 1929 (MBTC 6). See Moffat 2004: 67–69.
11. Goldsmith 2008: 11.
12. Fielding 1974: 112.
13. Maud Tree to Viola Tree, [1923] (MBTC 6).

APPENDIX

List of Theatre Roles

Date	Role and Play	Author	Theatre
30 Jan 1883	Jenny Northcott in *Sweethearts*	W. S. Gilbert	Gaiety
08 May 1883	Mrs Stern in *Knowledge*	Unknown	Gaiety
25 May 1883	Olivia in *Twelfth Night*	William Shakespeare	Gaiety
Sep 1883	Barbara Nugent in *Elsie*	Agnes Maitland	Globe
27 Sep 1883	Hester Gould in *The Millionaire*	G. W. Godfrey	Court
17 Feb 1884	Maud in *Six and Eightpence*	Herbert Tree	Prince's
18 Feb 1884	Margery Blackburn in *Margery's Lovers*	Henry Stephens	Court
02 Feb 1885	Thordisa in *The White Pilgrim*	Herman Merivale	Olympic
16 Feb 1885	Marie Graham in *In His Power*	Mark Quinton	Court
Aug 1885	Charlotte in *The Magistrate*	Arthur Pinero	Court
17 Feb 1886	Belinda Treherne in *Engaged*	W. S. Gilbert	Haymarket
17 May 1886	Oenone in *Helena in Troas*	John Todhunter	Hengler's Circus
23 Oct 1886	Miss Moxon in *The Hobby Horse*	Arthur Pinero	St. James's
03 Mar 1887	Lady Clencarty in *Clencarty*	Tom Taylor	St. James's
15 Sep 1887	Princess Claudia Morakoff in *The Red Lamp*	W. Outram Tristram	Haymarket
11 Jan 1888	Mlle de Florian in *Incognito*	Baron Josef von Eichendorff	Haymarket
31 Mar 1888	Marquise de Pompadour in *Pompadour*	H. G. Wells & Sydney Grundy	Haymarket
20 Jun 1888	Stella Darbishire in *Captain Swift*	C. Haddon Chambers	Crystal Palace
13 Sep 1888	Anne Page in *The Merry Wives of Windsor*	William Shakespeare	Crystal Palace

05 Dec 1888	Mabel Vane in *Masks and Faces*	Tom Taylor and Charles Reade	Haymarket
03 Apr 1889	Marguerite in *A Village Priest*	Sydney Grundy	Haymarket
27 Apr 1889	Edith Ruddock in *Wealth*	Henry Arthur Jones	Haymarket
12 Sep 1889	Henriette Laroque in *A Man's Shadow*	Robert Buchanan	Haymarket
16 Oct 1889	Lady Teazle in *The School for Scandal*	R. B. Sheridan	Crystal Palace
03 Nov 1890	Dorothy Musgrave in *Beau Austin*	W. E. Henley and Robert Louis Stevenson	Haymarket
09 Sep 1891	Ophelia in *Hamlet*	William Shakespeare	Theatre Royal, Manchester
21 Jan 1892	Ophelia in *Hamlet*	William Shakespeare	Haymarket
11 May 1892	Zanetto in *The Waif*	Cotsford Dick, adaptation of François Coppée's *Le Passant*	Haymarket
15 Aug 1892	Sybil Crake in *The Dancing Girl*	Henry Arthur Jones	Grand, Islington
19 Apr 1893	Mrs Allonby in *A Woman of No Importance*	Oscar Wilde	Haymarket
20 Sep 1893	Lady Avis Rougemont in *The Tempter*	Henry Arthur Jones	Haymarket
18 Jan 1894	Isabel Arlington in *The Charlatan*	Robert Buchanan	Haymarket
28 Mar 1894	Rita in *Once Upon a Time*	Adapted by Louis N. Parker and H. Tree from Ludwig Fulda's *Der Talisman*	Haymarket
25 Apr 1894	Mrs Murgatoyd in *A Bunch of Violets*	Adapted by Sydney Grundy from Octave Feuillet's *Montjoye*	Haymarket
02 Jul 1894	Vivien Hereford in *A Modern Eve*	Malcolm C. Salaman	Haymarket
28 Jan 1895	Princess Claudia in *The Red Lamp*	W. Outram Tristram	Abbey's, New York
02 Apr 1895	Kate Cloud in *John-A-Dreams*	C. Haddon Chambers	Haymarket
Jun 1895	Fedora in *Fedora*	Adapted by Herman Merivale from Victorien Sardou's *Dora*	Haymarket

27 Dec 1895	Hon. Nina Keith in *A Woman's Reason*	Charles Brookfield	Shaftesbury
08 May 1896	Lady Percy in *King Henry IV, Part I*	William Shakespeare	Haymarket
02 Sep 1896	Trilby in *Trilby*	George du Maurier's play, adapted by Paul M. Potter	Borough Theatre, Stratford
28 Apr 1897	Mme de Cournal in *The Seats of the Mighty*	Gilbert Parker	Her Majesty's
03 May 1897	Mrs Wilton in *John Gabriel Borkman*	Henrik Ibsen	The Strand
10 Jul 1897	Marquise de Prie in *The Silver Key*	Sydney Grundy	Her Majesty's
01 Nov 1897	Katharine in *Katharine and Petruchio*	Garrick's version of Shakespeare's *The Taming of the Shrew*	Her Majesty's
22 Jan 1898	Lucius in *Julius Caesar*	William Shakespeare	Her Majesty's
23 Jun 1898	Alison in *Ragged Robin*	Adapted by L. N. Parker from *Le Chemineau* by Jean Richepin	Her Majesty's
03 Nov 1898	Anne of Austria and Miladi in *The Musketeers*	Sydney Grundy, based on the Alexandre Dumas novel	Her Majesty's
Oct 1899	Recitation of *The Absent-Minded Beggar*	Rudyard Kipling	Alhambra and Palace
10 Jan 1900	Titania in *A Midsummer Night's Dream*	William Shakespeare	Her Majesty's
06 Sep 1900	Calpurnia in *Julius Caesar*	William Shakespeare	Her Majesty's
24 Jan 1901	Lady Summershire in *Last of the Dandies*	Clyde Fitch	Her Majesty's
28 Oct 1901	Mary in *The Likeness of the Night*	Mrs W. L. Clifford	St. James's
Mar 1902	Directing *Heard on the Telephone* (in which she played Marie Marex), *Irish Assurance* and *Caesar's Wife* (in which she played Léonore de Gourgiran)	André de Lorde; William Bernard; Paul Hervieu	Wyndham's
10 Jun 1902	Anne Page in the Coronation revival of *The Merry Wives of Windsor*	William Shakespeare	His Majesty's
17 Jan 1903	Mistress Ford in *The Merry Wives of Windsor*	William Shakespeare	His Majesty's

Date	Role	Author	Theatre
17 Sep 1903	Baroness Pitchioli in *The Flood Tide*	Cecil Raleigh	Drury Lane
Nov 1904	Henriette Laroque in *A Man's Shadow*	Robert Buchanan	Windsor Castle
27 Apr 1905	Ophelia in *Hamlet*	William Shakespeare	His Majesty's
28 Apr 1905	Beatrice in *Much Ado About Nothing*	William Shakespeare	His Majesty's
May 1905	Gertrude, Queen of Denmark, in *Hamlet*	William Shakespeare	His Majesty's
25 Jan 1906	Agrippina in *Nero*	Stephen Phillips	His Majesty's
22 May 1906	Mrs Seabrooke in *Captain Swift*	C. Haddon Chambers	His Majesty's
29 May 1906	Mrs Mackenzie in *The Newcomes*	Adapted by Michael Morton from Thackeray's novel	His Majesty's
Sep 1906	Paulina in *The Winter's Tale*	William Shakespeare	His Majesty's
11 Feb 1908	Clytemnestra in *Electra*	Hugo von Hofmannsthal	Garden Theatre, New York
28 May 1908	Mrs James in *The Grey Stocking*	Maurice Baring	Royalty
23 Jun 1908	Mrs Fitzgerald in *The Drums of Doom*	Hubert Woodyward	Scala
03 Sep 1908	Comtesse de la Brière in *What Every Woman Knows*	J. M. Barrie	Duke of York's
09 Dec 1908	Madame X in *The Stronger Woman*	August Strindberg	His Majesty's
31 Jan 1910	Biskra in *The Sirocco*	Arthur Scott Craven	Olympia, Liverpool
15 Oct 1910	Mrs Insole in *Grace*	W. Somerset Maugham	Duke of York's
28 Feb 1911	Olive in *The Great Man*	Unknown	His Majesty's
22 May 1911	Portia in *Julius Caesar*	William Shakespeare	His Majesty's
27 Jun 1911	Tilburnia in *The Critic*	R. B. Sheridan	Duke of York's
21 Oct 1911	Comtesse de la Brière in *What Every Woman Knows*	J. M. Barrie	Duke of York's
08 Jun 1912	Mistress Page in *The Merry Wives of Windsor*	William Shakespeare	His Majesty's
26 Mar 1913	Lady Henry Fairfax in *Diplomacy*	Clement Scott and Mrs Bancroft from Victorien Sardou's *Dora*	Wyndham's
28 Jan 1915	*Entente Matinée*	Various	His Majesty's
June 1915★	Lady Sorel in *The Angel in the House*	Eden Phillpotts and Basil Macdonald Hastings	Savoy

List of Theatre Roles

	Kate in *The Passing of the First Floor Back*	J. C. Jerome	Unknown
	The Countess in *The Admirable Crichton*	J. M. Barrie	Unknown
	Cynisca in *Pygmalion and Galatea*	W. S. Gilbert	Unknown
	Henrietta Lamson in *The Bill*	Lady Randolph Churchill	Prince of Wales's
02 May 1916*	*The Merry Wives of Windsor*	William Shakespeare	Drury Lane
16 May 1916*	Zelda Sears in *The Show Shop*	James Forbes	Globe
19 May 1916*	Hyged in *King Lear's Wife*	Gordon Bottomley	His Majesty's
July 1916*	*The Little Silver Ring*	Edward Knoblauch	Regent's Park
July 1916*	Lady Trent in *War Committee*	Edward Knoblauch	Haymarket
02 Feb 1917*	Mrs Candour in *The School for Scandal*	R. B. Sheridan	Unknown
22 Feb 1919	Queen Mother in *A Certain Liveliness*	Basil Macdonald Hastings	St. Martin's
Feb 1920	Lady Tonbridge in *The Young Person in Pink*	Gertrude Jennings	Prince of Wales's
9 Aug 1920	Mrs Wharton in *The Unknown*	W. Somerset Maugham	Aldwych
Nov 1920	Mrs Clandon in *You Never Can Tell*	George Bernard Shaw	Garrick
29 Oct 1921	The Countess of Crewkerne in *Araminta Arrives*	J. C. Snaith and Dorothy Brandon	Comedy
09 Mar 1922	Gabrielle in *Mayfair and Montmartre*	C. B. Cochran Revue	New Oxford
27 May 1922	Mrs Preen in *Shall We Join the Ladies?*	J. M. Barrie	RADA
Feb 1923	La Fronchard in *The Two Orphans*	Adaptation of Adolphe d'Ennery and Eugène Moar's *Les Deux Orphelines*	Lyceum
May 1923	Comtesse de la Brière in *What Every Woman Knows*	J. M. Barrie	Apollo

* Denotes performances given for charity. Often roles were from short scenes taken from a play. For instance, Maud abandoned her role in *The Show Shop* after only a few performances and was able to take on other work.

Mar 1924	Lady Henry Fairfax in *Diplomacy*	Clement Scott and Mrs Bancroft from Victorien Sardou's *Dora*	Adelphi
Dec 1924	'Comic Queen' in *A Kiss for Cinderella*	J. M. Barrie	St. James's
Sep 1925	Lady Maria in *The Last of Mrs Cheyney*	Frederick Lonsdale	St. James's
Aug 1926	Grand Duchess Emilie in *The Queen was in the Parlour*	Noel Coward	St. Martin's
Jun 1927	Baroness in *The Spot in the Sun*	Unknown	Ambassadors
May 1928	Mrs Ackroyd in *Alibi*	Michael Morton's adaptation of an Agatha Christie novel	Prince of Wales's
May 1933	Mrs Malaprop in *The Rivals*	R. B. Sheridan	Embassy
Jan 1934	Mrs Malaprop in *The Rivals*	R. B. Sheridan	Ambassadors
Jan 1935	Mrs Candour in *The School for Scandal*	R. B. Sheridan	Bournemouth
Feb–Apr 1935	Mistress Quickly in *King Henry IV, Part I*	William Shakespeare	His Majesty's
May 1935	Madame Duquesnoy in *The Mask of Virtue*	Carl Sternheim	Ambassadors
Nov 1935 to Jan 1936	The Duchess of Stroud in *Our Own Lives*	Gertrude Jennings	Ambassadors

Maud Tree's Film Appearances

1916 Mrs Sternhold in *Still Waters Run Deep* (dir. Fred Paul)
1920 Mrs Clennam in *Little Dorrit* (dir. Sydney Morgan)
1920 Granny in *Such is the Law* (dir. Sinclair Hill)
1932 Countess of Stokeshire in *Wedding Rehearsal* (dir. Alexander Korda)
1933 Grandma in *Her Imaginary Lover* (dir. George King)
1933 The King's Nurse in *The Private Life of Henry VIII* (dir. Alexander Korda)
1933 Madame Petypon in *The Girl from Maxim's* (dir. Alexander Korda)
1933 Widow Seidelblast in *Early to Bed* (dir. Ludwig Berger)
1936 Grigsby's Housekeeper in *The Man Who Could Work Miracles* (dir. Lothar Mendes)

BIBLIOGRAPHY

AGATE, JAMES. 1924. [Review of *A Kiss for Cinderella*], *Dramatic World* (28 December)
ANON. 1846. 'Modern Guardians of the Drama, their Qualifications and Attainments', *Theatrical Times* (25 July)
ANON. 1896A. 'Actress and Actress', *Theatre* (1 August), 58–61
ANON. 1896B. 'Female Dramatists of the Past', *Era* (23 May)
ANON. 1899. 'Model Mothers: Mrs Beerbohm Tree', *Home Chat* (4 March)
ANON. 1900. 'London's Lady Managers: A Chat with Miss Janette Steer', *Era* (2 June)
ARIA, ELIZA. 1906. *Costume: Fanciful, Historical and Theatrical* (London: Macmillan)
ASHWELL, LENA. 1936. *Myself a Player* (London: Michael Joseph)
AUERBACH, NINA. 1982. *Woman and the Demon: The Life of a Victorian Myth* (Cambridge, MA, & London: Harvard University Press)
—— 1987. *Ellen Terry: Player in Her Time* (Philadelphia: University of Pennsylvania Press)
BALL, ROBERT HAMILTON. 2013. *Shakespeare on Silent Film: A Strange Eventful History* (London: Routledge)
BAILEY, CATHERINE. 2012. *The Secret Rooms* (London: Viking)
BARRIE, J. M. 1926. *What Every Woman Knows* (London, New York, & Sydney: Samuel French)
BARTHOLOMEUSZ, DENNIS. 1982. *The Winter's Tale in Performance in England and America, 1611–1976* (Cambridge: Cambridge University Press)
BAUGHAN, E. A. 1902A. 'London Theatrical Topics', *New York Times*, 5 March
—— 1902B. 'London Theatrical Topics', *New York Times*, 16 March
BEERBOHM, MAX. 1924. *Herbert Beerbohm Tree — Some Memories of Him and of His Art Collected by Max Beerbohm* (London: Hutchinson)
BINGHAM, MADELEINE. 1979. *The Great Lover: The Life & Art of Herbert Beerbohm Tree* (New York: Atheneum)
BLATHWAYT, RAYMOND. 1898. *Does the Theatre make for Good: An Interview with Mr. Clement Scott* (London: A. W. Hall)
BOOTH, MICHAEL. R. 1981. *Victorian Spectacular Theatre, 1850–1910* (London: Routledge & Kegan Paul)
BOOTH, MICHAEL. R., and JOEL. H. KAPLAN, eds. 1996. *The Edwardian Theatre* (Cambridge: Cambridge University Press)
BRECHT, BERTHOLD. 1965. *The Messingkauf Dialogues*, trans. by John Willett (London: Methuen)
CAMPBELL, BEATRICE STELLA. 1922. *My Life and Some Letters* (London: Hutchinson)
CECIL, DAVID. 1985. *Max: A Biography* (New York: Atheneum)
CERASCO, G. A. 1993. 'Divorce: the 1890s', in *The 1890s: An Encyclopaedia of British Literature, Art and Culture*, ed. by G. A. Cevasco (New York: Garland)
CHISHOLM, HUGH. 1911. 'Paul Hervieu', in *Encyclopaedia Britannica*, 11th edn (Cambridge & New York: Cambridge University Press)
CLIFFORD, LUCY. 1900. *The Likeness of the Night* (London: A. & C. Black)
COLLIER, CONSTANCE. 1929. *Harlequinade: The Story of My Life* (London: Bodley Head)

Cooper, Diana. 1954. *Old Men Forget* (London: Rupert Hart-Davis)
—— 1958. *The Rainbow Comes and Goes* (London: Rupert Hart-Davis)
Cory-Wright, Susana. 2011. 'An Annotated Edition of the Selected Correspondence of Maud, Lady Tree: 1880–1917' (PhD thesis, De Montfort University, Leicester)
—— 2012. *Lady Tree: A Theatrical Life in Letters* (Lola Press)
—— 2017. *The London Wife* (Kindle Direct Publishing)
Cowman, Krista. 1998. 'A Party Between Revolution and Peaceful Persuasion: A Fresh Look at the United Suffragists', in *The Women's Suffrage Movement: New Feminist Perspectives*, ed. by Maroula Joannou and June Purvis (Manchester & New York: Manchester University Press), pp. 77–89
Craig, Edward Gordon. 1932. *Ellen Terry and Her Secret Self* (London: Sampson Low)
Crosse, Gordon. 1953. *Shakespearean Playgoing, 1890–1952* (London: A. R. Mowbray)
Davenport-Hines, R. 1988. *Ettie: The Intimate Life and Dauntless Spirit of Lady Desborough* (London: Weidenfeld & Nicolson)
Davis, Tracy C. 1991. *Actresses as Working Women: Their Social Identity in Victorian Culture* (London & New York: Routledge)
—— 1992. 'Indecency and Vigilance in the Music Halls in British Theatre in the 1890s', in *Essays on Drama and the Stage*, ed. by Richard Foulkes (Cambridge: Cambridge University Press), pp. 111–31
—— 2000. *The Economics of the British Stage 1800–1914* (Cambridge: Cambridge University Press)
Dibdin, Rimbault. 1905. *Frank Dicksee: His Life and Work* (London: [n.p.])
Donaldson, Frances. 1970. *The Actor-Managers* (London: Weidenfeld & Nicolson)
Donohoe, Joseph. 1996. 'What is Edwardian Theatre?', in *The Edwardian Theatre*, ed. by Michael R. Booth and Joel H. Kaplan (Cambridge: Cambridge University Press)
Dudgeon, Piers. 2009. *Captivated: J. M. Barrie, Daphne du Maurier & The Dark Side of Neverland* (London: Vintage Books)
du Maurier, George. 1895. *Trilby* (London: Osgood, McIlvaine)
Edwards, Dennis F. 1992. *Watford: A Pictorial History* (Chichester: Phillimore)
Eliot, George. 1954–78. *The George Eliot Letters*. ed. by Gordon S. Haight, 9 vols (New Haven, CT, & London: Yale University Press)
Ferrero, William. 1893. 'Woman's Sphere in Art', *New Review*, 9: 554–60
Fielding, Daphne. 1974. *The Rainbow Picnic: A Portrait of Iris Tree* (London: Eyre Methuen)
Fitzgerald, Percy Hetherington. 1881. *The World Behind the Scenes* (London: Chatto)
—— 1908. *Shakespearean Representation: Its Law and Limits* (London: E. Stock)
Flanders, Judith. 2001. *A Circle of Sisters* (London: Viking)
France, Peter. 2000. *The Oxford Guide to Literature in English Translation* (Oxford: Oxford University Press)
Glenn, Susan A. 2000. *The Politics of Comedy* (New Haven, CT: Harvard University Press)
Gray, Frances. 2003. *Women, Crime and Language* (Basingstoke: Palgrave Macmillan)
Gottlieb, Robert. 2010. *Sarah: The Life of Sarah Bernhardt* (New Haven, CT, & London: Yale University Press)
Grein, J. T. 1900. *Premieres of the Year* (London: Macqueen)
Grundy, Sydney. 1880. *A Debt of Honour* (London: Thomas Scott)
Grylls, Rosalie Glynn. 1948. *Queen's College 1848–1948* (London: George Routledge & Sons)
Hapgood, Norman. 1901. *The Stage in America, 1897–1900* (New York: Macmillan)
Henley, William Ernest, and Robert Louis Stevenson. 1907. *Beau Austin*, in *The Plays of W. E. Henley and R. L. Stevenson* (London: William Heinemann)
Hilbert, H. 1914. 'Unknown', *Westminster Gazette* (3 January)

HINDSON, CATHERINE. 2008. 'Maud Beerbohm: Performing the Actor-Manager's Wife; Disrupting the Actor-Manager?' (Leeds: TaPRA)
HOGARTH, BASIL. 1936. *Trial of Robert Wood* (London: William Hodge & Co. Ltd.)
HOLLEDGE, JULIE. 1981. *Innocent Flowers: Women in the Edwardian Theatre* (London: Virago)
JALLAND, PAT. 1988. *Women, Marriage and Politics 1860–1914* (Oxford: Oxford University Press)
JAMES, HENRY. 1908. *The Portrait of a Lady*, in *The Novels and Tales of Henry James*, New York Edition (London: Macmillan), III & IV
—— 1890. *The Tragic Muse* ((London: Macmillan)
—— 1948. *The Scenic Art: Notes on Acting and Drama 1872–1901* (London: Rupert Hart-Davis)
JAY, HARRIET. 1883. *Through the Stage Door: A Novel* (London: White)
JOHN, ANGELA V. 1995. *Elizabeth Robins: Staging a Life* (London & New York: Routledge)
KACHUR, B. A. 1992. 'Shakespeare Politicized: Beerbohm Tree's King John and the Boer War', *Theatre History Studies*, 12: 25–44
KENDAL, MADGE. 1933. *Dame Madge Kendal, by Herself* (London: John Murray)
KENNEDY, DENNIS. 1996. 'The New Drama and the New Audience', in *The Edwardian Theatre*, ed. by Michael R. Booth and Joel H. Kaplan (Cambridge: Cambridge University Press)
KENNEY, ANNIE. 1924. *Memories of a Militant* (London: Edward Arnold)
KIPLING, RUDYARD. 2005. *Something of Myself: For My Friends Known and Unknown* (Rockville, MD: Wildside Press)
LAMBERT, ANGELA. 1984. *Unquiet Souls: The Indian Summer of the British Aristocracy, 1880–1918* (London: Macmillan)
LEASK, MARGARET. 2000. 'Lena Ashwell 1869–1957: Actress, Patriot, Pilgrim' (University of Sydney, New South Wales, unpublished doctoral thesis)
LERNER, GERDA. 1976. 'New Approaches to the Study of Women in American History', in *Liberating Women's History: Theoretical and Critical Essays*, ed. by Berenice A. Caroll (Urbana & London: University of Illinois Press)
LEWES, G. H. 1875. *On Actors and the Art of Acting* (Leipzig: Bernard Tauchnitz)
LONGAKER, JOHN MARK. 1945. *Ernest Dowson* (Pennsylvania: University of Pennsylvania Press), M. 1884. 'Platform Women', *Nineteenth Century*, 15: 409–15
LYNN LINTON, E. 1885. 'The Stage as a Profession for Women', *National Review*, 5: 8–19
MARSH, EDWARD. 2009. *Rupert Brooke: A Memoir* (Charleston, SC: BiblioBazaar)
MARSHALL, GAIL. 1998. *Actresses on the Victorian Stage: Feminine Peformance and the Galatea Myth* (Cambridge: Cambridge University Press)
MOFFAT, IVAN. 2004. *The Ivan Moffat File: Life Among the Beautiful and Damned in London, Paris and Hollywood*, ed. by Gavin Lambert (London: Pantheon Books)
MOORE, GEORGE. 1891. *Impressions and Opinions* (New York: Scribners)
MORTON, EDWARD. 1909. 'A Queen's Love Romance,' *The Playgoer and Society Illustrated*, 2: 61–78
NELSON, CLAUDIA, and ANN SUMNER, EDS. 1997. *Maternal Instincts: Visions of Motherhood and Sexuality in Britain 1875–1925* (London: Palgrave Macmillan)
NEVINSON, H. W. 1935. *Fire of Life* (London: Nisbet)
OFFICER, LAWRENCE H., and SAMUEL H. WILLIAMSON. 2010. 'Measures of Worth', <https://www.measuringworth.com/worthmeasures.php> [accessed 6 September 2017]
OWEN, DAVID. 1964. *English Philanthropy 1660–1960* (Cambridge, MA: Belknap Press)
PEARCE, BRAIN. 1995. 'Beerbohm Tree's Production of *The Tempest* 1904', *New Theatre Quarterly*, (November), 299–308
PEARSON, H. 1940. *The Last Actor-managers* (London: Methuen)
—— 1988. *Beerbohm Tree, His Life and Laughter* (London: Columbus Books)

PEARSON, ROBERTA E., and WILLIAM URICCHIO. 1994. 'Shriekings From Below the Gratings: Sir Herbert Beerbohm Tree's Macbeth and His Critics', in *Reclamations of Shakespeare*, ed. by A. J. Hoenselaars (Amsterdam: Rodopi)

POLLOCK, F., ED. 1875. *Macready's Reminiscences*, 2 vols (New York: Harper)

POMERANZ, VICTORY. 1971. 'O'Callaghan on His Last Legs', *James Joyce Quarterly*, 9 (1): 136–39

POWELL, KERRY. 1997. *Women and the Victorian Theatre* (Cambridge: Cambridge University Press)

PROCHASKA, FRANK K. 1988. *The Voluntary Impulse* (London: Faber & Faber)

PYE, DEBORAH. 2003. 'Irreproachable Women and Patient Workers: The Memoirs of Victorian Leading Ladies', *Texas Studies in Literature and Language*, 45 (1): 73–79

REED, DONALD. 1994. *The Age of Urban Democracy: England 1868–1914* (London & New York: Longman)

REES, T. 1978. *Theatre Lighting in the Age of Gas* (London: Society for Theatre Research)

REYNOLDS, K. D. 1998. *Aristocratic Women and Political Society in Victorian Britain* (Oxford: Clarendon Press)

RICHARD, JEFFREY. 2005. *Sir Henry Irving: A Victorian Actor and His World* (New York & London: Hambledon)

ROBINS, E. 1940. *Both Sides of the Curtain* (London: William Heinemann)

—— 1928. *Ibsen and the Actress* (London: Hogarth Press)

ROWELL, GEORGE. 2009. 'Sardou on the English Stage', *Theatre Research International*, <https://doi.org/10.1017/S0307883300003412> [accessed 11 September 2017]

SCHAFER, ELIZABETH. 2003. *Playing Australia: Australian Theatre and the International Stage* (Amsterdam: Rodopi)

SCHULZ, DAVID. 1995. 'Spectacular Feasts: Herbert Beerbohm Tree and the Mise-en-Scène of Consumption' (University of Washington, unpublished PhD thesis)

SHAW, GEORGE BERNARD. 1931. *Our Theatre in the Nineties*, 3 vols (London: Constable)

—— 1958. *Shaw on Theatre*, ed. by E. J. West (New York: Hill & Wang)

—— 1961. *Platform and Pulpit*, ed. by Dan H. Lawrence (New York: Hill & Wang)

—— 1993. *The Drama Observed*, 4 vols (University Park: Pennsylvania State University Press)

SHELLARD, DOMINIC. 2004. *The Lord Chamberlain Regrets: British Stage Censorship and Readers' Reports from 1834 to 1968* (London: British Library)

SMITH, JACOB. 2008. *Vocal Tracks: Performance and Sound Media* (Berkeley: University of California Press)

SMITH, MALVERN VAN WYK. 1978. *Drummer Hodge: Poetry of the Anglo-Boer War, 1889–1902* (Oxford: Oxford University Press)

SOROS, SUSAN WEBER, ED. 1999. *E. W. Godwin: Aesthetic Movement Architect and Designer*, ed. by Susan Weber Soros (New York: Yale University Press)

Hamish Hamilton)

STEVENSON, ROBERT LOUIS. 1929 [1868]. *The Charity Bazaar: An Allegorical Dialogue* (Westport, CT: Georgian Press)

SWINBURNE, ALGERNON CHARLES. 1866. *A Ballad of Burdens* in *Poems and Ballads*, (London: J. C. Hotten)

SYMONS, ARTHUR. 1903. *Plays, Acting, and Music* (New York: Dutton)

—— 1977. *The Memoirs of Arthur Symons: Life and Art in the 1890s* (University Park & London: Pennsylvania State University)

TERRY, ELLEN. 1908. *The Story of My Life* (London: Hutchinson)

TOLLES, WINTON. 1940. *Tom Taylor and the Victorian Drama* (New York: Columbia University Press)

TRAUB, VALERIE. 1992. *Desire and Anxiety: Circulations of Sexuality in Shakespearean Drama* (London & New York: Routledge)
TREE, HERBERT BEERBOHM. 1913. 'Votes for Women', *London Budget* (2 May)
—— 1915A. *Thoughts and After-Thoughts* (London: Cassell)
—— 1915B. 'Constantinople of the Stage', *Allies in Art* (11 February) and *Irish Times* (5 March)
TREE, MAUD. *Our Little Life*. Unpublished manuscript (Bristol Theatre Collection)
TREE, VIOLA. 1926. *Castles in the Air: A Story of My Singing Days* (London: George H. Doran)
—— 1937. *Can I help you?* (London: Hogarth Press)
TRUMAN, OLIVIA. 1984. *Beerbohm Tree's Olivia* (London: André Deutsch)
TYLEE, CLAIRE M. 1998. 'A Better World for Both: Men, Cultural Transformation and the Suffragettes', in *The Women's Suffrage Movement,* ed. by Maroula Joanou & June Purvis (Manchester: Manchester University Press)
VANBRUGH, IRENE. 1948. *To Tell My Story* (London: Hutchinson)
VANBRUGH, VIOLET. 1925. *Dare to be Wise* (London: Hodder & Stoughton)
VICINUS, M. 1977. *A Widening Sphere: Changing Roles of Victorian Women* (Bloomington: University of Indiana Press)
WALBROOK, H. M. 1922. *J. M. Barrie and the Theatre* (London: Duckham)
WALWORTH, JANETTE H. 1895. 'Garnered in Feminine Fields', *New York Mail and Express* (16 February); *Pioneer Press* (17 February); *Chicago Evening Post* (2 March)
WEBSTER, JOHN. 1970. *The White Devil*, ed. by J. R. Mulryne (Lincoln: University of Nebraska Press)
WILDE, OSCAR. 1886. 'Helena in Troas', *Dramatic Review* (22 May), 161–62
WILLIAMS, GARY JAY. 1997. *Our Moonlight Revels: A Midsummer Night's Dream in the Theatre* (Iowa City: University of Iowa Press)
WINTER, JOHN STRANGE. 1902. *Connie, The Actress: A Novel* (London: White)
YOUNG, SIR CHARLES. 1881. [REVIEW OF *Shadows*], *Era* (22 January)
ZIEGLER, PHILIP. 1982. *Diana Cooper* (New York: Alfred A. Knopf)

INDEX

Abbey's Theatre 36, 45
The Absent-Minded Beggar 67–79, 94, 147, 170, 181
Académie Française 138
Achurch, Janet 28, 32, 57–58, 61
Actors Benevolent Fund 67, 125, 137
Actresses' Franchise League (AFL) 46, 135
Adams, Maude 129
The Admirable Crichton 159, 183
AFL, *see* Actresses' Franchise League
Agate, James 167, 170, 185
Aglavaine 60
Aïdé, Hamilton 16, 21, 64, 113
Ainley, Henry 170
Alexander, George 16, 60, 117, 149
Alexandra, Queen 144, 158
Alhambra Theatre 72, 77, 137, 181
Alibi 171, 173, 178, 184
Alma-Tadema, (Sir) Lawrence 4, 16, 26, 35, 63, 108
American Easter Council 145
American Women's War Hospital 139
Anderson, Mary 24
Anderson, Percy 119, 130
Androcles and the Lion 129
The Angel in the House 182
Anglo-Boer War 188
Anti-Suffrage League 46–47, 49
Apples 13
Araminta Arrives 164, 183
Archer, William 44, 53, 58–59, 62, 105
Asche, Oscar 147
Ashwell, Lena (Lady Simson) 31, 47, 49, 95, 99, 108, 118, 126, 130, 135, 137, 142, 185, 187
Asquith family:
    Elizabeth 135
    Herbert Henry 7, 9, 24, 27, 47–48, 118, 125, 137–38, 140, 144, 149, 167
    Katharine 124
    Margot (*née* Tennant) 48, 122, 132, 140–41
    Raymond 124, 141
Athenaeum 15, 80, 89, 110
Australian Red Cross Ball 142

Baird, Dorothea 55, 76
Balfour, Arthur 41, 149
Balmer, Edwin 148
Balmoral 45, 178
Bancroft, Marie 8, 16, 21, 28, 51, 59, 69, 76, 108, 182, 184

Bancroft, (Sir) Squire 122, 138
Baring, Maurice 163, 182
Barker, Granville 66
Barrie, J. M. 4, 108, 118–19, 127, 129–31, 136, 147, 159, 164, 167–68, 173, 182–86, 189
Battle of Jutland 148, 178
Beardsley, Aubrey 44, 49
Beau Austin 35, 180, 186
Beauté 171
Bechstein Hall 31, 144
Becky Sharp 100–01, 148
Beecham, (Sir) Thomas 122, 124
Beerbohm family:
    (Sir) Max (Tree's half-brother) 15–16, 19–20, 31, 46, 80–81, 91, 138, 156–59, 185
    Agnes Mary 15
    Claude (Reed) 142, 149, 162–63
    Constance (Tree's sister) 15, 22, 134
    Constantia (*née* Draper) (Tree's mother) 15
    Dora 15
    Eliza (*née* Draper) (Tree's step-mother) 15
    Ernest 8, 11, 15, 19, 27, 36, 48–49, 60–61, 66, 77, 109–10, 115, 130–31, 134–35, 152, 156, 170
    Herbert, *see* Tree
    Julius (Tree's brother) 8, 11, 15, 19, 27, 36, 48–49, 60–61, 66, 77, 109–10, 115, 130–31, 134–35, 152, 156, 170
    Julius Ewald (Tree's father) 11, 15
Beerbohm household 15
Begbie, Harold 74
Bell, Florence 44, 49
Bell, Vanessa 125
The Bells 5
Belvoir Castle 7, 23, 33, 47, 50, 159
Benckendorff, Count Constantine 124
Benson, Frank 26–27, 177
Benvenuto Cellini 58
Berger, Ludwig 174, 178, 184
Bernhardt, Sarah 31, 52, 60, 67, 88, 107, 137–38, 163, 186
Besant, Walter 43
Bijou Comedy Company 12
The Bill 183
The Blind Man's Eyes 148
Blinded Soldiers' Association 141
Boer War 71, 74, 103, 187
Bons Frères Club 70
Boscawen, Pamela 172

Boucicault, Dion 16, 36
Bourchier-Wrey, (Sir) Philip 164
Boyne, Leonard 91–93, 181
Braithwaite, Lillian 126
Brecht, Bertolt 99
British Legion 163
Brooke, Rupert 140–41, 187
Brookfield, Charles 32, 60, 94–95, 181
Brown Potter, Cora 31, 64–66, 76
Buchanan, Robert 30, 43, 180, 182
Bulwer-Lytton, Edward 170
A Bunch of Violets 43–44, 180
Burne-Jones, (Sir) Edward 13–14, 19, 35, 64, 66, 71
Burne-Jones, (Lady) Georgiana 74, 157, 159
Burne-Jones, (Sir) Philip 71, 77, 162, 170
Butt, Clara 69, 102

Caesar's Wife 16, 89–99, 111, 181
Called Black 22
Calvert, Louis 57, 61, 63
Camden Town Murder 117
Campbell, Mrs Patrick (*née* Beatrice Stella Tanner) 5, 51, 57, 60, 62, 115–16, 125, 129, 185
Captain Swift 32, 36, 179, 182
Carlton Hotel 22, 55
Carnac Sahib 53, 65
Carrington, Dora 125
Caruso, Enrico 137
Cassel, Ernest 55, 61, 92, 123, 189
Cavendish, (Lady) Lucy 48, 50
Cavendish-Bentinck, Winifred Anna (Duchess of Portland) 41
Cecil, Eleanor 19, 27, 47, 49–50, 185
A Certain Liveliness 157, 183
Chambers, Haddon 32, 36, 53, 158, 179–80, 182
Chambers, Montpellier 125, 130
Charing Cross Bazaar 68–70, 76, 88, 137
The Charlatan 43–44, 180
Charley's Aunt 22
Christie, Agatha 166, 171, 184
Chu Chin Chow 130, 147, 156, 159, 162
Churchill, Winston 70, 77, 108, 126, 170
Cinematography Film Act 172
Clarke, (Sir) Edward 130
Cockayne-Cust, Henry John ('Harry Cust') 73, 77
Collier, Constance 102, 104–05, 107–09, 147, 149
Collins, Arthur 121–22, 130, 144
Colonel Newcome 130
Comédie Française 105, 137–38
Comedy Theatre 28, 164–65
Comyns Carr, Alice 113, 115, 126
Comyns Carr, Joseph William 21, 28, 110, 112
Contagious Diseases Act 61
Cooper, (Lady) Diana 134, 172–73, 189
Cooper, (Sir) Duff 124, 128, 140
Cooper, Gladys 60, 125–26, 135
Cordova, Rudolph 163

Corrupt Coterie 123–24, 140
Cory-Wright, (Lady) Felicity, (*née* Tree) 110, 139, 186
Cosmo, Stuart 101
Costume Society 17
Council of Jews 145
Coward, Noel 126, 168–69, 184
Craig, Edith 'Edy' 142, 186
Craig, Edward Gordon 108
The Critics 182
Cumberland, Stuart 43
Cunard, Maud, (Lady) 'Emerald' 102, 118
Cunard, Nancy 123–24, 135

Dana, Henry 57, 61, 148
The Dancing Girl 180
Daudet, Alphonse 30
Delysia, Alice 166, 170
Desborough, (Lady) Ettie 7, 133, 158–59, 161, 173, 186
Dick, Charles George Cotsford 41
Dickens, Charles 4, 23, 142, 163
Dicksee, (Sir) Frank 10
Diplomacy 122, 125–29, 144, 167, 182, 184
Disraeli 121
Ditrichstein, Leo 148
Douglas, (Lord) Alfred 41, 151
The Drums of Doom 182
Drake 132
du Maurier, George 76, 181
du Maurier, (Sir) Gerald 6, 126, 138–39, 164, 167, 171
The Duke's Motto 2
Duse, Eleonora 31, 107

Early to Bed 174, 184
Electra 115, 182
Elgar, (Sir) Edward 59, 102, 138, 144
Elliot, Maxine 125, 129, 133, 140
Elsie 21
Empire Picture Hall 142–43
Engaged 24, 179
Enoch Arden 3
Entente Matinée 137–39, 163, 182
The Erratics 11

Fedora 2, 5, 31, 51–53, 60, 126–27, 180
Feuillet, Octave 43, 180
The First Floor Back 183
Fitch, Clyde 181
The Flood Tide 182
Floyd ('Flordyce') Bertha (*née* Holt) (Maud's sister) 2, 8, 161
    Gwendolyn (Maud's niece) 161
Forbes, James 183
Forbes-Robertson, Norman 6, 9, 60, 127, 129–31, 144, 164
Forgotten 58
Franco-British Women's Exhibition 118
French Red Cross 146–47

Fripp, (Sir) Alfred 113–14, 149, 151
Frohman, Charles 129
Fulton, Charles 63

The Gadfly 69–70
Gamblers All 139
Garden Theatre New York 115, 182
George, Lloyd 144, 149
George Washington 135
Gielgud, John (Sir)113, 170
Gielgud, Val 174
Gilbert, (Sir) William Schwenck 12, 22–23, 30, 52, 64, 108, 179
The Girl from Maxim's 168, 173, 184
Gladstone, William 10, 16, 24, 35, 39, 50
The Glass of Fashion 21
Glottenham House 120, 125, 136, 156–57
Glynn, Rosalie 186
Godard, Claude 178
Godwin, Edward William 16–18, 24–27, 188
Gordon-Cumming, (Sir) William 130
Grace 120
Grand-Guignol 93, 99
The Great Lover 148–49, 185
The Great Man 182
Greek Theatre 24–25
Grey Stocking 163, 182

Hamlet 37–38, 40, 48, 180, 182
Hanbury, Hilda 41, 44, 49
Hanbury, Lily 36, 44, 63
Harding, Lyn 43–44, 53, 57, 61, 64, 85–86, 88, 122, 179–81, 186
Harmsworth, Alfred (1st Viscount Northcliffe) 71, 77
Harris, Frank 91, 96
Hart-Davis, Sybil 128
Hawtrey, Charles 129
Haymarket Theatre 28, 32–33, 36–39, 41–43, 49, 51, 53, 55, 58, 76, 88, 110, 121, 179–81, 183
Heard on the Telephone 39, 91, 93, 155, 181
Helena in Troas 25–27, 179, 189
Hengler's Circus 24–25, 27
Henry Hall, (Sir) Thomas 129
Henry V 36
Henry VIII 8, 49, 140, 173, 184
Henson, Leslie 170
Her Imaginary Lover 172, 184
Hervieu, Paul 181, 185
Hichens, Robert Smythe 101, 148, 151
His Last Legs 92–93, 188
The Hobby Horse 26, 179
Hofmannsthal, von Hugo 182
Holloway, Stanley 173
Holt family:
    Bertha 2–6, 17, 19, 21, 32, 102, 120
    Emma (*née* Brown) 2

Emmie 2–4, 7, 17–18, 20
Hellen Maud *see* Tree, Maud 2–9
Henrietta (Harriet, 'Harrie') 2–3, 102, 120, 154, 158–59
Horace 2
William 2–4, 8
Horner, Edward 124, 140
Howard, Leslie 160

Ibsen, Henrik 46, 51–62, 94, 117, 171, 176, 178, 181, 188
In His Power 24, 179
Incognito 179
Irish Assurance 91–93, 181
Irving, (Sir) Henry 69, 188

James, Henry 4, 8, 13–14, 35, 187
Jennings, Gertrude 160–61, 171, 174, 183–84
John, Augustus 125
John-A-Dreams 180
John Gabriel Borkman 59, 93, 181
John the Penman 26
Joseph and His Brethren 40, 128
Julius Caesar 8, 41, 60, 63–66, 69, 99, 181–82
The Jungle Book 77, 169

Katharine and Petruchio 181
Kean, Charles 111
Keep the Chaperones 170
Kendal, Madge 26, 76, 102, 108, 114, 138, 187
Keppel, Violet 138, 144
King Henry IV 174–75, 181, 184
King John 8, 49, 70–72, 77, 103, 144
King Lear's Wife 183
Kingsway Theatre 99
Kipling, Rudyard 53, 60, 70–72, 74–75, 77, 81, 169–70, 181, 187
A Kiss for Cinderella 167, 184–85
Knoblock, Edward 144, 147, 183
Knowledge 21
Korda, Alexander 172–73, 177, 184
KOW (Keen on Waller) 63

Lady Clancarty 27, 53, 179
Lady Windermere's Fan 41
Langtry, Lily 5, 76, 89
The Last of the Dandies 181
The Last of Mrs Cheyney 168, 184
Laughton, Charles 169, 171, 173
Lawrence, Gertrude 169
Le Passé 60
League of Mercy 67, 160, 169
Ledebur, Iris (Countess) *née* Tree 138
Lee, Sydney 80
Leigh, Vivien 174, 178
Lewis, Edith 61

Lewis, George 35, 56
The Likeness of the Night 44, 85–88, 91, 181, 185
Lindsay, Charles 7
Lindsay, Norah 56, 61
Lindsay, Violet (Duchess of Rutland) 7, 11, 19, 21–22, 27, 31, 36–37, 40–41, 45, 47–49, 57, 63, 65–66, 68–69, 73, 77, 85, 88, 100, 108, 115, 118, 124, 132, 134, 140, 156, 158–59, 161, 167–68, 177
Lipton Expedition 134
Lister, Charles 140
Little Dorrit 163, 184
Little Eyolf 61
Little Silver Ring 183
The Little Silver Ring 183
Llewelyn Davies, Sylvia 4, 35, 127
Lohr, Marie 164
London Film Productions 172
Lonsdale, Frederick 168, 184
Lusitania 118
Lyttelton, Edith 162
Lyttleton, Alfred 24

Macbeth 61, 142, 147, 154, 167
Macquoid, Percy 103, 110–11
The Magistrate 24, 179
Manners, Henry John (8th Duke of Rutland) 7–8, 19, 27, 48-9, 56, 61, 66, 69, 88, 113, 115, 125, 132, 136, 138, 140, 148, 159
A Man's Shadow 58, 144
Marbury, Elisabeth 61, 148
Margery's Lovers 22, 179
Marie Odile 144
Marshall, Robert 101
Mayson, Emily ('Emmie') *see* Holt
The Mask of Virtue 115, 174
Masks and Faces 32, 109, 142, 180
Maude, Cyril 121
Mayfair and Montmartre 166, 183
McCarthy, Lillah 129–30
Melba, Nellie 69, 89
Merivale, Herman 23, 51, 151, 179–80
The Merry Wives of Windsor 102, 113, 144, 179, 181–83
Meyer, Carl 55, 57, 61, 92, 123
A Midsummer Night's Dream 8, 61, 79–88, 93, 96, 103–04, 130, 181, 189
The Millionaire 21
Moby Dick 125
A Modern Eve 180
Moffat, Curtis 19, 148, 151, 170, 178, 187
Moffat, Ivan 116, 178, 187
Moffat, Iris *see* Ledebur
Moore 8, 10, 22, 76, 148, 187
Morrell, (Lady) Ottoline 53, 135
Montjoye 43, 180
Much Ado about Nothing 11, 16, 159, 182–83
A Mummer's Wife 8

The Murder of Roger Ackroyd 171, 184
The Musketeers 64, 73, 181

Nares, Owen 142
Neilson, Julia 69, 79
Nelkie, Maud 128
Nero 102–04, 109–10, 182
Neville, Vera 157
New Century Theatre 58
NKG (Nice Kind Gentleman) 12, 95
NKL (Nice Kind Lady) 12
Novello, Ivor 169

Oberon, Merle 172–73
Ogden's Guinea Gold Cigarettes 34
Ogilvie, Stuart 28, 157, 159
Once Upon a Time 180
Otello 17
Othello 26–27, 53
Our Own Lives 171, 174, 178, 184

Paderewski, Ignacy 88, 102
Paget, (Lady) Muriel Evelyn DBE 134, 139, 144
The Palace of Truth 12
Parker, Louis N. 139, 158, 180
Parsons, Alan 123, 140
Parsons, David 139, 161
Parsons, Viola *see* Tree
Partners 30
Pavlova, Anna 125
Pemberton, Max 156, 159
Peter Pan 127, 129
Philothespians 11
Phipps, Charles J. 55
Pinero, Arthur 24, 26, 28, 51, 104, 108, 117, 174, 179
Pinney, Beatrice May *see* Reed
Pinney, Henrietta L. 84, 88
Pinney, William 61
Playgoers' Club 90
Pompadour 64, 179
Ponsonby, Claude 21, 27
Porto-Riche, Georges de 60, 62
Potter, Paul M. 181
Poynter, Edward 4, 33
Prinsep, Val 145
The Private Life of Henry VIII 173, 184
Pygmalion and Galatea 24, 173, 183

Queen's College 4–6, 8, 10, 17, 19–20, 160, 163, 186
Quiller-Couch, Arthur 119, 130

Ragged Robin 181
Reade, Charles 32, 109, 180
Red Cross 133–34, 139, 160
The Red Lamp 28, 45, 61, 179–80
Reed, Beatrice May *see* Pinney

Reed, Carol (Sir) 56, 163
Reed, Claude *see* Beerbohm 56
Reed, Oliver 56
Rehearsal Club 67, 121, 126, 141
Reinhardt, Max 168
Rennie, Michael 177
Ridley, Muriel 145, 149
Risler Aîné 30
Robey, George 174
Robins, Elizabeth 32, 36, 58–62, 93–94, 120, 136, 187–88
Rorke, Kate 56
Routledge, George 16, 28, 185–87, 189
Russell, Charles 85, 88, 159

Salaman, Malcolm C. 180
Salome 122
Sardou, Victorien 2, 51–62, 127, 180, 182, 184, 188
Sargent, John Singer 35
Sassoon, Siegfried 125
The School for Scandal 26, 35, 137–38, 174, 180, 183–84
Scott, Clement 16, 39, 89, 92, 99, 101, 126, 182, 184–85
The Seats of the Mighty 59, 62, 181
Shadows 11
Shall We Join the Ladies? 166, 183
Shaw, George Bernard 5, 8
  on acting 26, 33, 51, 59, 63–64, 107
  '...the Beerbohm Trees' 109, 112
  advice to Viola Tree 124, 115, 117, 124, 129, 140, 142–43, 151, 157–58, 162, 183, 188
Shaw-Stewart, Patrick 140
Shoreham Beach Studio 163
The Show Shop 76, 145, 183
Sickert, Walter 15, 117
Siddons, Henry 115
The Silver Key 118, 181
Sirocco 120, 182
Six and Eightpence 22, 179
Society for the Prevention of Cruelty to Children (SPCC) 76, 78
Smith, Dorothy Gladys 'Dodie' 171, 174
Somerset Maugham, William 15, 120–21, 130, 161, 182–83
'The Souls' 12, 15, 114, 123, 163, 168
Spencer-Churchill, Jennie (Lady Randolph) 68, 133, 183
St John, Christopher 119
Sternheim, Carl 174, 184
Stevenson, Robert Louis 35, 68, 180, 186
Still Waters Run Deep 142–43, 184
Stoll Film Company 120
Strauss, Richard 122–23
Strindberg, August 119, 182
The Stronger Woman 182
Sturgis, Julian 13, 39, 48, 52–53, 60
Such is the Law 172, 184
Sullivan, (Sir) Arthur 12, 67, 77
Sutro, Alfred 58

Sweethearts 21, 56, 126, 179
Swinburne, Algernon Charles 3, 23, 88, 188

The Tale of Troy 11
Taylor, Tom 3–4, 27, 32, 59, 109, 142, 179–80, 188
The Tempest 40, 42, 49, 94, 102, 187
The Tempter 42, 44, 180
Tennant, Charles 23
Tennant, Margot (see Asquith) 9, 23–24, 45, 102, 140
Terriss, Ellaline 113
Terry family:
  Edward 90
  Ellen 8–9, 16–17, 21, 23, 26, 31, 35, 39–40, 48, 60, 67, 102, 108–13, 119, 125, 130, 142–43, 151, 155, 185–86, 188
  Kate 170
  Marion 28, 30
Théâtre Antoine 93
Théâtre Libre 94
Theatre Regulation Act 99
Thorndike, Sybil 164, 177
Thursby, Charles 119, 130
Transvaal War Fund Café 70

Trilby 55, 57, 61, 76, 127, 181, 186
Tristram, William Outram 28, 36, 52, 60, 179–80
Truman, Olivia 105, 110, 112–13, 115–16, 145, 149, 151, 189
Tweedie, Ethel Brilliana (Mrs Alec) 163, 170
Twelfth Night 21, 179
The Two Orphans 166, 183
Tree family:
  Tree, (Sir) Herbert Beerbohm:
    takes name of Tree 11
    meets Maud, act together 12
    friendship with E.W. Godwin 17–20
    marriage 20
    birth of Viola 22
    husband and wife play onstage Sir Peter and Lady Teazle 26
    becomes manager of the Comedy Haymarket Theatres 28
    plays Triplet and initiates matinee performances on a Wednesday 32
    encounter with Gladstone 35
    plays Hamlet 37
    Tree's lighting and stage effects 40–42
    commissions Oscar Wilde to write *A Woman of No Importance* 41–42
    first American Tour 45–46
    buys *Trilby* and plans for Her Majesty's Theatre 55–60
    produces *Julius Caesar* 63
    rivalry with Lewis Waller 64–65
    King John and 70–72
    plays Oberon 79

philosophy on management 79–81
criticism of Tree as theatre manager 94
Colonel Newcome 130
production of *The Tempest* 40, 42, 49, 94
as Nero 103–04, 109
produces *The Winter's Tale* 111
Joseph and His Brethren 128
makes war time speeches 132, 137, 139
writes *Thoughts and Afterthoughts* 136
leaves for America with Iris 142
Tree's German ancestry questioned in the press 144–45
Shylock in America 146
Tree's film of *Macbeth* 142
Barrie's spoof of *Macbeth* 147
Tree in Hollywood 142, 163
acts as King's Messenger 149
birth of Tree's son Paul Ridley 145
success of *Chu Chin Chow* 156, 162
operation to knee and death 149–51
funeral 153, 157
Tree, (Lady) Maud (née Holt):
upbringing 1–7
friendship with Violet Lindsay 7
model for *Harmony* 10
early acting ambition 10–11
meets Herbert Beerbohm 11–12
betrothal to Herbert 13
wedding 17–20
birth of Viola 22
befriends Margot Asquith 23
visits Egypt 28
Maud's homes 28
professional disagreement with Herbert 30
voice technique, elocution and maternal instincts in acting 30–32, 69, 187
as Mabel Vane 32
as Ophelia 38
entertaining Oscar Wilde 41–43
birth of Felicity 44
performs Balmoral and the White House 45
anti-suffrage position, New Woman 48–50
plays Fedora 51–52
acts with Lewis Waller in *A Woman's Reason* 53–54
involvement with finance, build and furnishing of Her Majesty's Theatre 55
birth of Iris 58
plays Ibsen, friendship with Elizabeth Robins and William Archer 58–59
philanthropy and the actress 67–68
Charing Cross Hospital Bazaar 68–69
recites *The Absent Minded Beggar* 70–76
plays Titania 79–81
discovers Tree's relationship with May Pinney 81–84
success of *The Likeness of the Night* 86–87
becomes 'wo-manager' 90–92, 114

plays Agrippina 102, 104–07
plays Paulina 111
relationship with Lewis Waller 113
car accident 112–16
reports on Camden Town Murder 117–18
Viola's wedding 123
speeches to raise money for charity 126, 142, 169
plays Lady Henry Fairfax 126–27
outbreak of war 132
Trees' joint war effort 135–38
film debut in *Still Waters* 142
anonymous blackmailer 145
purchases rights to *The Blind Man's Eyes* 148
Herbert's death 153
writes 'Herbert and I' for anthology 157–58
sale of His Majesty's Theatre 158
charity work and OBE 160
writes articles 163, 167
appears in revue *Mayfair to Montmartre* 166
plays in Alexander Korda's *Wedding Rehearsal* 172
death and tributes 177
Tree, Felicity (daughter) 9–13, 49–50, 56, 152, 154–55, 159, 161, 170, 173, 177
Venice with Herbert Asquith and Lord Vernon 122–24
Maud's advice on singing career and future 13, 85, 122–25, 133–34, 149
war work 134–36
marriage 139
and Rupert Brooke 140
birth of Felicity's sons 161
Tree, Iris (daughter) 11, 56–57
friendship with Nancy Cunard 102, 135
accident on Serpentine and court appearance 110
Man Ray, *La Dolce Vita, Moby Dick* 123–25
Herbert Asquith requests poetry 128
outbreak of war 132
friendship with Lady Ottoline Morrell 135
visits Hollywood with Tree 140
marriage to Curtis Moffat 142, 148–49
The Miracle with Diana Cooper 168, 172, 177, 186
Tree, Viola (daughter):
birth 22
friendship with Herbert Asquith 27
acting debut as Ariel 102
singing career, failed attempt to sing Salome, visits Richard Strauss 122–24
marriage to Alan Parsons 123
as Perdita in *The Winter's Tale* 111
on acting 139, 144, 177
Women's Emergency Corps 135
writing as Hubert Parsons in collaboration with Gerald du Maurier 127
birth of daughter Virginia 149
death of Herbert 159
Maud's death 173

The Unknown 161, 183

Vanbrugh, Irene 8, 49, 116, 125, 158, 164, 189
Vanbrugh, Violet 8, 23, 114, 138
Vanity Fair 100
Venne, Lottie 21, 144
Vernon (Lord) George Francis 140
Vezin, Herman 21, 23, 26–27, 59, 62
The Vicar of Wakefield 11
Victoria, Queen 10, 45, 48, 88, 160
Victoria League 162
A Village Priest 35, 180
Voluntary Aid Detachment (VAD) 134, 140
Voynich, Ethel Lilian 69, 77

The Waif 41, 94, 180
Waller, Florence (née West) 58, 89, 96
Waller Lewis, William 2, 19, 53-4, 58, 63–6, 79, 84-5, 88, 94, 96, 98-9, 105, 113-15, 119, 122, 139
   acts with Maud in *Lady Clancarty* 53
   plays Brutus 63
   rivalry over *The Three Musketeers* 64
   relationship with Maud 113
   death 139
Walpole House 100
War, outbreak of 9, 70–71, 118, 128, 132–33, 135–37, 139–40, 142, 145, 148–49, 154–56, 159, 161–62, 187
War Committee 183
Ward, Genevieve 59
Ward, Mary Augusta (Mrs Humphry) 49

Warner Brothers 172
Waugh, (Rev.) Benjamin 76
Wealth 24, 33, 103, 180
Wedding Rehearsal 172–73, 184
Wells, Honor 111
West, Florence *see* Waller
Whistler, James 16
White House 45, 178
Wilhelm II, Kaiser 121–22, 139
The White Pilgrim 23–24, 151, 179
The Who Could Work Miracles 177, 184
Wilde, Constance 26, 42, 49
Wilde, Oscar 4, 7, 16, 22, 26–28, 41–42, 104, 118, 122, 151, 180, 189
Wilkie Collins, William 21, 124
The Winter's Tale 113, 182, 185
A Woman of No Importance 41–42, 46, 49, 180
A Woman's Reason 53–54, 60, 78, 181
WFL (Women's Freedom League) 46, 49
WSPU (Women's Social and Political Union) 46
Wyndham, Charles 60, 91–92, 95, 97, 99, 128, 139, 181–82
Wyndham's Theatre 40, 89, 92, 95, 99, 122, 127

You Never Can Tell 162, 183
Young, (Sir) Charles 19, 26
The Young Person in Pink 160, 183

Zanetto (*The Waif*) 44, 180
Zuleika Dobson 19, 129, 156